PICTURING INDIAN TERRITORY

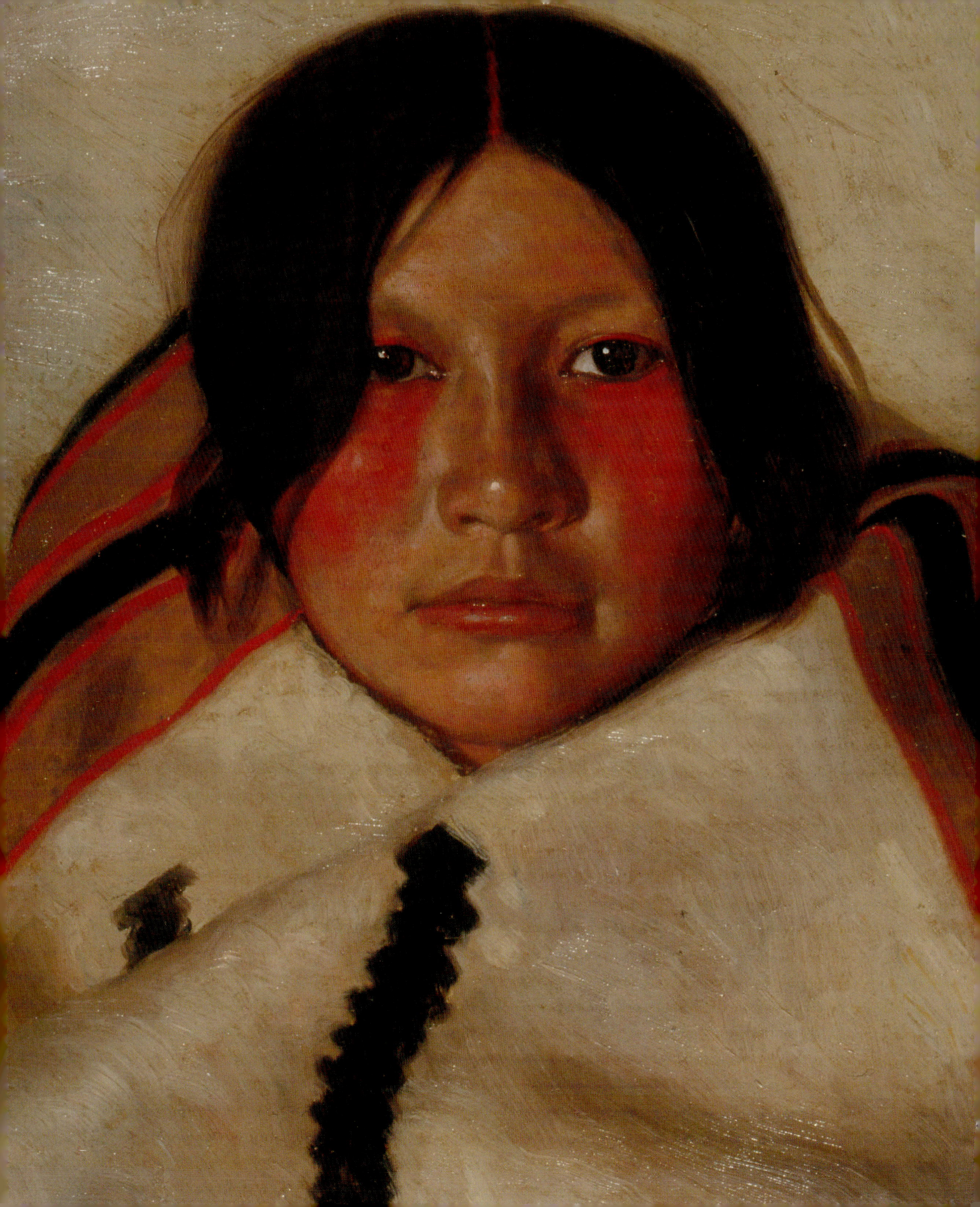

PICTURING INDIAN TERRITORY

Portraits of the Land That Became Oklahoma, 1819–1907

Edited by B. Byron Price | Foreword by John R. Lovett

CONTRIBUTIONS BY JAMES PECK, B. BYRON PRICE, AND MARK ANDREW WHITE

UNIVERSITY OF OKLAHOMA PRESS : NORMAN

This book is published with the generous assistance of the Charles M. Russell Center for the Study of Art of the American West and the Edward Everett Dale Society of the Western History Collections, University of Oklahoma.

The following images appear uncaptioned on the pages noted:

Page ii: (detail) Elbridge Ayer Burbank, *Gi-aum-e Hon-o-me-tah (Young Woman), Kiowa, Fort Sill, Oklahoma Territory*, 1899. (See figure 2.26, page 62)

Page iv: (detail) Thomas Croft and P. A. Miller, associates of William S. Prettyman, Cherokee Outlet, *At the Starting Signal at High Noon*, September 16, 1893. (See figure 3.1, page 79)

Pages xii–1: (detail) Thaddeus Mortimer Fowler and James B. Moyer, *Fort Reno, Oklahoma Territory*, 1891. Color map, 21 5/16 × 28 1/16 inches. Library of Congress, Geography and Map Division, Washington, D.C. (G4024.E34:2F6A3 1891.F6)

Library of Congress Cataloging-in-Publication Data
Name: Price, B. Byron, editor.
Title: Picturing Indian Territory : portraits of the land that became Oklahoma, 1819–1907 / edited by B. Byron Price ; foreword by John R. Lovett ; contributions by James Peck, B. Byron Price, and Mark Andrew White.
Description: Norman : University of Oklahoma Press, 2016. | Series: Charles M. Russell Center Series on Art and Photography of the American West ; volume 26 | Includes bibliographical references and index.
Identifiers: LCCN 2016008830 | ISBN 978-0-8061-5577-7 (hardcover : alk. paper)
Subjects: LCSH: Oklahoma—In art. | Indians in art.
Classification: LCC N8214.5.U6 P49 2016 | DDC 704.03/97—dc23
LC record available at http://lccn.loc.gov/2016008830

Picturing Indian Territory is Volume 26 in the Charles M. Russell Center Series on Art and Photography of the American West.

The paper in this book meets the guidelines for permanence and durability of the Committee on Production Guidelines for Book Longevity of the Council on Library Resources, Inc. ∞

1 2 3 4 5 6 7 8 9 10

CONTENTS

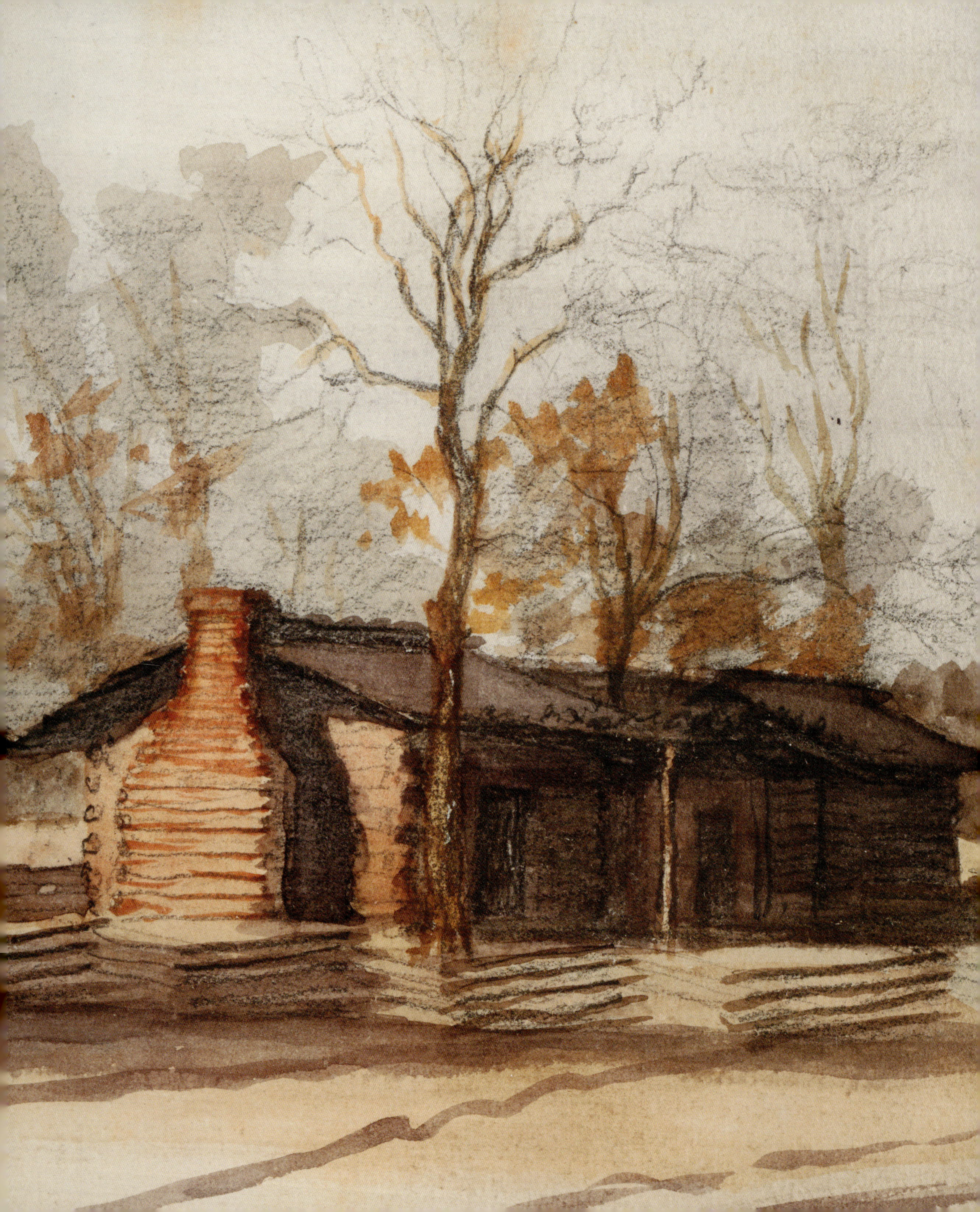

FOREWORD

JOHN R. LOVETT

Picturing Indian Territory: Portraits of the Land That Became Oklahoma, 1819–1907 captures a rich visual record. Drawn, painted, and photographed by both professional and amateur non-Native artists, these works portray a distinctive landscape populated by diverse cultures, troubled by frequently changing political boundaries, and transformed by historical events that were colorful, dramatic, and sometimes tragic. This book and the exhibit it accompanies are a collaboration of the University of Oklahoma's Charles M. Russell Center for the Study of Art of the American West, Fred Jones Jr. Museum of Art, and Western History Collections. The images included in this show span nearly nine decades and range from the scientific illustrations rendered in the journal of the English naturalist Thomas Nuttall to the easel paintings of such late-nineteenth- and early-twentieth-century American artists as Frederic Remington, Henry Farny, and Charles Schreyvogel. Some of the images are the product of more than one artist, and in a few cases the creator is anonymous. Other original works of art have not survived and are known to us only because they were converted for publication into wood engravings, chromolithographs, and halftones. Many of the pictures were completed by illustrators onsite in Indian Territory. Other visual reporters relied on written accounts and vivid imaginations. For better or worse, and whatever their origin or quality, these depictions of people, places, and events helped define Indian Territory for American and European audiences.

The Western History Collections is pleased to lend to the exhibit many of the primary source materials and magazine illustrations that are also included in this book. In some cases, this is the first time these works have ever been displayed or exhibited. One example is a sketch of a Caddo village in Indian Territory drawn by U.S. Army

FACING
(Detail) Vincent Colyer, *Residence of the Chief of the Seminoles Indian Territory in 1867*, 1867. Watercolor on paper, 5¾ × 9¾ inches. Gilcrease Museum, Tulsa, Oklahoma (0226.1371)

surgeon James Regale, Jr., in his diary while he served with the 10th U.S. Cavalry in 1867. The Western History Collections is also the source of a rare bird's-eye map of Fort Reno, published in 1891; a well-preserved copy of A. P. Jackson and E. C. Cole's *Oklahoma! Politically and Topographically Described*, published in 1885; and a program cover from 1884 for *Buffalo Bill's Wild Wes*t show.

In the pre-photography era of Indian Territory, and for many years after photography's advent, the artists and illustrators of Indian Territory created a vivid, if sometimes fanciful, visual record for those who could not visit the region. In these artworks they have provided a lens through which current and future generations may view the past.

INTRODUCTION

B. BYRON PRICE

In the nearly two decades since its founding in 1998, the Charles M. Russell Center for the Study of Art of the American West at the University of Oklahoma has undertaken a number of special research projects that have produced new scholarship in the field. The first and most significant of these efforts created an online catalogue raisonné devoted to the art of Charles M. Russell and included publication of a companion book on the artist by the University of Oklahoma Press in 2007. This book became the first of the more than two dozen volumes that now constitute the Press's Charles M. Russell Center Series on Art and Photography of the American West.

By the time *Charles M. Russell: A Catalogue Raisonné* reached publication, the Russell Center had already embarked on another long-term research project, this one devoted to documenting the artistic heritage of the State of Oklahoma. Over the past decade a series of graduate students holding art history fellowships, funded by the Robert S. and Grayce B. Kerr Family Foundation and working from the Charles M. Russell Center, have identified and documented nearly six hundred Oklahoma-related two-dimensional works of art created by non-Native artists between 1819 and Oklahoma statehood in 1907. This research contributed significantly to the content of this volume, and the Kerr Fellows who conducted it are recognized with gratitude in the acknowledgments section.

Picturing Indian Territory and the museum exhibition that accompanies it not only draw from the Russell Center's database of Oklahoma art but also build upon a pair of pioneering articles written in the early 1950s by art historians Oscar Brousse Jacobson and Jeanne d'Ucel and published in the Oklahoma Historical Society's quarterly journal, the *Chronicles of Oklahoma*. These articles, arranged chronologically, consist of brief biographical sketches of some of the better-known non-Native artists who left a visual record of Oklahoma in the nineteenth and early twentieth centuries. Since the publication of Jacobson and d'Ucel's articles, however, relatively little has been written about art pertaining to Oklahoma before statehood. Moreover, most recent scholarship on the subject is narrowly biographical rather than interpretive and rarely relates the art to the larger history of the state.

The essays in the present volume not only strive to achieve a more complete and useful synthesis of the subject than is currently available, but also seek to contextualize the work of individual artists and incorporate that work into the swiftly moving panorama of regional history. James Peck, a former Kerr Fellow and the present director of the Oceanside Museum of Art in Oceanside, California, for example, examines a group of government-funded artist-explorers who employed art in the service of science in what became Oklahoma between 1819 and the American Civil War. Peck also describes the work of a few adventuresome artists who, motivated by the trope of the "vanishing race," independently produced images of Native Americans living in a vast and imperfectly known region north of the Red River and west of American settlements in Arkansas and Missouri.

As director of the Charles M. Russell Center, I pick up the story at the advent of the Civil War and follow its thread to Oklahoma statehood in 1907. My essay focuses primarily on the work of a steady stream of outsiders—newspaper and magazine reporters, government functionaries, and artist-travelers—drawn to the region by the rapidly changing fortunes of the region's traditional Indian cultures in the wake of war and non-Indian settlement.

Mark Andrew White, the Wylodean and Bill Saxon Director of the Fred Jones Jr. Museum of Art at the University of Oklahoma, examines the art and illustration resulting from the unrelenting efforts of outsiders who settled Oklahoma Territory in the four decades following the Civil War. He demonstrates the crucial role that writers and artists played in constructing a mythical image of Oklahoma as an American Canaan and as the apex of the nation's imperial dreams.

Although the narrative that follows is more complete than anything attempted previously, it is necessarily limited by the extent and quality of the material that was produced and that has survived. In addition, the artists who addressed Oklahoma people, places, and events produced their work randomly over time and in response to specific personal interests or field assignments. In crafting their images, they relied, in at least a few cases, on written accounts and fertile imaginations rather than personal experience. Whether or not they were eyewitnesses to scenes they portrayed, they painted, sketched, and photographed what interested them, and admittedly, some were more skilled or motivated than others. What we are left with as a result is therefore not a comprehensive record, but a valuable one nonetheless.

The chaos and discord that accompanied the late-nineteenth-century effort to introduce white settlers into a region formerly the exclusive province of Indians were reflected in the frequently changing geographic and political boundaries. To accommodate this complexity and to avoid omitting artwork that appropriately relates to the state's history, the contributors to this volume occasionally use the term "Indian Territory" outside its strict historical or legal definition to embrace the entirety of the region that now forms the State of Oklahoma.

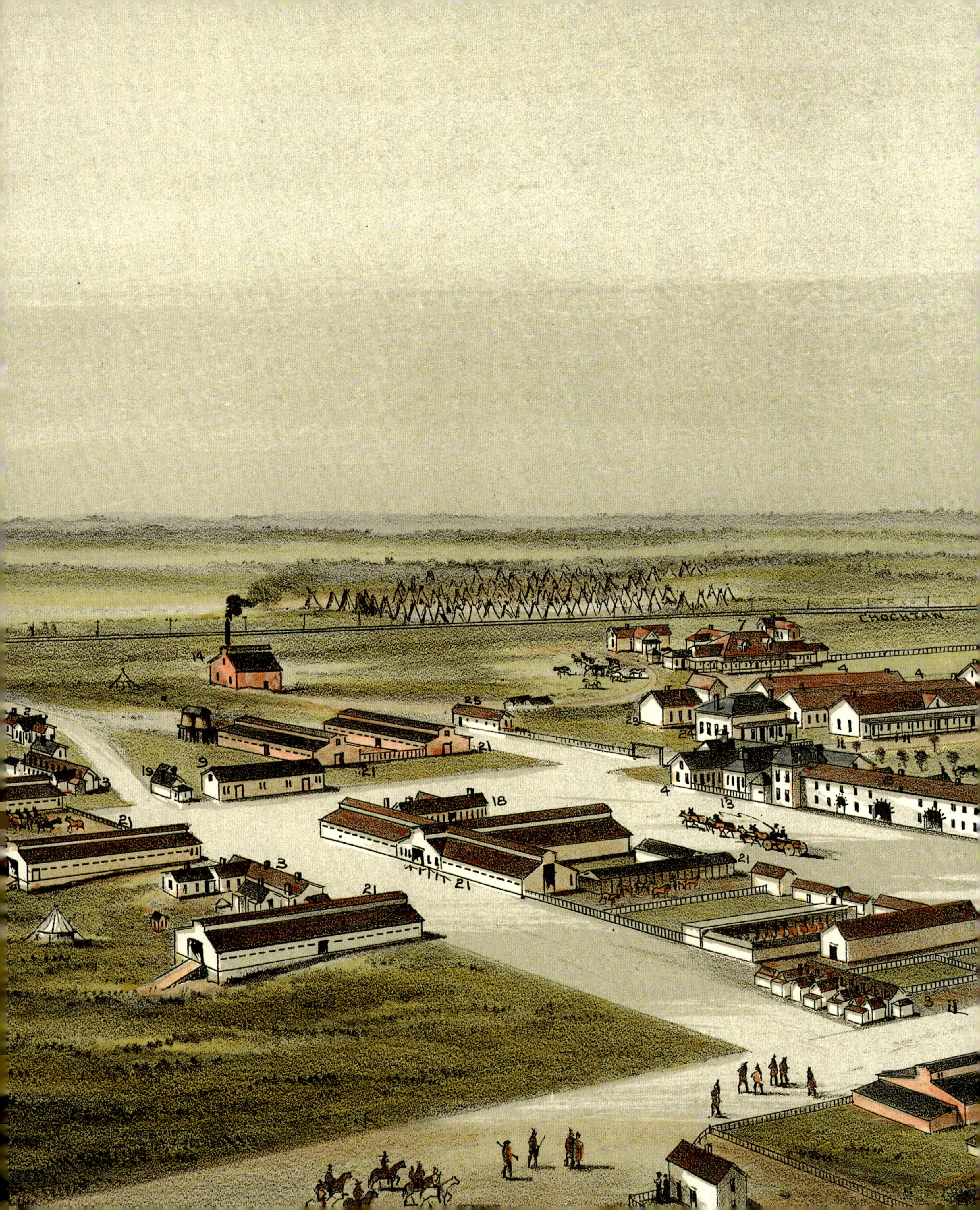
CHOCKTAW

PICTURING INDIAN TERRITORY

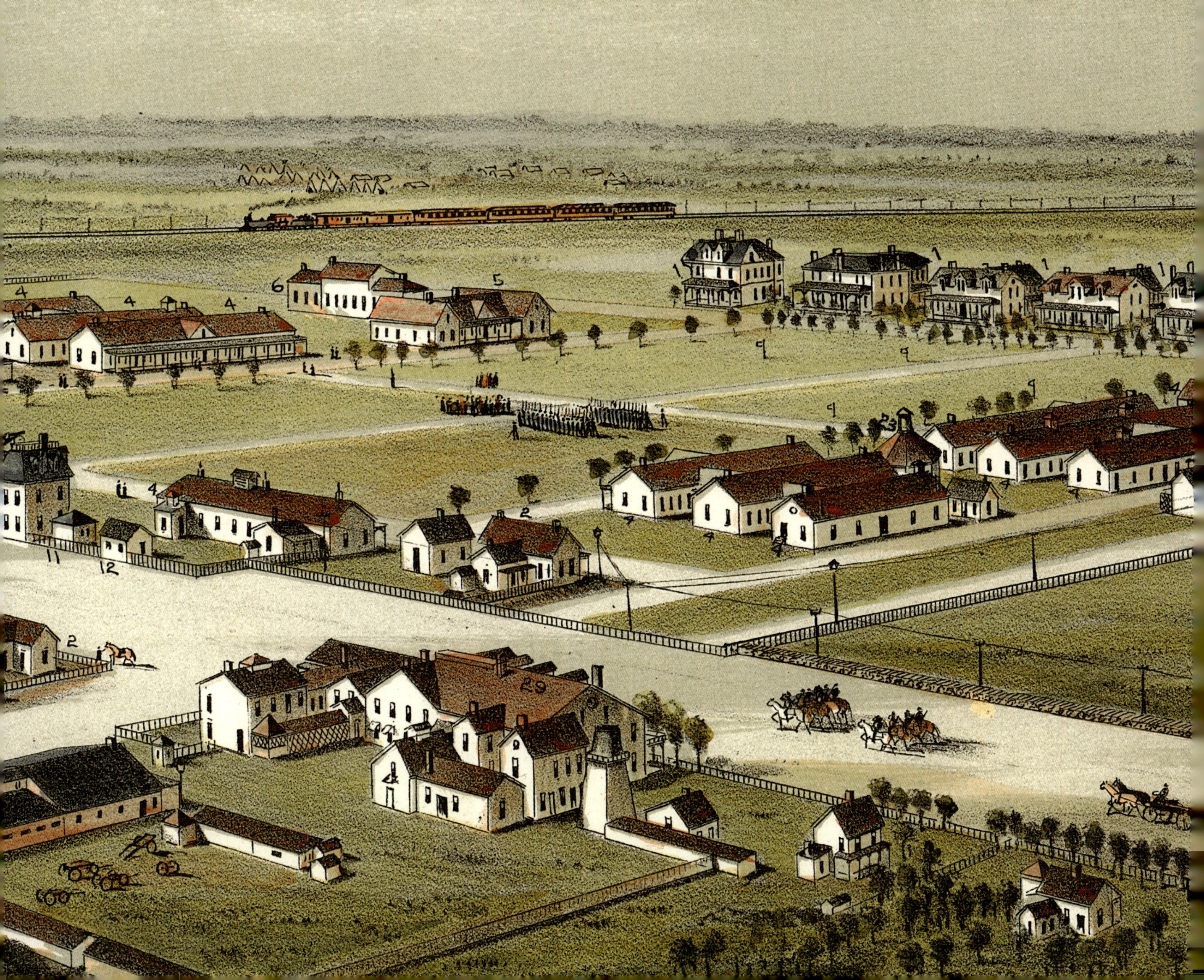

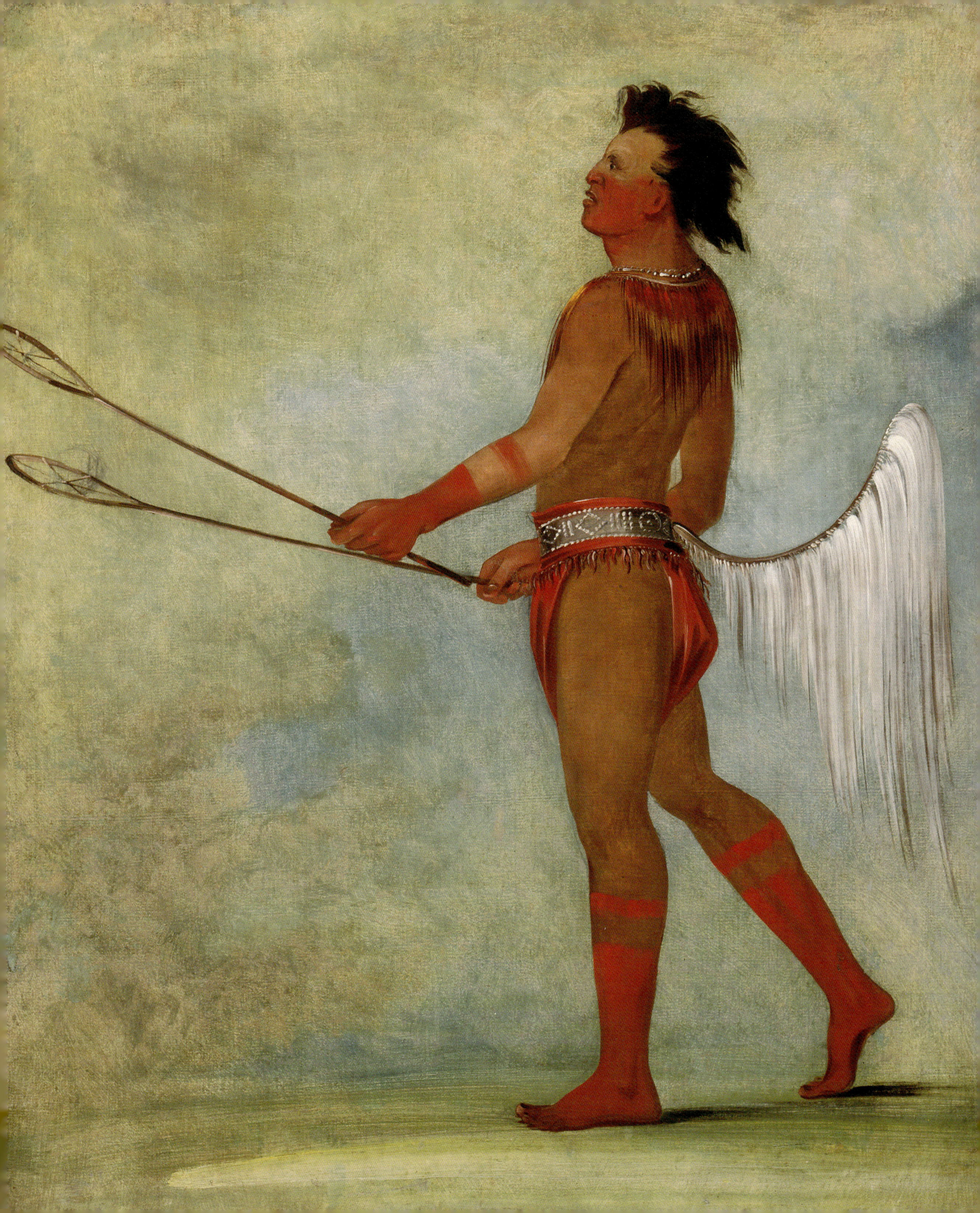

1 INDIAN TERRITORY, 1819–1861

Romanticism and the Spirit of Discovery

JAMES PECK

Around the time of the Louisiana Purchase of 1803, "Indian country" was a poorly defined, sprawling, inchoate area that ranged south to Texas, north to Canada, east to Arkansas Territory, and west to present-day Montana and Wyoming. By the late 1830s, however, the U.S. government had forcibly relocated tens of thousands of Indians from dozens of eastern tribes to "Indian Territory," land set aside in present-day Oklahoma, Kansas and Nebraska. Most of this region was already claimed by the Comanche, Osage, Kiowa, and other Plains tribes. Inevitably, tensions soon developed between the residents and the new arrivals. In response, the U.S. government built and manned a series of military forts to keep the peace between the competing groups. The result was a quasi-territorial military zone meant to separate Indians from the rest of America.

Isolated by both geography and the U.S. military, Indian Territory was little known to the world at large. The only way for a non-Indian to see the territory was to travel through it, a feat that required a valid scientific, political, or strategic reason—and typically, a military escort. In a time before the widespread use of cameras, it fell to artists to draw and paint this remote land. Unsurprisingly, few images were made of Indian Territory in the first half of the 1800s. Those images that survive portray the area as a liminal place, a fragile, transitory amalgam of displaced Indians, the American soldiers sent west to control and protect them, and the few non-Indian traders and missionaries allowed to live there. The land is variously presented to American audiences as strange, beautiful, distant, and, ultimately, abundant and available.

The context in which these images came to be reflects not the hopes and aspirations of Native peoples, but rather the ideology of colonial desire inherent in the creation of

FACING

(Detail) George Catlin, *Tul-lock-chísh-ko, Drinks the Juice of the Stone, in Ball-player's Dress*, 1834. Oil on canvas, 29 × 24 inches. Smithsonian American Art Museum, Washington, D.C. Gift of Mrs. Joseph Harrison, Jr. (1985.66.299)

this place. The output of the three most prodigious Indian Territory artists—George Catlin, John Mix Stanley, and Henrich Balduin Möllhausen—was made possible in part or in total through the aid of the U.S. military. The images these artists produced are of a contact zone, a space "in which peoples geographically and historically separated come into contact with each other and establish ongoing relationships, usually involving conditions of coercion, racial inequity, and intractable conflict."[1] It was a place defined by asymmetrical power, occupied by the dispossessed, controlled by colonial forces, and surveyed and studied ultimately as a precursor to white settlement. The images made describe a place that was hardly known to the American government or to the eastern Indians forcibly moved there, a place that nevertheless radically altered the history of a vast number of Native peoples and profoundly reshaped America.

Because Indian Territory was a physical manifestation of an ideology that advocated the separation, deprivation, and assimilation of indigenous people, it would be easy to categorize early images as vignettes illustrating this ideology. Yet they offer much more; they provide the earliest visual descriptions of the flora, fauna, and geological features of the area that would become Oklahoma. These images also offer portraits of Indian tribes who resisted, adapted, and ultimately survived. Indian Territory remains an important cultural crossroads of vital historical importance to Americans and to Native people, and as such, these images reward careful consideration.

Early Sightings

Thomas Nuttall, Titian Ramsay Peale, and the Art of Exploration

In 1819, the English naturalist Thomas Nuttall traveled with a military expedition to the Three Forks area near present-day Fort Gibson, Oklahoma, at the confluence of the Grand, Verdigris, and Arkansas Rivers. There he made extensive observations of the Osage Indians he encountered, collected floral specimens, and wrote comprehensive journal records. He also took a separate trip in the company of traders and a guide through parts of the central Oklahoma plains. Two years after his adventures, Nuttall published *A Journal of Travels into the Arkansas Territory during the Year 1819*.[2] Nuttall, a respected botanist with connections to the intelligentsia of London and Philadelphia, wrote a text rich in scientific and ethnographic detail. Even so, his prose sometimes slips into the language of colonial desire; he often evaluated prairies, geological formations, and rivers for their utility to future settlers.[3]

In the one image of Indian Territory illustrated in Nuttall's journal (figure 1.1), language and imagery reinforce each another. The engraving is a picturesque image of Cavanal Mountain, part of the Ouachita Mountain Range near present-day Poteau,

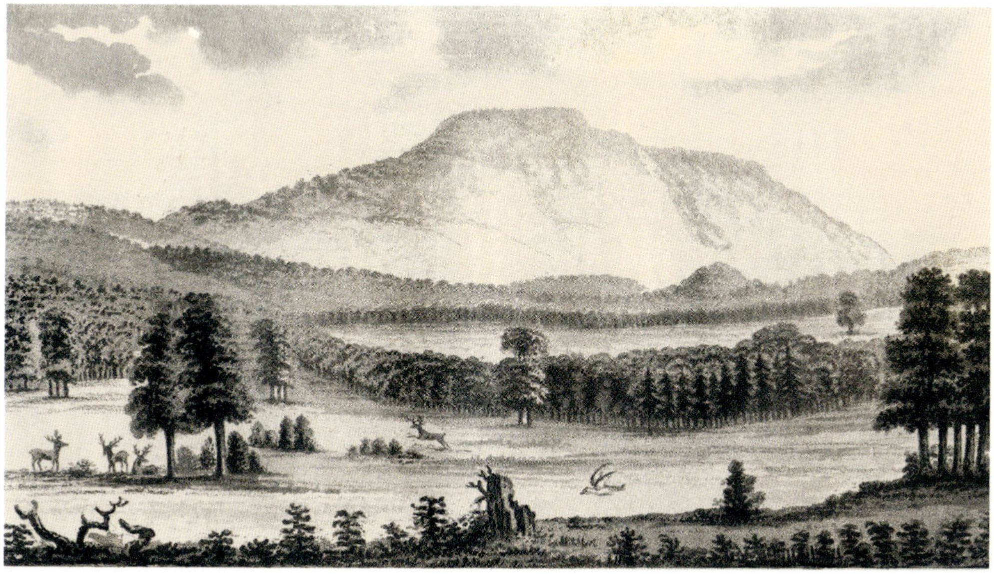

1.1. Thomas Nuttall, *Cavaniol* [Cavanal] *Mountain*, 1819. Engraving, from Thomas Nuttall, *A Journal of Travels into the Arkansas Territory during the Year 1819* (Philadelphia, Pa.: T. H. Palmer, 1821), opposite p. 144. Western History Collections, University of Oklahoma Libraries, Norman, Oklahoma

Oklahoma. The mountain, at nearly 2,400 feet above sea level, was a well-known geological feature used by travelers as a landmark. Yet the image, which features the tabular-topped mountain framed by a lush, verdant landscape flush with deer, birds, trees, and grass, suggests untapped potential; it visualizes the unspoken aspirations of Europeans and Americans wishing to exploit the land. Nuttall underlines this point in the text, noting that the mountain "lacked nothing but human occupation to reclaim it from barren solitude, and cast over it the air of rural cheerfulness and abundance."[4] The civilizing influence of European and American settlers would, therefore, turn the "barren solitude" into a bucolic English pastoral scene. Such civilizing efforts would of course exclude the local Native peoples as well as those displaced tribes that would soon start pouring into the land.

In 1819, the same year of Nuttall's travels, Lieutenant Stephen Harriman Long led a scientific expedition through a vast area of the Louisiana Purchase. The purpose of the expedition was twofold: to discover the sources of the Platte, Arkansas, and Red Rivers, and to explore the newly defined border between the United States and New Spain, which had been delineated and clarified by the Adams-Onís Treaty of 1819. The expedition traveled from St. Louis, Missouri, to the front range of the Rocky Mountains, before returning east toward Fort Smith, Arkansas Territory, along the Platte and Arkansas Rivers. On July 24, 1820, after reaching the front range of the Rockies, Long split his party into two groups. Long led his group, which included the naturalist-artist Titian Ramsay Peale, south toward the source of the Red River. The second group, led by Long's second-in-command, Captain John R. Bell, went east and south along the Arkansas River toward Fort Smith. Bell's group included the landscape painter Samuel

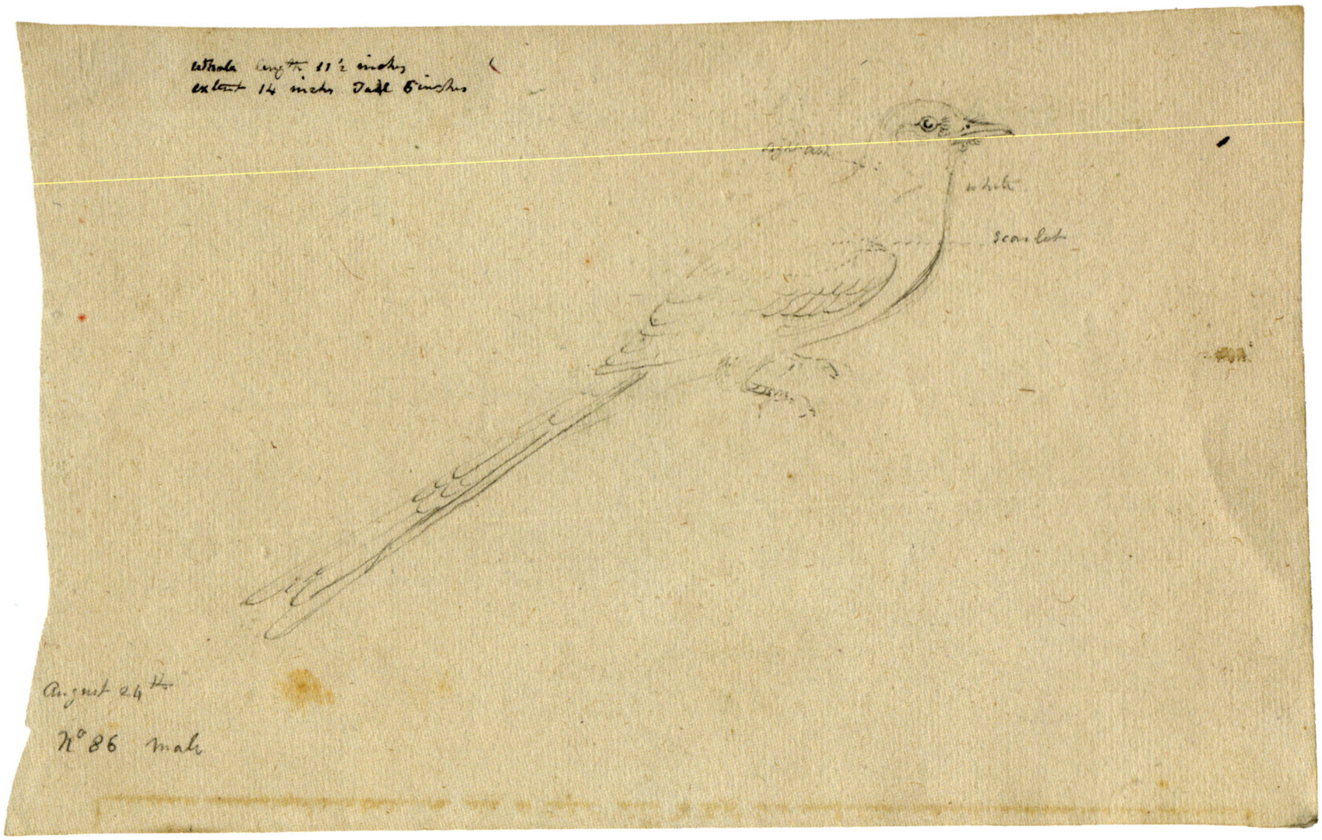

1.2. Titian Ramsay Peale, *Bird (unidentified)*, August 24, 1820. Ink on paper, 5 × 8¼ inches. American Philosophical Society, Philadelphia, Pennsylvania (APSimg5687)

Seymour. Long's party got lost searching for the origin of the Red River and ended up following the Canadian River east. On August 17, Long's party entered Indian Territory about thirty miles south-southeast of present-day Arnett, Oklahoma. That same day, Bell's party crossed from the north into Indian Territory about ten miles north of present-day Newkirk, Oklahoma. On September 13, the two groups rendezvoused at Fort Smith.[5]

During this two-year odyssey, Peale and Seymour produced hundreds of sketches, drawings, and watercolors of the people, places, and events they experienced.[6] Yet each artist spent less than a month, from August 17 through September 12, 1820, in present-day Oklahoma, and only one drawing, by Peale, can be definitively linked to this period. Peale did not identify the genus and species of the bird in his highly detailed drawing (figure 1.2), but it is easily identifiable as a scissor-tailed flycatcher, *Tyrannus forficatus*.[7] Peale's field notes indicate the specimen's length and coloration, as well as the date, August 24. The bird seems alive, perched on an unseen branch, as if it might launch skyward at any moment. The pose and detail aid in the illusion of life. In keeping with the practices of the day, however, Peale almost certainly killed and arranged the bird for study and reproduction.

The act of preparing *Bird* for display, for visual consumption, bears metaphorical similarity to the formation of Indian Territory itself. Shot, killed, stuffed, and manipulated to seem vibrant and alive, Peale's scissor-tailed flycatcher is presented without *context*—no foreground, no background, nothing to indicate the past or the future. *Bird* lives only in the present tense. Likewise, whatever Indian Territory was, and whatever it might become, what the artist-naturalist presents speaks only to the current situation. *Bird* is also emblematic of the larger motive behind the expedition—discovery. Looking, cataloging, drawing, and writing about the unknown conferred mastery over the unknown to the expedition members.[8] Their cataloging would in time lead early American settlers to view the Oklahoma plains as a bountiful promised land.

Catlin and Stanley

From Chaos to Order

More than a decade after the Long expedition, in 1834 the painter George Catlin arrived in Indian Territory. Catlin was disillusioned with the Indians in the east, who had generally lived among whites for generations and therefore did not meet the young artist's romantic notion of "real" Indians. Catlin wanted to meet, and to paint, "authentic" Indians not tainted by what he saw as corrupting white influences. Catlin, like so many of his contemporaries, was involved in salvage work; he tried to preserve, in paint and in text, what he saw as a dying race. That U.S. government policies were largely to blame for the disappearance of Indians and Indian culture was an irony largely lost on those like Catlin. The progress of the entire continent toward Western civilization was the only outcome most Americans could foresee.

During the 1830s, Catlin found his "real" Indians among the Osages and Comanches, and to a lesser extent, in the recently relocated Cherokees, Choctaws, and Creeks, in Indian Territory. Catlin arrived there in 1834, just as Indian removal and relocation efforts ratcheted into full effect. Catlin spent two months painting the likenesses of Creeks, Cherokees, Choctaws, and Osages at Fort Gibson. Later that summer, the artist traveled with the Dodge-Leavenworth expedition, accompanied by U.S. Dragoons under the command of General Henry Leavenworth, from Fort Gibson to the Wichita Mountains in southwestern Indian Territory to meet with Plains tribes, who were opposed to the government's resettlement policy and resentful of eastern Indians being moved into their territory. Disease struck the command before it reached its destination, however, incapacitating Leavenworth, Catlin, and about one third of the troops. Colonel Henry Dodge continued on and carried out the mission, but Catlin was too sick to go farther. Instead, Catlin's assistant Joe Chadwick accompanied Dodge and generated sketches from which Catlin later produced paintings of the Comanche and Wichita villages and other scenes as though he had been an eyewitness.

The views Catlin created of the region and its people, later widely exhibited and published, were the first to be made by any artist. Although he was in Indian Territory for just a few months, Catlin made, over the next six years, about 450 paintings based on his time there, and throughout his career, he created more than 1,000 works based on his encounters with Indians in the West. Taken together, Catlin's paintings made in or of Indian Territory form a vast and important archive, which can be divided into two broad categories. The first, and by far the largest, category consists of individual portraits of Indians. The second, much smaller category consists of images representing Indian lifeways or Indian interactions with the U.S. Dragoons in the summer of 1834. Both offer significant insight into a transitory time.

Catlin's portraits, at their best, show him to be a talented and sensitive artist. In *Ha-Tchoo-Tuck-Nee, the Snapping Turtle (Peter Pitchlynn)* (figure 1.3), the subject's active pose, elaborate dress, and realistic likeness animate the portrait with a spark of life. Snapping Turtle's asymmetrical body posture, crooked left arm and leg, cockeyed collar, disheveled coat, and freely drawn details of his costume give him an unmistakable immediacy not evident in earlier Indian portraits made by leading artists Charles Bird King or James Otto Lewis. The immediacy of the Snapping Turtle portrait reads like a snapshot. While ethnographic details, such as the Choctaw sash and headdress, are suggestive markers of traditional Indian culture, the sitter's western shirt and pants, short haircut, and purposeful off-center gaze lead back to his mixed-blood status. Snapping Turtle, also known as Peter Pitchlynn, was a graduate of the University of Nashville and had reluctantly relocated to Indian Territory. As one of Catlin's principal informants on the Choctaw Nation, Pitchlynn would both prosper and make a name for himself in the years that followed.[9] Placed before an abstract background and removed from chronology and geography, however, Catlin's finely rendered, humane portrait of the future Choctaw leader reads as a portrait of a man from two worlds, yet with no real home.

His-Oo-San-Chees, The Little Spaniard (figure 1.4) contrasts in significant ways with the portrait of Snapping Turtle. Little Spaniard stands, face turned to one side, holding a large shield, bow, and arrows in one hand, and a lance in his other hand. He wears a loincloth, leggings, moccasins, body paint, and little else. His accoutrements of war and his strongly built legs and torso confirm that Little Spaniard was a warrior. Here was Catlin's wild Indian. Unlike Snapping Turtle, Little Spaniard has been placed on firm ground in front of teepees. He is a fully human subject, engaged and engaging, who is nonetheless rendered in precise ethnographic details. Little Spaniard, a true "wild"

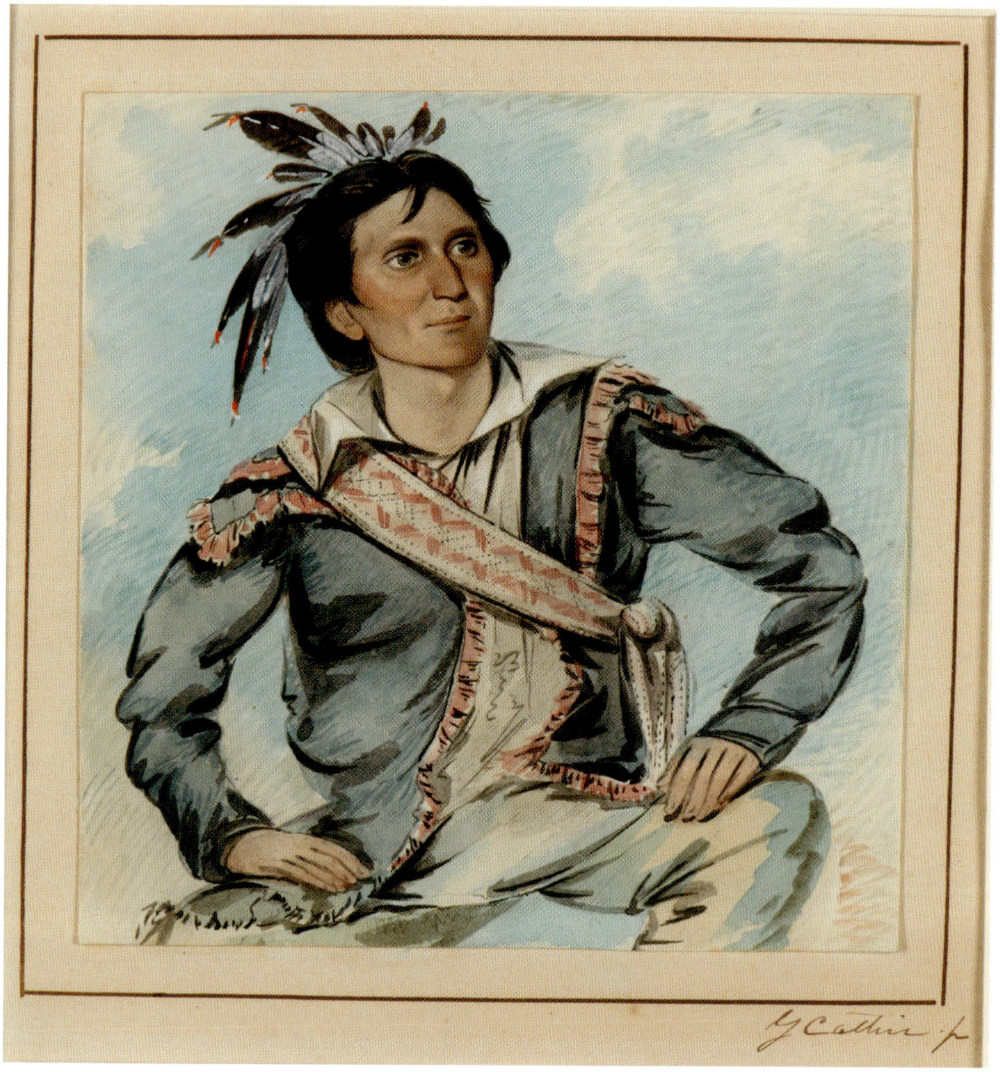

1.3. George Catlin, *Ha-Tchoo-Tuck-Nee, the Snapping Turtle (Peter Pitchlynn)*, 1836. Watercolor on paper, 19 ⅜ × 14 ⅜ inches. Gilcrease Museum, Tulsa, Oklahoma (0226.1573)

Comanche Indian, belongs, emphatically, to the place where he stands.[10] In contrast, Snapping Turtle has no such connectedness.

Painting by painting, Catlin reveals a portrait of an indigenous population thrown together—eastern Indian tribes, long acculturated to white ways, living in an uneasy tension with Plains tribes—Comanches, Kiowas, and Osages—who had experienced relatively less contact with Americans. The Comanches, particularly, had very little exposure to Americans until 1820. Although Catlin had been ill and did not witness the historic meeting between Comanches and Dragoons near present-day Fort Sill, his interpretation is based on the sketches of an assistant who was present. In *Comanche Warriors, with White Flag, Receiving the Dragoons* (figure 1.5), the left half of the composition is divided between a tall peak of the Wichita Mountains (background) and the undulating green expanse of the prairie (mid- and foreground). On the right, the mountains, characterized by a series of lower peaks, are visually equated with the

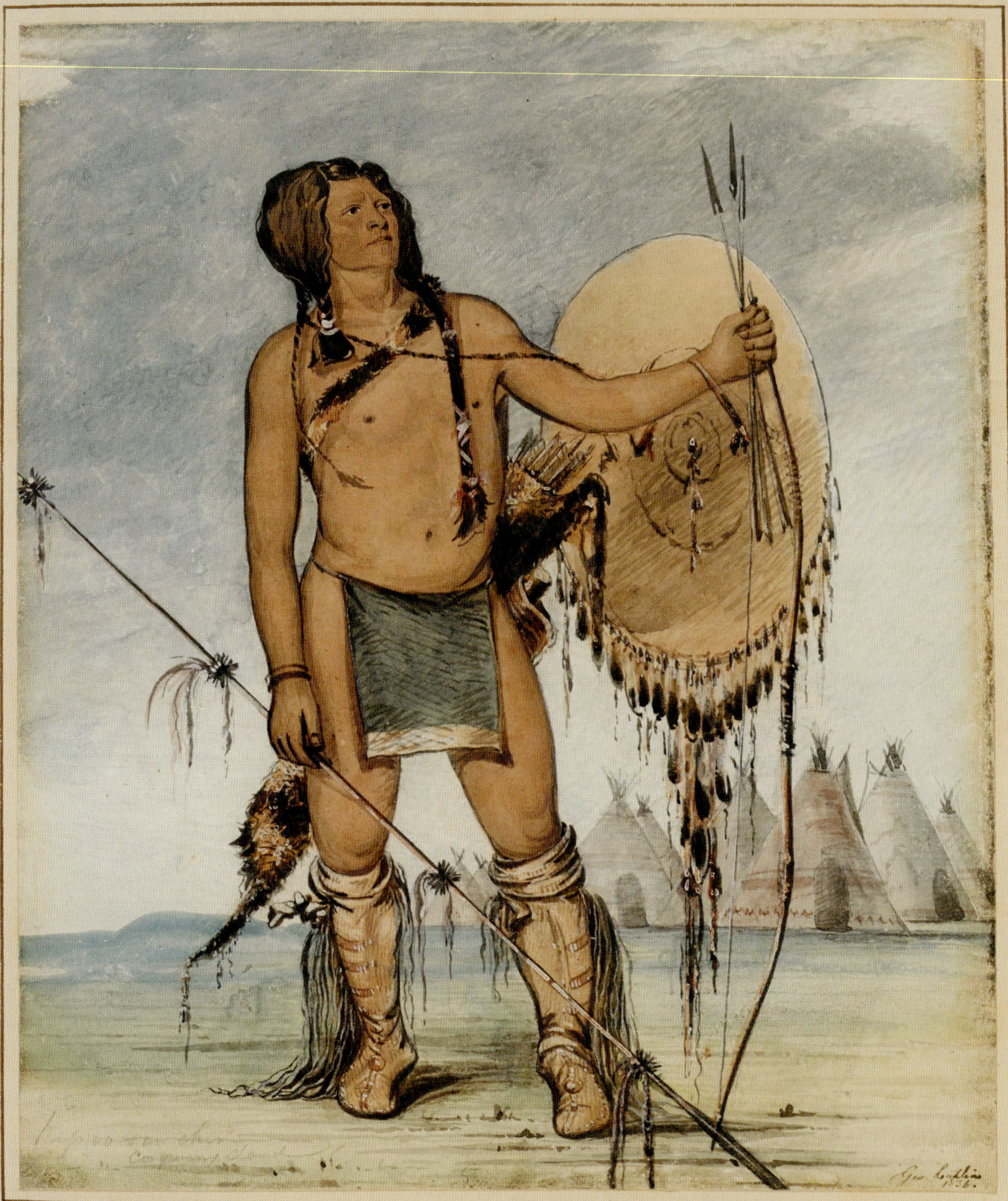

No 8.

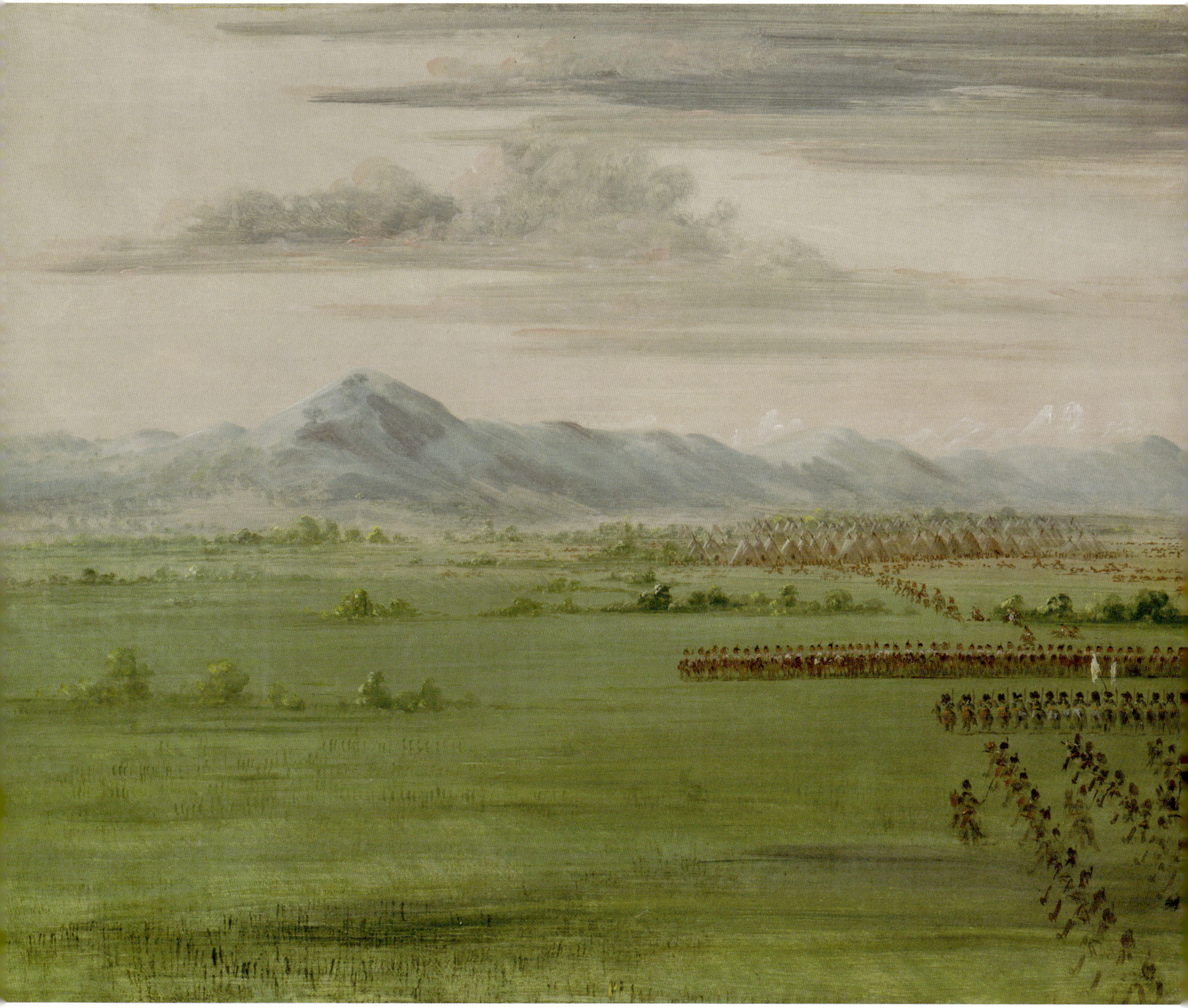

1.5. (Detail) George Catlin, *Comanche Warriors, with White Flag, Receiving the Dragoons*, 1834. Oil on canvas, 24 × 29 ⅛ inches. Smithsonian American Art Museum, Washington, D.C. Gift of Mrs. Joseph Harrison, Jr. (1985.66.353)

FACING

1.4. George Catlin, *His-Oo-San-Chees, The Little Spaniard*, 1836. Watercolor on paper, 10 × 8 ¼ inches. Gilcrease Museum, Tulsa, Oklahoma (0226.1534)

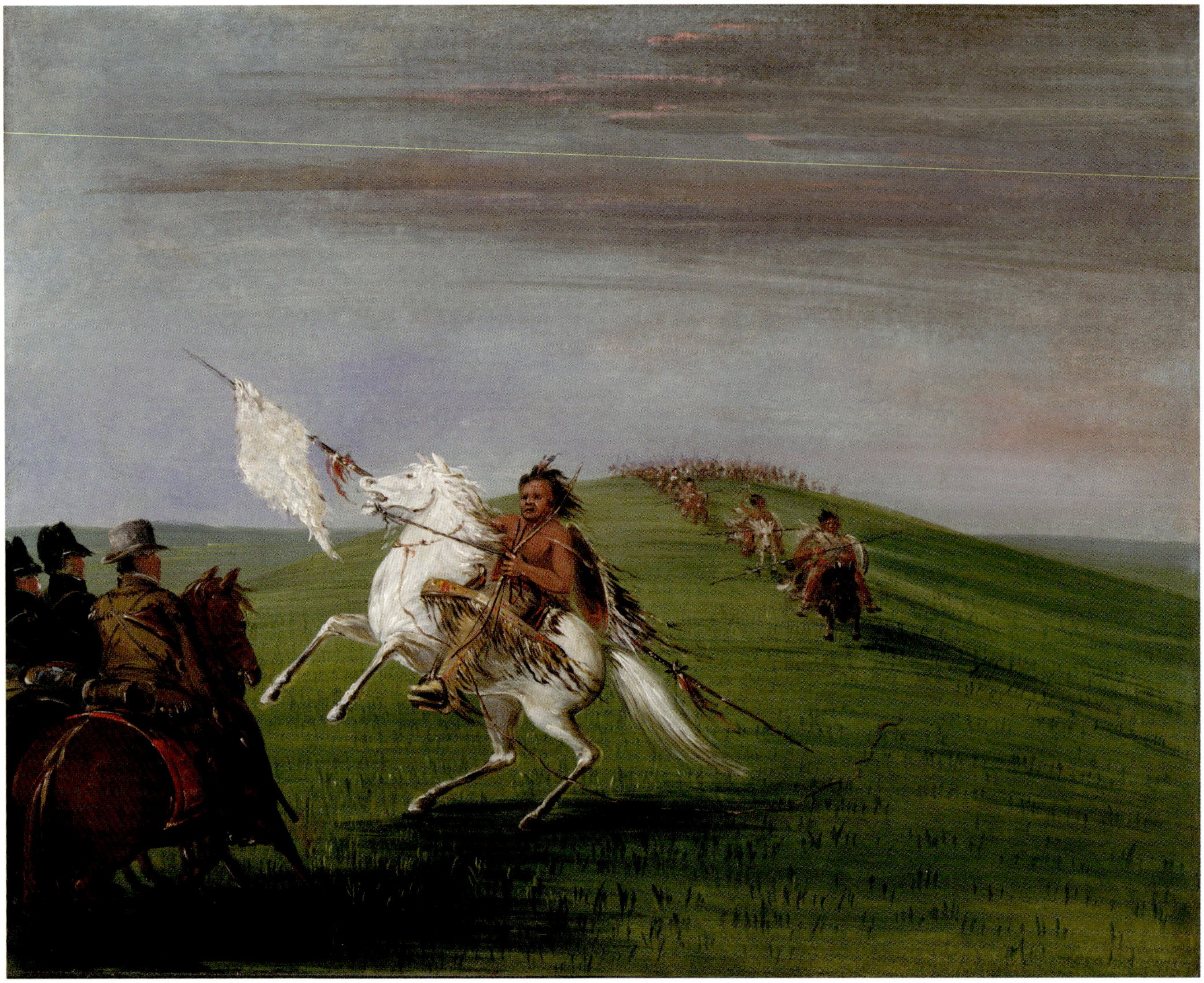

1.6. George Catlin, *Comanche Meeting the Dragoons*, 1834. Oil on canvas, 24 × 29 inches. Smithsonian American Art Museum, Washington, D.C. Gift of Mrs. Joseph Harrison, Jr. (1985.66.488)

teepees of a Comanche encampment. Comanche horsemen ride, fast and free, from a herd of wild horses toward the encampment. They join a single line of riders in the midground headed toward the Dragoons. Nearer the Dragoons, several Comanche riders break into a disorganized sprint toward the American cavalry. The Comanches race from their wild past (the horses) toward their uncertain future among Americans (the Dragoons).

The foreground is defined by the precise linear pattern made by the Dragoons marching in formation. The crisp lines and formal uniforms contrast with the Comanche riders and the soft undulations of the verdant prairie. Here, then, is a visual representation of two worlds colliding. In the second row of Dragoons, two soldiers hold out white flags. *Comanche Meeting the Dragoons* (figure 1.6) can be read as the second act of this drama. A Comanche horseman, Little Spaniard, is shown leading a charging line

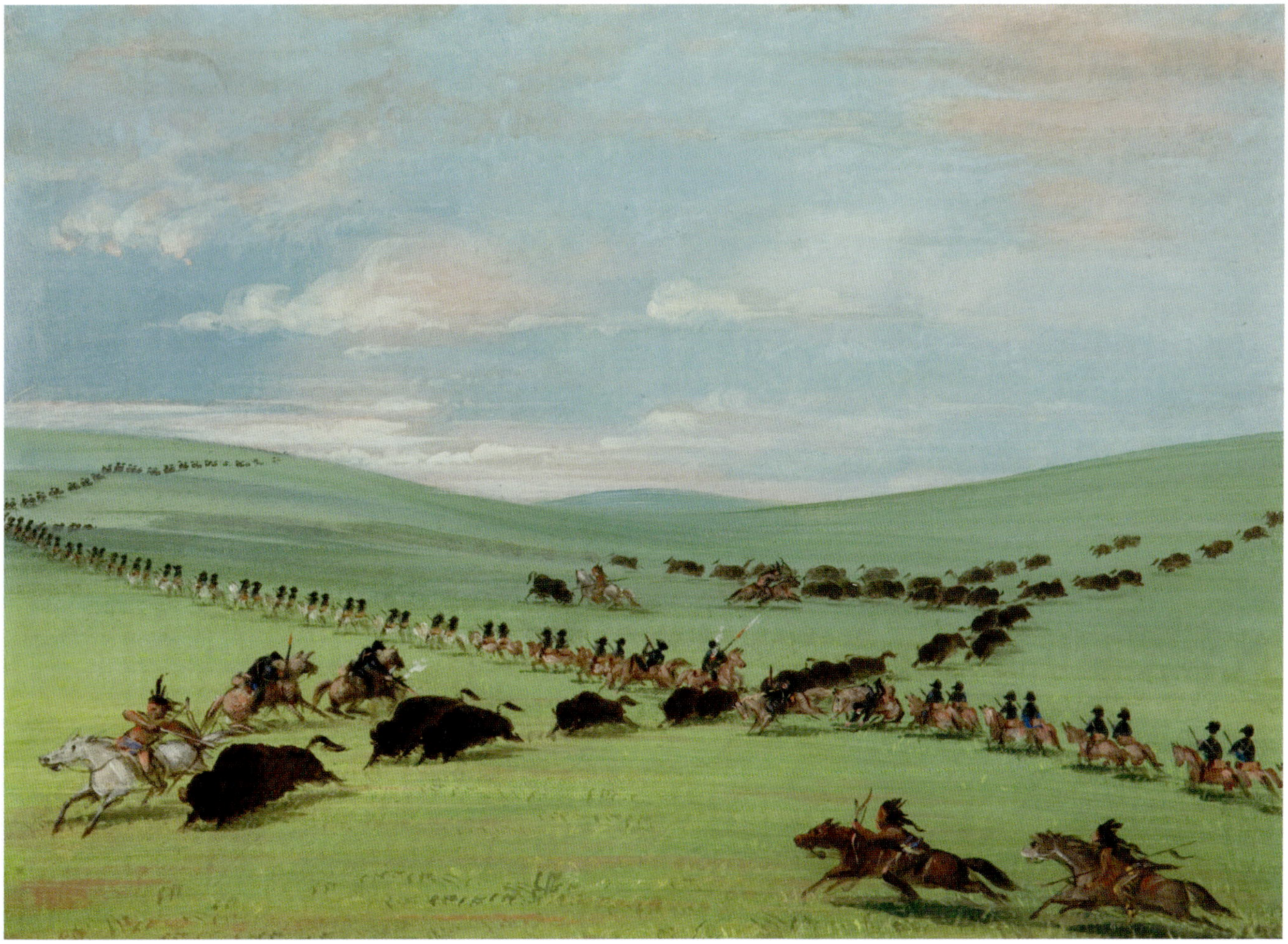

1.7. George Catlin, *The 1st Regiment of the United States Dragoons with Several Indian Hunters and Guides Meeting a Herd of Buffaloes in Texas,** 1852. Oil on canvas, 13¹³⁄₁₆ × 17 inches. Gilcrease Museum, Tulsa, Oklahoma (0176.2157)

*[Indian Territory]

of Indians. He rears up on his white horse; his barely controlled forward movement and exaggerated gestures are met with mild surprise in Catlin's group of three, emphasized by the backward movement of the Americans' horses. Catlin, positioned at the epicenter of the historic meeting, is closest to Little Spaniard, who proffers a white buffalo robe flag, confirming a peaceful encounter.

In *The 1st Regiment of the United States Dragoons* (figure 1.7), Catlin illustrates the Comanches as they chase buffalo through the column of Dragoons. The image conveys an uneasy humor colored by very real danger. On the one hand, Catlin offers the viewer a bit of fun, high jinks on the high plains. On the other, the Comanches, by breaking protocol and joining in the hunt, confirm how little the two sides really knew each other. Though long in contact and confrontation with the Spanish, the Comanches had had little contact with Americans. *The First Regiment of the U.S. Dragoons* is a visual

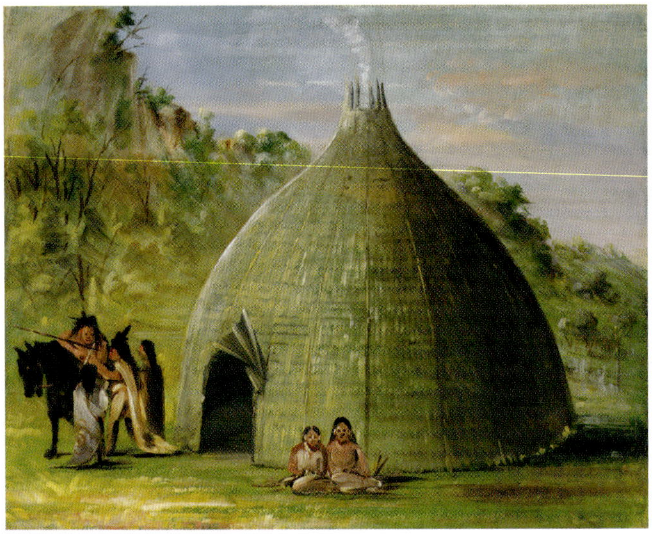

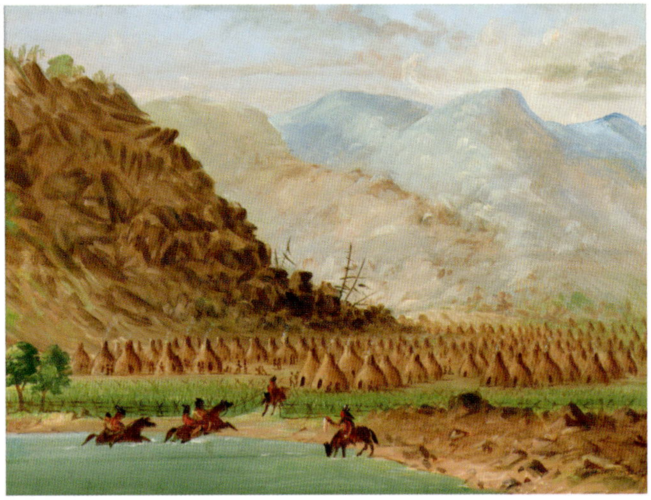

1.8. George Catlin, *Wichita Lodge, Thatched with Prairie Grass*, 1834. Oil on canvas, 24 × 29 inches. Smithsonian American Art Museum, Washington, D.C. Gift of Mrs. Joseph Harrison, Jr. (1985.66.492)

1.9. George Catlin, *Village of the Pawnee Picts, at the Base of the Rocky Mountains, Western Texas*,* 1852. Oil on canvas, 13½ × 17 inches. Gilcrease Museum, Tulsa, Oklahoma (0176.2124)

*[Indian Territory]

reminder of just how tenuous the situation was in Indian Territory in 1834. Considering the purpose of the meeting and the Comanches' animosity toward both eastern American Indians and their would-be foreign rulers, it is easy to read against the playful nature of the hunt and see instead a feint, a mock battle, and a contest of wills and lifestyles.

Catlin also produced ethnographic paintings of Indians at work and play. In *Wichita Lodge, Thatched with Prairie Grass* (figure 1.8), Catlin frames a typical thatched Wichita grass lodge against distant mountains. A familial vignette unfolds to the left. A warrior figure on horseback, either arriving or taking leave, is in conversation with figures on the ground next to the hut. Dead center, two small figures, perhaps children, look directly out from the picture, specimens captured by the artist's gaze. In *Village of the Pawnee Picts* (figure 1.9), Catlin captures a portrait of an entire Wichita village nestled at the base of the Wichita Mountains. Painted some years after his Indian Territory adventure, *Village of the Pawnee Picts* shows Catlin's loose, expressive brushwork building up the mountain. Indians on horseback ford a river near the village, where the inhabitants, unaware of them, go about their daily routines.

Far from "civilization," Catlin finds Indians worthy of study as objects of curiosity and difference. The paintings discussed above as well as other, similar paintings reveal less about the Indian villages pictured than about Catlin's intentions. Catlin had in mind creating and touring an Indian cabinet of pictures, from which he would make his fame and fortune. His success depended on the pictures showing difference between whites and Indians, so Catlin's images of "wild" Indians, who were almost unknown to eastern audiences, were essential to the positive reception of his cabinet. Yet Catlin, like others before and after him who made pictures of Indians, also recorded Indian lifeways, in paintings that have historical utility in and of themselves. *Tul-lock-ch'ísh-ko, He Who Drinks the Juice of the Stone, Choctaw* (figure 1.10) records the likeness of a great Choctaw ball player; *Ball Play* (figure 1.11) shows the game itself. A ceremonial version of warfare and a precursor to modern-day lacrosse, this ball game had been played by Native tribes for centuries throughout the east.[11] When the Choctaws moved west, they brought this important ritual game with them. Times were hard, but not everything changed for these eastern tribes stuck in Indian Territory. These paintings also show acculturation to be an uneven, nonlinear, messy process.

By the time John Mix Stanley traveled to Indian Territory in 1842, much had changed since Catlin's sojourn eight years earlier. Stanley arrived just a few years after the conclusion of the Cherokee Trail of Tears, a ruinous event in which two thousand to six thousand Cherokees had perished. During this time, all inhabitants of the territory—eastern transplants, western locals, and the U.S. military—were busy trying to make the best of a bad situation. For the eastern Natives, this meant trying to reestablish the government, commerce, educational system, and tribal customs they had been forced to give up during the great migration west. Stanley seems to have sensed his fortuitous timing, because he stayed in the territory, on and off, from 1842 to 1845, longer than any other non-Native artist before or after him. During his time there, Stanley set up a portrait studio at Fort Gibson; traveled twice to the Texas border to meet and paint Comanche, Seneca, and Delaware representatives; painted portraits of Cherokee principal chief John Ross and his family at Bayou Menard; and visited Creek settlements on the North Canadian River.

Yet his most important painting was completed in Tahlequah, in June 1843, where he attended a grand council of tribes called by Chief John Ross. There, Stanley painted *International Indian Council (Held at Tallequah [sic], Indian Territory, in 1843)* (figure 1.12). This was the first political painting made in Indian Territory since Catlin's Dragoon paintings a decade earlier. What was almost certainly a chaotic scene of hundreds of Indian delegates from more than a dozen tribes in a multitude of dress and poses crowded

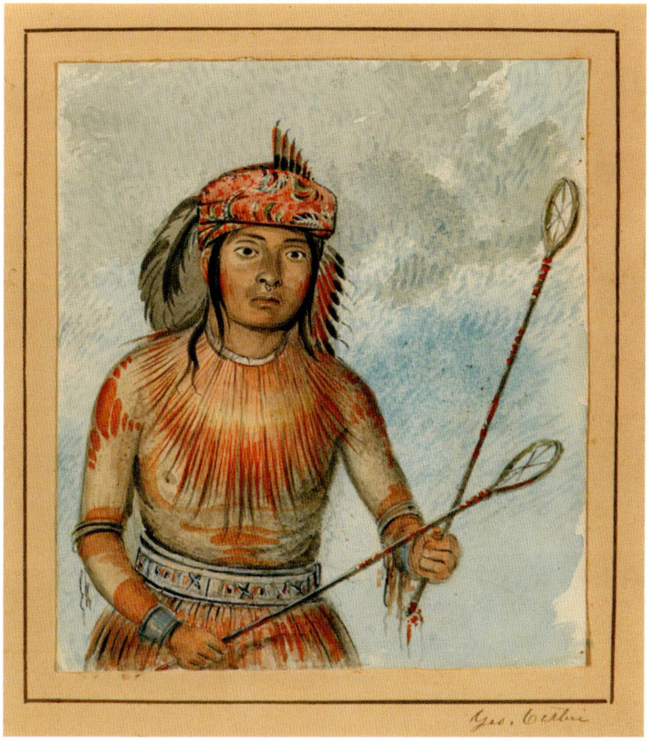

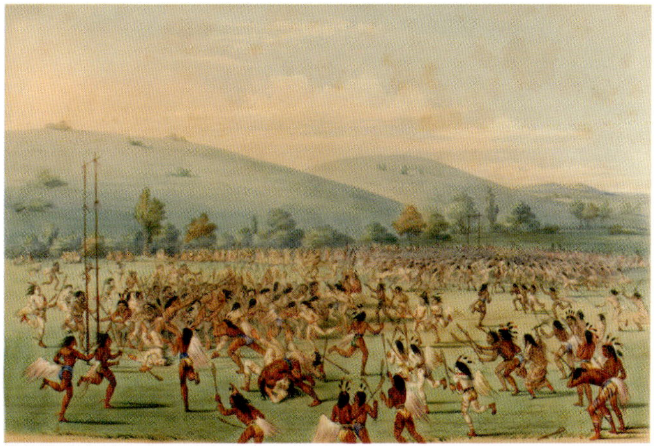

1.10. George Catlin, *Tul-lock-ch'ísh-ko, He Who Drinks the Juice of the Stone, Choctaw,* n.d. Watercolor on paper, 19⅜ × 14⅜ inches. Gilcrease Museum, Tulsa, Oklahoma (0226.1512)

1.11. George Catlin, *Ball Play,* 1841. *Plate 23 of George Catlin, North American Indian Portfolio,* 17½ × 23¾ inches. Gilcrease Museum, Tulsa, Oklahoma (4576.93.23)

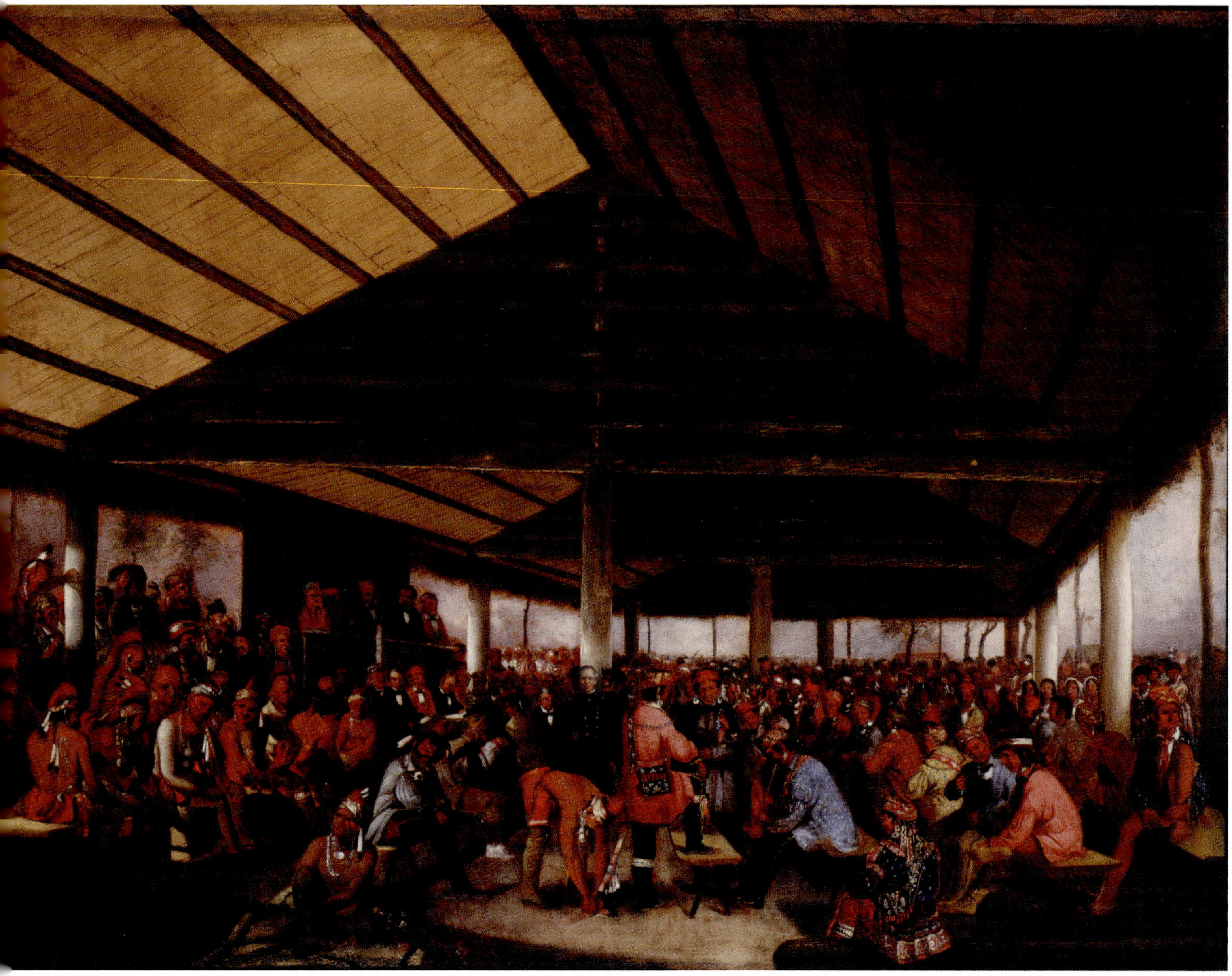

1.12. John Mix Stanley, *International Indian Council (Held at Tallequah [sic], Indian Territory, in 1843)*, 1843. Oil on canvas, 31 ½ × 40 ½ inches. Smithsonian American Art Museum, Washington, D.C. Gift of the Misses Henry (1985.66.248,934B)

into a small area is made orderly through Stanley's composition. The painting forces order from chaos and visually dovetails closely with the goals of the council's organizer, Chief John Ross. Stanley's painting records and comments on a contemporary historic event. Yet Stanley's ambition went further—he used visual devices borrowed from the Renaissance to expand the appeal of the painting beyond reportage and into the realm of history painting.

International Indian Council is organized by the roof of the shedlike structure that houses the council. The roof expands into the viewer's space, and allowing us to see into and through the open-air structure. The orthogonal lines of the roof provide the perfect organizational conceit—an inverted one-point linear-perspective scheme. Much as Luciano Laurana used street pavers in his *View of an Ideal City* (figure 1.13) to convey a

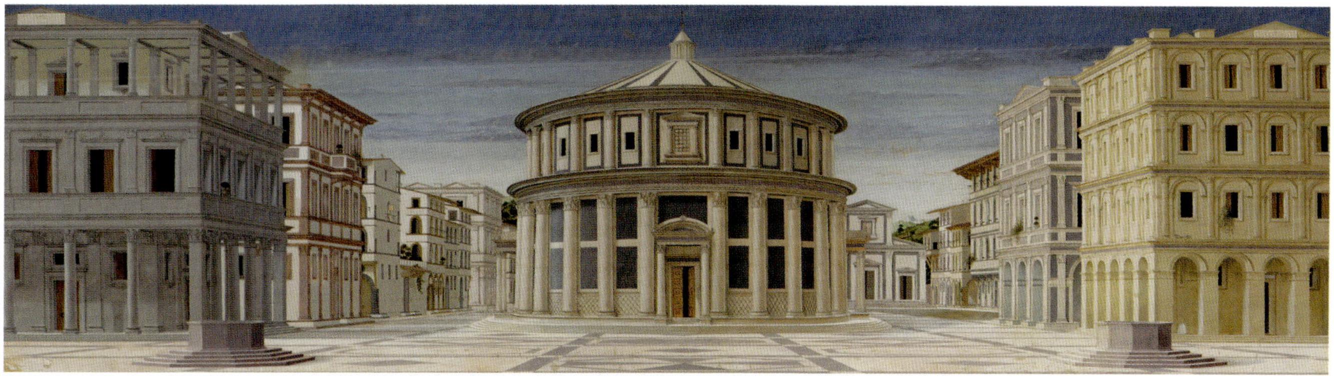

1.13. Attributed to Luciano Laurana, *View of an Ideal City, or The City of God*, after 1470. Oil on panel, 23½ × 78⁷⁄₁₀ inches. Galleria Nazionale delle Marche, Urbino, Italy. Photograph courtesy Bridgeman Images

sense of order and three-dimensional depth, Stanley used the orthogonals of the roof to similar effect. As the orthogonal roof lines converge toward a single vanishing point, the structure orders the space into foreground, midground, and background.

The space is further defined by three large bays supported by wooden posts. Each post terminates in triangular joists, or supports. While the orthogonal lines move the viewer's eye toward the distance, the vertical supports stop this movement. The vertical support closest to the picture plane splits the structure in two, breaking the space into left and right halves. Standing erect in front of the central vertical support post is General Zachary Taylor, a future hero of the Mexican-American War who would become president of the United States. John Ross, principal chief of the Cherokees and the man who called the grand council, sits directly to Taylor's left, his characteristic black coat and bow tie in evidence. Other attendees, mostly anonymous today, were clearly portraits made by Stanley and inserted into the complex scene. Portraits in the foreground give way to barely defined masses farther into the distance. By their dress, the Indians to the left represent western Plains Indians, while those on the right side represent eastern Indians. Taylor, the only American military or government official in evidence, is conspicuous by both his central location and his status as an outsider. His dress, demeanor, posture, position, and likeness mark him as the most important attendee. He stands erect at the center of the council and looks out toward the viewer. Ross echoes Taylor's direct gaze, yet he is seated, subordinate to Taylor. Overall, the painting reveals much about Ross's political aspirations and his goals for hosting the grand council. It even hints that Indian Territory might be emerging from the chaos caused by forced migrations. Even so, Taylor's presence underscores the tenuous nature of Indian self-governance and sovereignty.

When John Ross arrived in Indian Territory in 1839, having walked the Trail of Tears, he was greeted by several thousand Cherokee settlers who had been coerced to move west years earlier. They had been established in Indian Territory for more than a decade by this point, and they had their own leaders and their own ideas about how to move forward; few old settlers felt any allegiance to Ross.[12] Ross realized that his power was based in numbers; more than ten thousand Cherokees had arrived with him. The new arrivals, making up more than two-thirds of the Cherokee population and under the leadership of John Ross, set out to reestablish the legal, governmental, and social institutions they knew from their homelands in Georgia. Ross's efforts met repeatedly with challenges from the old settlers and tribal members who had supported the Treaty of New Echota in 1835. The murders of treaty adherents Major Ridge, his son John, and Elias Boudinot in 1839 had further divided the tribe. Against this tumultuous backdrop, Ross convened the grand council to publically demonstrate and consolidate his power.

At the same time, Ross was trying to avoid a war with the Osages and other established western tribes, attempting to establish law and order in a chaotic time, and combating disease and poverty among his people. He was also battling the U.S. government for the political and territorial future of his tribe and, more broadly, for Indians throughout the territory. Ross wanted to renegotiate treaties so that the Cherokees could receive more money. He also argued for the complete removal of U.S. military from all Indian lands.[13] Chief Ross understood that true sovereignty could not be achieved with a foreign military stationed throughout Indian Territory. In many respects, Stanley's painting dovetails with Ross's goals, so much so that it seems almost like propaganda. Yet Taylor's presence, and Ross's visual subjugation to Taylor, makes it clear what a difficult task lay ahead for the Indians in the territory. While *International Indian Council* presents an orderliness unthinkable during Catlin's visit, it also subtly undermines the progress to which it bears witness. Compared with Catlin's Dragoon paintings of the previous decade, however, Stanley's painting clearly shows that the tribes were trying to make life work in the territory.

Samuel Washington Woodhouse and Heinrich Balduin Möllhausen

A Naturalist, a Railroad Survey, and the Beginning of the End

In 1849–50, the surgeon-naturalist Samuel Washington Woodhouse accompanied the Creek Indian boundary survey led by Captain Lorenzo Sitgreave. While in Indian Territory, Woodhouse kept journals, collected natural flora and fauna samples, and made drawings of specimens as well as of significant landmarks. On August 14, 1849, Woodhouse drew *Home of the Cherokee, Elijah Hicks* (figure 1.14). Hicks was the brother-in-law of Cherokee principal chief John Ross, and thus was well-placed in the Cherokee hierarchy. Notwithstanding Hicks's societal standing, Woodhouse thought the house "an old shanty and in want of much repair." Indeed, most everyone in Indian

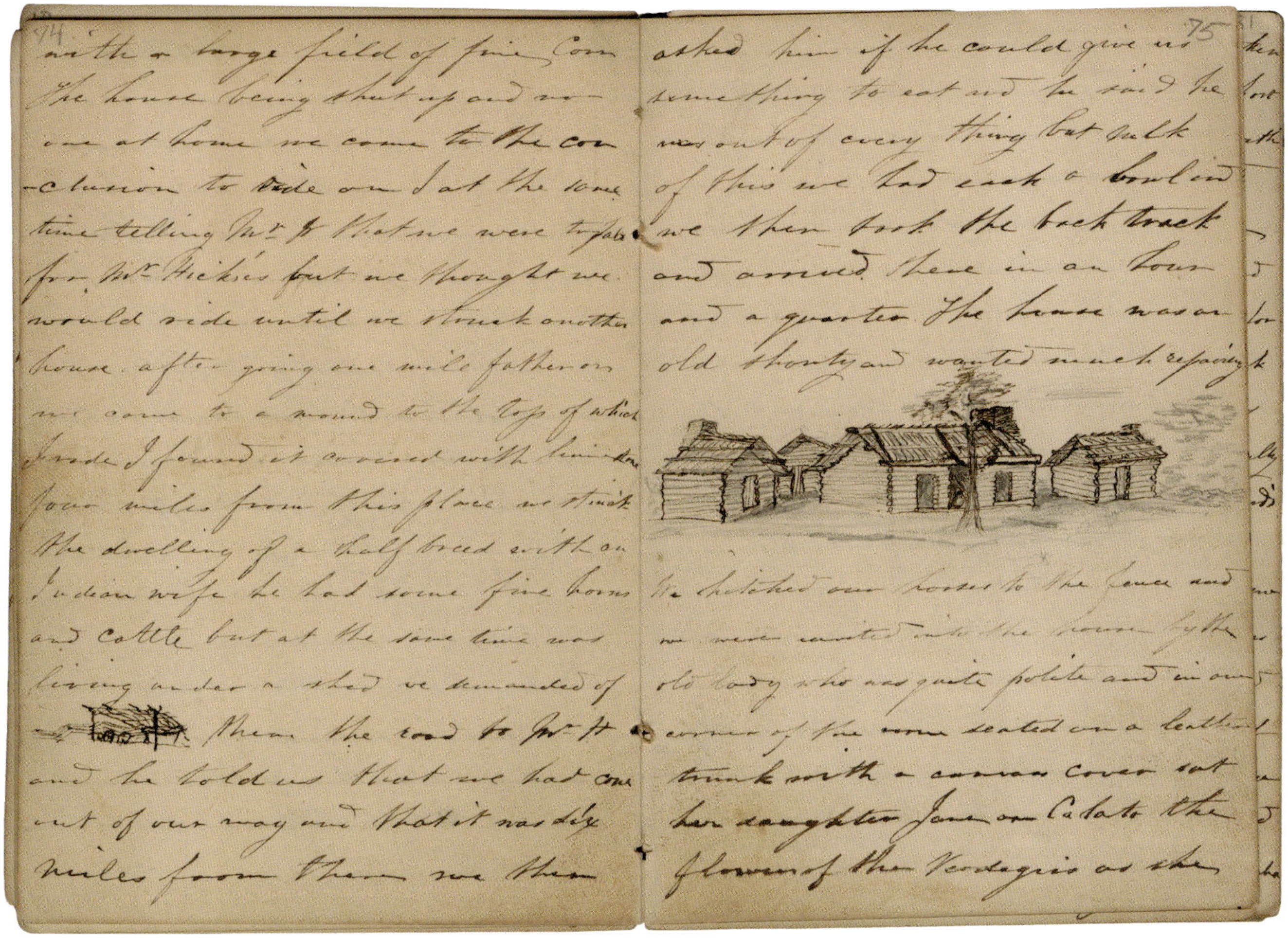

1.14. Samuel Washington Woodhouse, *Home of the Cherokee, Elijah Hicks*, 1849. Journal page, graphite on paper, 4 × 6 inches. Academy of Natural Sciences, Drexel University Archives Collection, Philadelphia, Pennsylvania (387)

Territory was poor by American standards. Woodhouse found a young lady at home, perhaps one of Hicks's daughters, and thought her "a perfect beauty, a lady," who, he opined, "did not look as if she belonged in such a cabin. She was dressed neatly."[14] In comparing Hicks's ramshackle house with his well-kept daughter, Woodhouse captured a central contradiction of life for postremoval Indians: the desire to succeed in their new land, despite their impoverishment, while holding fast to the accoutrements of the Americanized lifestyle they had grown accustomed to in the Southeast.

Woodhouse's other sketches note landmarks of interest. On August 22, 1849, near the Cross Timbers in central Oklahoma, Woodhouse discovered "some curious looking hills which I found to contain great quantities of gypsum" (figure 1.15). About a month later, on September 15, west of Tallassee (an archaic name for Tulsa), the naturalist sketched limestone outcrops, known collectively as Lost City, on the Arkansas River. In his journal, he described his impressions of the limestone structure: "It presented a strange appearance, looking at a short distance like an old fortification and when you

1.15. Samuel Washington Woodhouse, *Gypsum Hills Near the Cross Timbers*, c. 1849. Journal page, graphite on paper, 4 × 6 inches. Academy of Natural Sciences, Drexel University Archive Collection, Philadelphia, Pennsylvania (387)

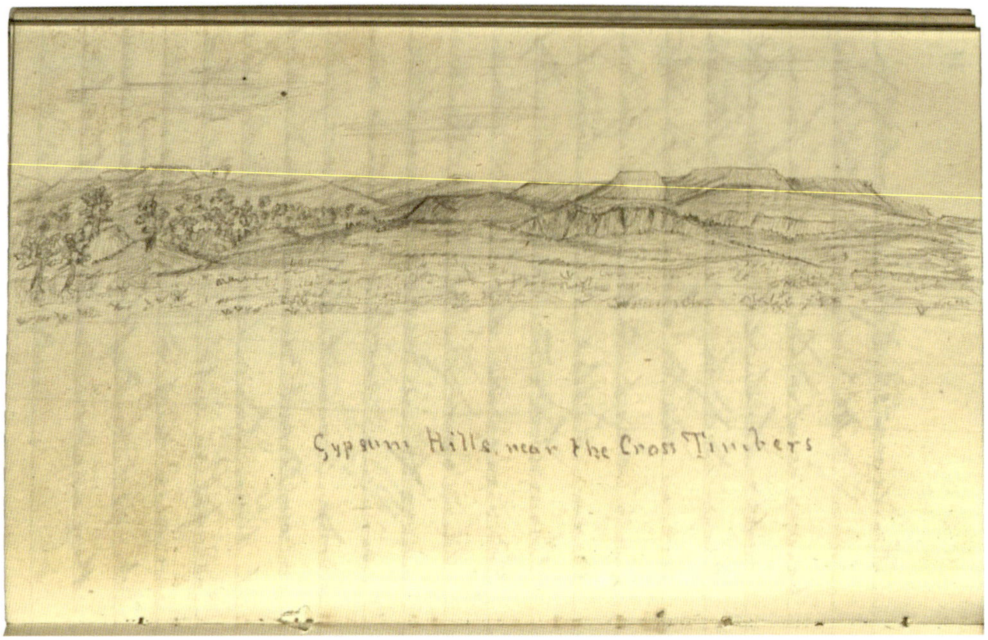

got near they looked as though they had been raised up out of the earth."[15] Woodhouse was trained, as all naturalists are, to note the odd, the useful, and the picturesque in an uncharted land. His drawings were few and personal, and thus only a minor contribution to the visual archive of pre-1860 Indian Territory. The next artist to follow Woodhouse, however, would have a far bigger impact.

Born in 1825 in Germany, Heinrich Balduin Möllhausen traveled to the United States in 1849. In 1853, he was appointed, at the recommendation of famed German naturalist Alexander von Humboldt, to be a draftsman and topographer on First Lieutenant Amiel W. Whipple's transcontinental railroad survey along the 35th Parallel. From Fort Smith, Arkansas, the Whipple party traveled westward across Indian Territory, Texas, New Mexico, Arizona, and California. Of the drawings Möllhausen produced while in Indian Territory, about half are individual portraits of Indians he encountered, while the other half are landmarks, geological formations, or flora he found to be of interest. Generally, Möllhausen's reductive, linear style is less suited to portraiture; as a group, his portraits are far less interesting and informative than the landscapes, particularly in comparison with Catlin's rich examples.

In sympathy with the purposes and goals of the expedition, Möllhausen's style and sensibilities were better suited for depicting land and geology. One such illustration, *Ring's Farm, Camp No. 1* (figure 1.16), shows the Whipple expedition's first camp after entering the Indian Territory from Fort Smith. Möllhausen demonstrates a keen ability to distill visual information down to a few salient points. The farmhouse, shown nearly parallel to the picture plane, fills the center of the drawing. Doors, windows, and even

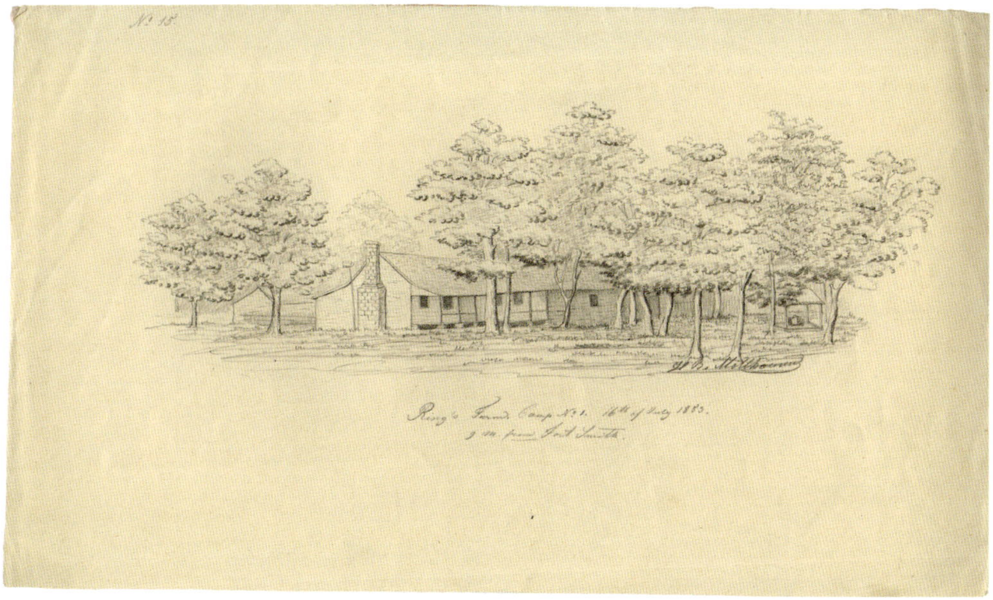

1.16. Heinrich B. Möllhausen, *Ring's Farm, Camp No. 1, 9 Miles from Fort Smith*, July 16, 1853. Graphite on paper, 8 × 14 inches. Oklahoma Historical Society, Oklahoma City, Oklahoma (1982_091_20_022_9256.OD15)

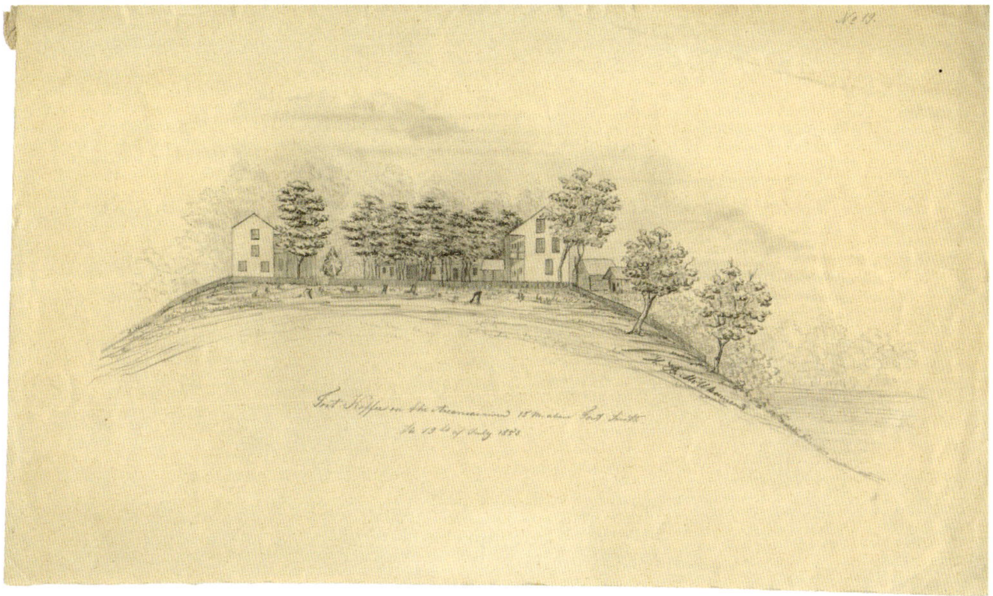

1.17. Heinrich B. Möllhausen, *Fort Koffee* [Coffee] *on the Arkansas River 15 Miles Above Fort Smith*, July 19, 1853. Graphite on paper, 9 × 14 inches. Oklahoma Historical Society, Oklahoma City, Oklahoma (1982_091_20_027_9256.OD19)

the chimney are meticulously rendered, as are the full trees that dot the flat land. Möllhausen provides a detailed portrait of a place that might be of tactical use to future expeditions. Similarly, his visual description of Fort Coffee (figure 1.17) conveys key features meant to differentiate the fort from the surrounding landscape. The background, minimal in *Ring's Farm*, is here nonexistent. Instead, Möllhausen focuses on the curvature of the hill, perhaps exaggerated, which identifies the location. The scene is about land, available resources, and defensibility. Even though by 1853, Fort Coffee had been converted into the Choctaw Boys School, the fort was still seen as a strategic and

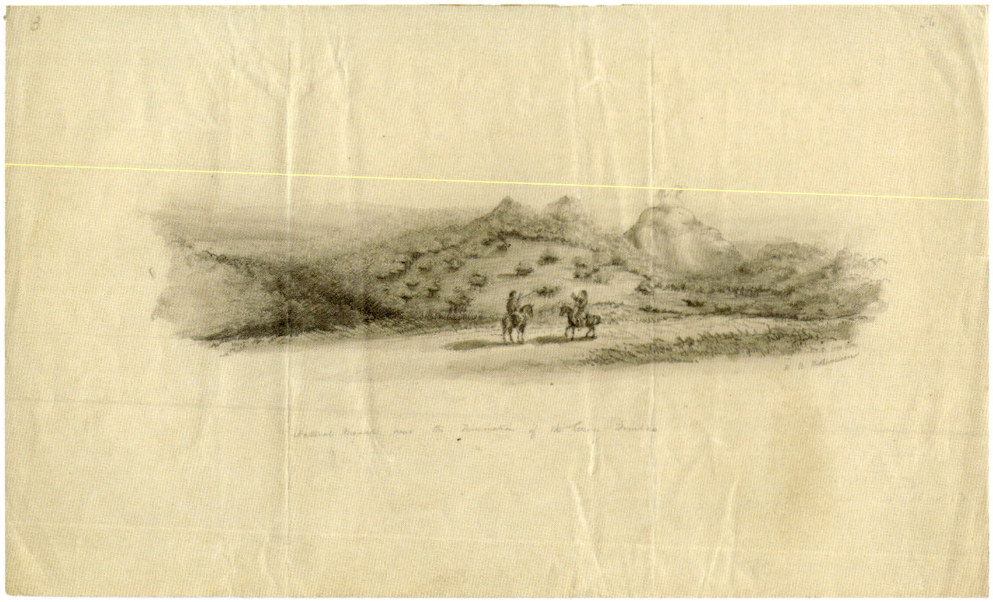

1.18. Heinrich B. Möllhausen, *Natural Mound Near the Termination of the Cross Timbers (Rock Mary)*, 1853. Graphite on paper, 9 × 14 inches. Oklahoma Historical Society, Oklahoma City, Oklahoma (1982_091_20_031_9256.OD36)

practical, rather than romantic, subject matter choice. Not surprisingly, during the Civil War, Confederate soldiers occupied the old fort.

Many of Möllhausen's drawings are the pragmatic output of an explorer surveying the land for suitable railroad passage. His drawing of Rock Mary (figure 1.18) provides a profile of the landmark made famous by Lieutenant James H. Simpson, who accompanied Captain R. B. Marcy in escorting settlers west, toward California, in 1849. Simpson was struck by a set of oddly unique rock formations on the plain west of present-day Oklahoma City. Upon discovery of one particular fascinating rock formation, he notes, "the novel character of the hill; its contorted appearance; its sudden emergence from the plain around it; my having reached its pinnacle; it being an object of interest to beholders in the distance;—all this had its complex influence upon me, and I felt correspondingly elated."[16] At the suggestion of Captain Marcy, Simpson planted an American flag on top of the rocky outcropping. Someone else in their party then suggested he name his find after Mary Conway, governor of Arkansas and cousin of President James Madison. "Rock Mary, then, is the name of this fantastic formation—at least until it can be authenticated that some prior explorer had assumed the prerogative to call it something else." Simpson goes on for some time in his journal describing Rock Mary, "situated solitarily in a prairie plain; its height some sixty feet; its base some two hundred feet in diameter. In form it is like a pound-cake well puffed up and partially broken at its centre. Two turret-like projections are seen protruding from its top."[17]

Simpson's description was so good that Lt. Whipple used it to find the formation on his travels: "Have travelled to-day nineteen miles, passing 'Rock Mary' and other mounds accurately described by Simpson and others."[18] Möllhausen's drawing echoes and adds to Simpson's description. In the foreground, two travelers on horseback greet each other, face to face, in front of the oddly shaped landmark. The trail they follow is well worn, and their postures and hand gestures are that of a friendly rendezvous. The central mound has only sparse grass until the top of the incline. The top of the central mound terminates into two peaks. The smaller mound to the right is grassless and tops off in a strange gnarled formation.

Simpson's description and Möllhausen's drawing suggest much about the nature of their missions and the fate of Indian Territory. In 1848, gold was discovered in California, prompting the famous Gold Rush of 1849. Simpson's task—securing passage for a group of American settlers traveling the arduous overland route to California—was a symptom of this larger push westward. Just a few years later, the Whipple expedition was traveling through Indian Territory looking for a potential route to build a transcontinental railroad that would link East to West. Möllhausen's drawing of Rock Mary takes for granted that Indian Territory would, at some point, be breached by settlers and subsequently be absorbed into the United States. The drawing features two travelers, headed in opposite directions, meeting in the middle, a visual portent of the coming connection of the country by railroad. The drawing of Rock Mary was created as a strategic reference point more than as a picturesque point of interest. From the point of view of the U.S. government, if not the American public, the question was when, not if, Indian Territory would be folded into the larger continental aspirations of the young nation. The fact that the government ultimately chose another transcontinental route hardly matters; by 1872, a branch of the regional Missouri-Kansas-Texas (MKT) rail line (the Katy line) spanned the territory north and south, from Chetopa, Kansas, to Denison, Texas.

The War before the Storm

Möllhausen was the last nonnative artist of any merit or distinction to make images of Indian Territory before the start of the Civil War in 1861. A few drawings were made on the eve of the Civil War by military draftsmen in the forts of southern Indian Territory and northern Texas. Used as illustrations for an article published in the March 16, 1861, issue of *Harpers Weekly*, detailing the loss of Fort Davis (Texas) and Forts Arbuckle and Washita (Indian Territory) to Confederate forces (figure 1.19), the reductive topographical line drawings echo Möllhausen's minimalist approach to landscape-and-architecture vignettes.

The text of the article retells how the forts were surrendered to the Confederates by General David E. Twiggs, commander of the Texas region and Southern sympathizer.

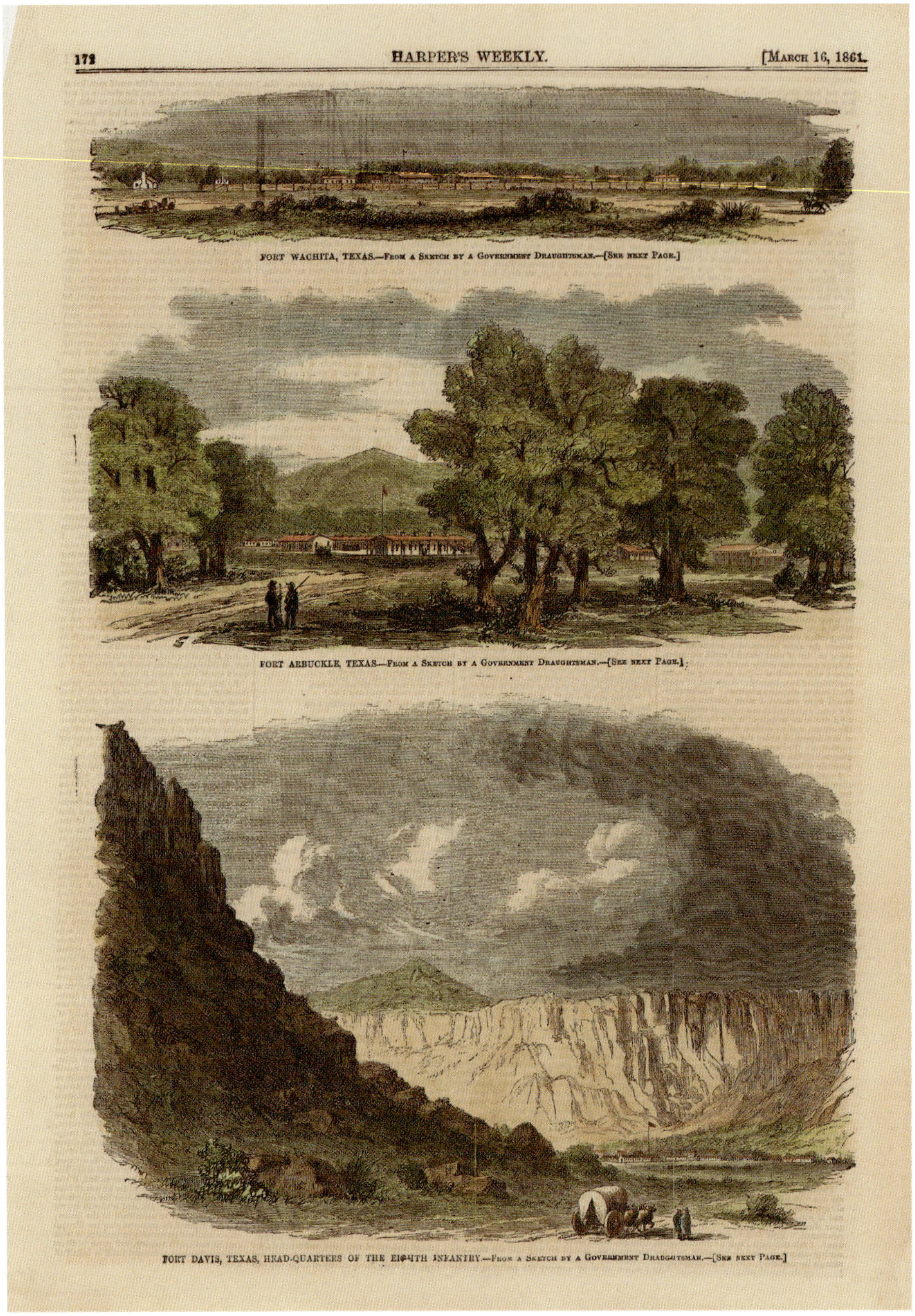
172 HARPER'S WEEKLY. [March 16, 1861.

FORT WACHITA, TEXAS.—From a Sketch by a Government Draughtsman.—[See next Page.]

FORT ARBUCKLE, TEXAS.—From a Sketch by a Government Draughtsman.—[See next Page.]

FORT DAVIS, TEXAS, HEAD-QUARTERS OF THE EIGHTH INFANTRY.—From a Sketch by a Government Draughtsman.—[See next Page.]

1.19. Unknown government draftsmen, *Fort Wachita, Texas* [Fort Washita, Indian Territory], *Fort Arbuckle, Texas*, and *Fort Davis, Texas, Head-quarters of the Eighth Infantry*, in *Harper's Weekly* 5, no. 220 (March 16, 1861): 172. Color added. Oklahoma Historical Society, Oklahoma City, Oklahoma (21563.PE.HW.61.3.16)

The strategic significance of the Union's loss of the forts is the central theme of the article; the engravings serve as little more than illustrations. Like these military forts, Indian Territory was temporary, built of military strife, hastily thrown together, and ultimately ceded to hostile forces. Although Indian Territory would survive for another forty years after the Civil War, the repercussions of the railroad and the war tore holes in the territory too wide to heal.

Notes

1. Mary Louise Pratt, *Imperial Eyes: Travel Writing and Transculturation*, 2nd ed. (London: Routledge, 2008), 8.
2. Thomas Nuttall, *A Journal of Travels into the Arkansas Territory during the Year 1819* (Philadelphia, Pa.: T. H. Palmer, 1821). The title of Nuttall's book can be confusing for contemporary readers. In 1819, most of present-day Oklahoma became part of Arkansas Territory. Between 1824 and 1828, this land mass separated from Arkansas Territory and reverted back to Indian Territory.
3. William V. Lombardi, review of *A Journal of Travels into the Arkansas Territory during the Year 1819*, by Thomas Nuttall, *Interdisciplinary Studies in Literature and Environment* 20, no. 1 (Winter 2013): 195–96.
4. Nuttall, *Journal of Travels*, 144–45.
5. See John R. Bell, *The Journal of Captain John R. Bell, Official Journalist for the Stephen H. Long Expedition to the Rocky Mountains, 1820*, vol. 6 of The Far West and the Rockies Historical Series, ed. Harlan M. Fuller and LeRoy R. Hafen (Glendale, Calif.: A. H. Clark, 1957); and Edwin James, comp., *Account of an Expedition from Pittsburgh to the Rocky Mountains, Performed in the Years 1819 and 20 by Order of The Hon. J. C. Calhoun, Sec'y. of War, Under the Command of Major Stephen H. Long*, vols. 14–17 of *Early Western Travels*, ed. Reuben G. Thwaites (Cleveland, Ohio: A. H. Clark, 1905).
6. For an excellent analysis of many surviving images, see Kenneth Haltman, *Looking Close and Seeing Far: Samuel Seymour, Titian Ramsay Peale, and the Art of the Long Expedition, 1818–1823* (University Park: Pennsylvania State University Press, 2008).
7. Peale did not identify the bird by common name either. My thanks to Sydney Peck and Brian Cross, who independently confirmed the bird's species. The scissor-tailed flycatcher is the state bird of Oklahoma.
8. David Spurr, *The Rhetoric of Empire: Colonial Discourse in Journalism, Travel Writing, and Imperial Administration* (Durham, N.C.: Duke University Press, 1993), 16–27.
9. For an extended biography of Peter Pitchlynn, see Joan Carpenter Troccoli, *First Artist of the West: George Catlin Paintings and Watercolors* (Tulsa, Okla.: Gilcrease Museum, 1993), 124–25.
10. Catlin's phonetic rendering of the Little Spaniard's name, Jesus Sanchez, suggests that Sanchez may have been a Mexican captive raised as a Comanche.
11. Thomas Vennum, *American Indian Lacrosse: Little Brother of War* (Baltimore, Md.: Johns Hopkins University Press, 2007).
12. For an account of the political differences between Cherokee factions at this time, see Tim Garrison, "Pan-Nationalism as a Crisis Management Strategy: John Ross and the Tahlequah Conference of 1843," in *Between Indigenous and Settler Governance*, ed. Lisa Ford, Tim Rowse, and Anna Yeatman (London: Routledge, 2012), 48–59, esp. 49–50.
13. Ibid., 49–50.
14. John S. Tomer and Michael Brodhead, eds., *A Naturalist in Indian Territory: The Journals of S. W. Woodhouse, 1849–50* (Norman: University of Oklahoma Press, 1992), 131.
15. Ibid., 132.
16. "Rock Mary Report," *Chronicle of Oklahoma* 38 (Summer 1960): 130, 132, http://digital.library.okstate.edu/Chronicles/v038/v038p130.pdf.
17. Ibid., 132.
18. Ibid.

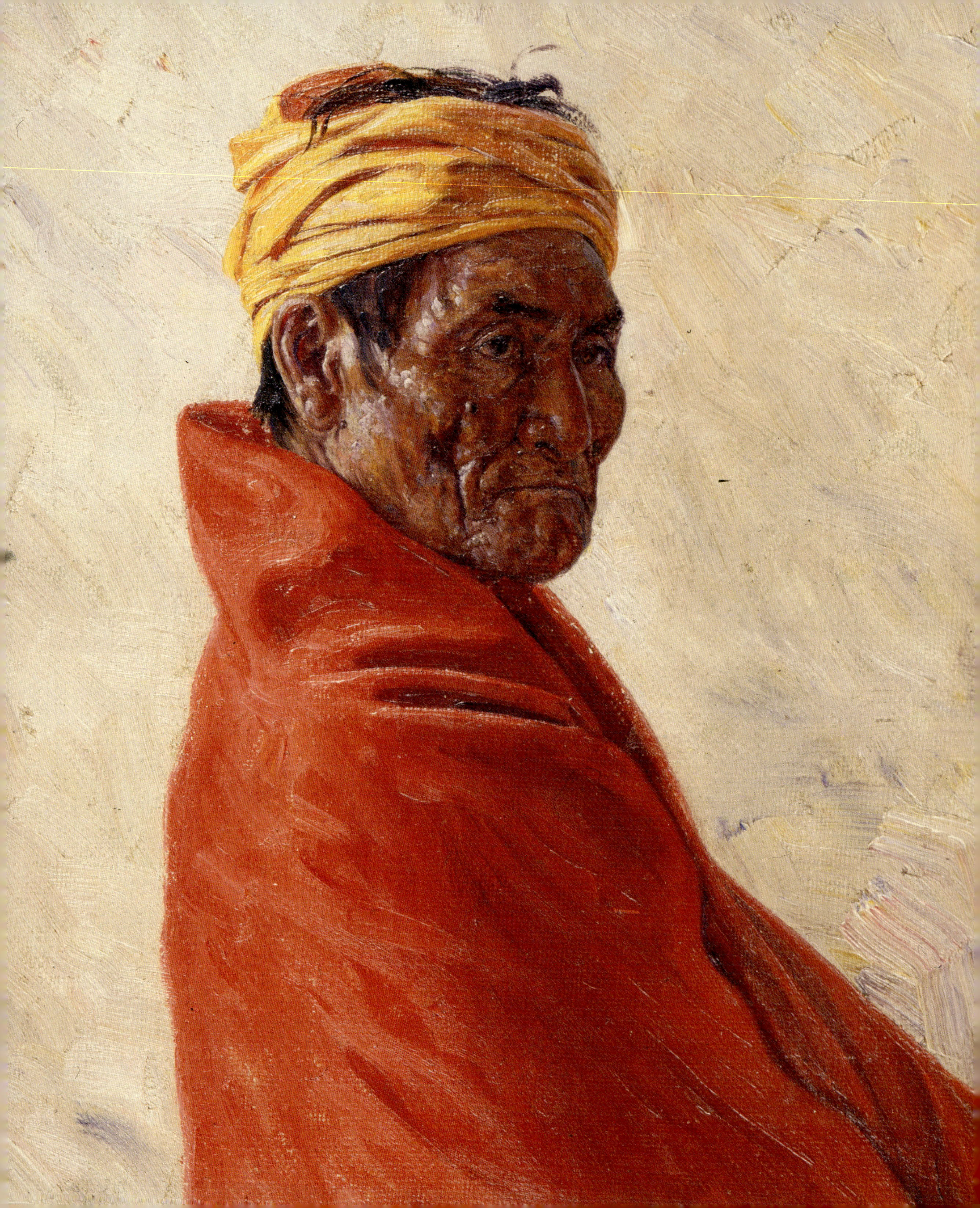

2 INDIAN TERRITORY, 1861–1907

Turmoil and Transition

B. BYRON PRICE

In the quarter century before the Civil War, a handful of Euro-American artists visually defined the region west of the Mississippi River that was set aside for Indian tribes displaced from their ancestral lands by the U.S. government in the 1830s. The colorful ethnographic portraits and genre scenes that compose the "Indian Galleries" of artists George Catlin and John Mix Stanley portrayed Indian Territory as a wilderness filled with a noble and vanishing race of savages. Although neither of these image makers possessed superior training or technical ability and never offered viewers more than selective glimpses of the land and its new residents, through energy and entrepreneurship, their pictorial vision of the area gradually spread throughout the United States and Europe.

During the same period, explorer-artists such as Samuel Washington Woodhouse and Heinrich Balduin Möllhausen, working with teams of government surveyors, portrayed the region's flora, fauna, and geology. Their efforts, too, were piecemeal at best, never approaching a comprehensive scientific understanding of the region. Nevertheless, the romanticism and spirit of discovery that characterized their work stirred the imaginations of early nineteenth-century Americans.

The onset of the Civil War in 1861 brought a brief hiatus to visual depiction of Indian Territory by professional artists. Confederate authorities seized control of federal military installations in the district without bloodshed and signed treaties of alliance with each of the Five Tribes and with several smaller Indian nations, despite considerable pro-Union sentiment among them. For much of the war, this remote area was of little strategic value to either side and was the scene of scant fighting.

FACING
(Detail) Elbridge Ayer Burbank, *Chief Geronimo; Apache (Chiricahua) (Fort Sill, O.T.)*, 1899. Oil on canvas, 13 × 9 inches. The Butler Institute of American Art, Youngstown, Ohio (912-O-582)

2.1. James R. O'Neill, *The War in Arkansas, the Battle of Honey Springs, July 17, 1863*, in *Frank Leslie's Illustrated Newspaper*, August 29, 1863, 364. Oklahoma Historical Society, Oklahoma City, Oklahoma (20655-63-364)

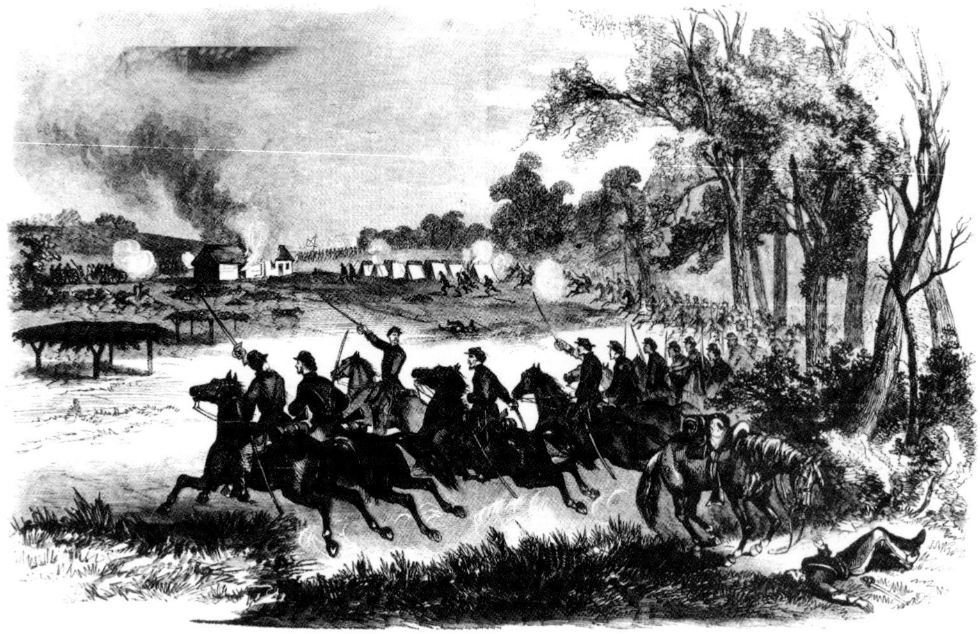

In early 1863, however, Union troops under the command of General James Blunt had recaptured Fort Gibson, near Tahlequah, hoping to use the post as a springboard to retake the entire region. On July 17, in an effort to secure their supply line, federal forces attacked Confederates at nearby Honey Springs. Fort Leavenworth, Kansas, resident James O'Neill (1833–1863), an Irish-born actor and sometime artist-correspondent for *Frank Leslie's Illustrated Newspaper*, witnessed the action. A woodcut derived from his drawing of a Union cavalry charge on the rebel camp during the battle, filled a double-page spread in the August 29 issue of the popular publication (figure 2.1). It would be the sole artistic representation of Indian Territory published during the Civil War. Unfortunately, the illustration's caption mislocated the engagement as occurring in Arkansas.[1]

The image itself likely stretched the truth as well. Blunt's cavalry fought dismounted during most of the engagement and does not appear to have conducted a mass saber assault of the sort portrayed in O'Neill's drawing. Nor did the illustrator's spirited representation of the largest Civil War battle fought in Indian Territory reflect the predominance of American Indian and African American units involved.[2]

In the wake of the fight at Honey Springs, O'Neill remained with Blunt's Army of the Frontier, filling his sketchbook with military imagery. The artist was killed, however, on October 6, 1863, by Confederate irregulars led by Colonel William C. Quantrill at Baxter Springs, Kansas, near the Cherokee Strip. He would be the only fatality among the more than three hundred artist-correspondents who covered the Civil War for *Leslie's Illustrated* and its competitors.

The end of the Civil War and the reestablishment of federal control brought momentous changes to Indian Territory. Peace treaties signed with the U.S. government in 1866 cost Indian slaveholders their human property and deprived the Five Tribes the western half of their lands. In addition to surrendering some of their autonomy and independence to the U.S. government, these tribes were also forced to cede the right-of-way for two railroads through their holdings.

The lawlessness and unceasing agitation over white settlement on unassigned Indian lands, which accompanied these developments, grabbed national attention, as did the hostilities that developed over the U.S. government's efforts to confine nomadic Native tribes on reservations in western Indian Territory.[3]

In late 1865, *Harper's Weekly* dispatched a Bostonian, Theodore A. Davis (1840–1894), to cover the U.S. Army campaign to subdue the Arapaho and Southern Cheyenne people. During the Civil War, Davis had become one of the newspaper's most reliable artist-correspondents. He was wounded twice while covering the Vicksburg Campaign and Sherman's famed March to the Sea.[4]

Between 1865 and 1867, he made three trips to the southern Great Plains. On his last and longest visit to the area, the "special artist" spent four months covering General Winfield Scott Hancock's unsuccessful punitive expedition against the Cheyenne tribe in Kansas and Indian Territory. Although Davis witnessed little actual bloodshed, his illustrations sensationalized events in the region and consistently portrayed Indians as brutal savages. They also burnished the image of Civil War hero Lieutenant Colonel George Armstrong Custer, as yet untested as an Indian fighter.[5]

Davis continued to illustrate news reports in Harper's publications into the 1870s, though never from firsthand experience. In December 1868, for example, he rendered several drawings of events surrounding Custer's successful November 27 attack on Cheyenne and Arapaho camps on the Washita River, in northwestern Indian Territory. These works portrayed the army's snow-impeded trek to the battleground, the early morning assault on Chief Black Kettle's unsuspecting village (figure 2.2), and the plight of the more than fifty women and children taken prisoner during and after the engagement. Subsequent issues of *Harper's Weekly* carried similarly imagined depictions by Davis of U.S. troops killing "worthless" Indian horses, and Custer's Osage Indian scouts celebrating the victory.[6]

Not to be outdone, *Leslie's Illustrated*, the principal competitor of *Harper's Weekly*, on January 9, 1869, carried Custer's own account of the Washita fight, under the

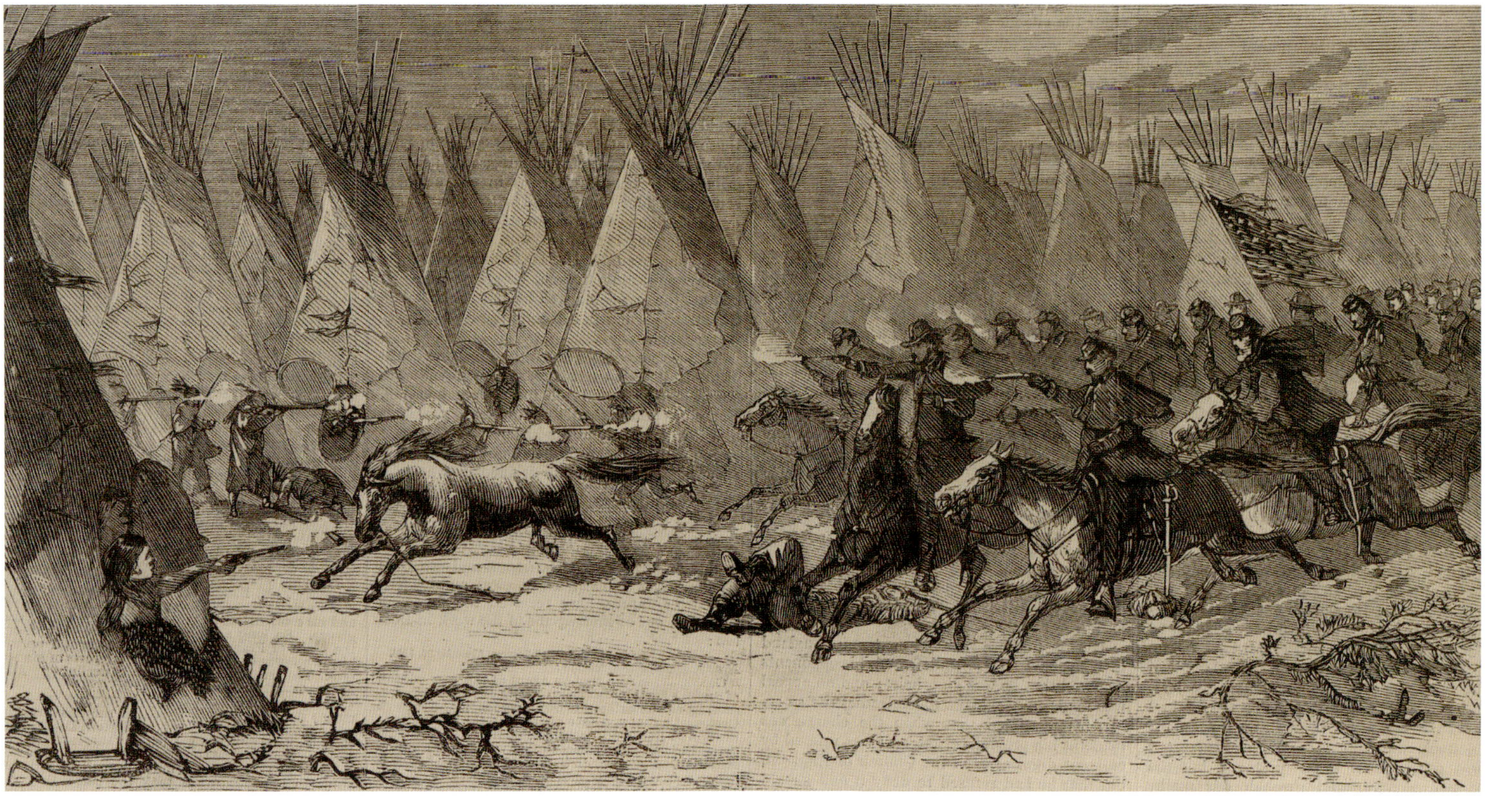

2.2. Theodore A. Davis, *The Seventh U.S. Cavalry Charging into Black Kettle's Village at Daylight, November 27, 1868*, *Harper's Weekly* 12, no. 625 (December 19, 1868): 804. University of Oklahoma Libraries, Norman, Oklahoma

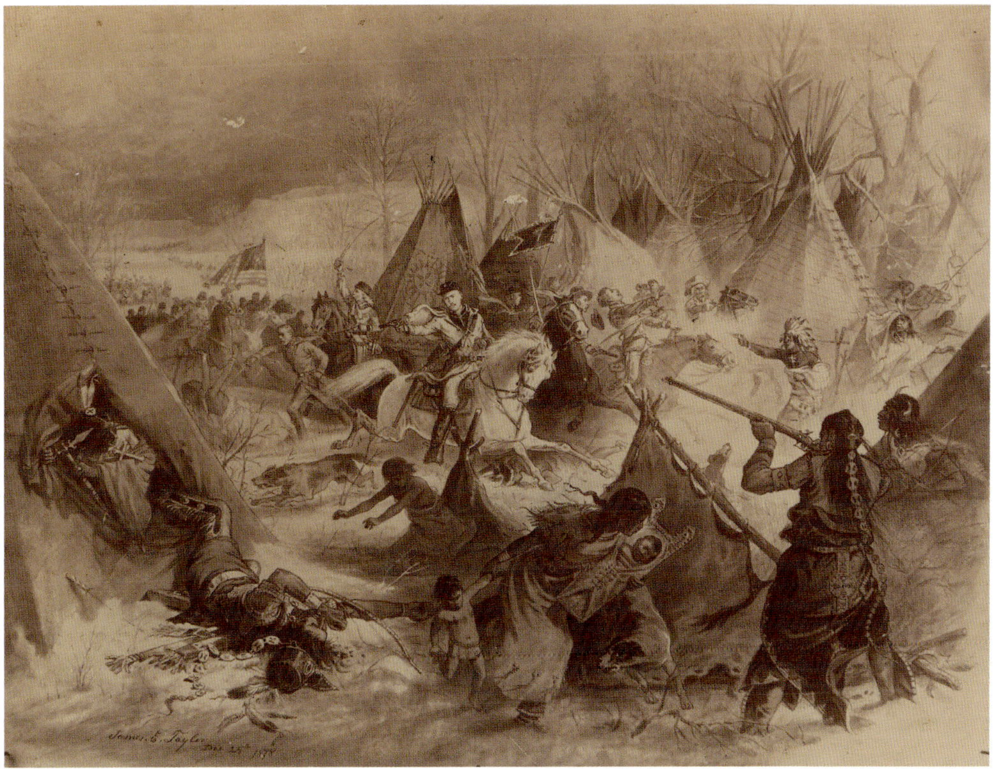

2.3. James E. Taylor, *Battle of Washita, Nov. 27, 1868*, 1878. Photoprint of painting, 9 × 12 inches. National Anthropological Archives, Smithsonian Institution, Washington, D.C. (MS 4605 01604407)

sensational title "Vengeance on the Trail," with an accompanying illustration of the action by an unnamed artist. In contrast to Davis's bird's-eye view of the cavalry's surprise assault on Black Kettle's village, *Leslie's* image pictured hand-to-hand combat at close quarters, with Custer in the center of the action.[7]

In the four decades that followed, Custer's attack at the Washita inspired a host of visual interpretations. Alfred Kappes (1850–1894) contributed one of the first, portraying the opening moments of the attack from inside Black Kettle's camp, for Custer's 1874 memoir, *My Life on the Plains*.[8]

James E. Taylor (1839–1901), a Civil War veteran and special artist for *Leslie's*, rendered two scenes of the battle in the early 1870s, both of them eventually published in Colonel Richard I. Dodge's popular book, *Our Wild Indians: Thirty-three Years' Personal Experience among the Red Men of the Great West*, in 1882. Taylor's *Battle of Washita* (1878; figure 2.3), set during the cavalry assault on Black Kettle's village, placed the artist's brother, Richard, a cavalry trooper in the engagement, center stage on a white horse. To his left rear, George Armstrong Custer urges his troops on, and to his right ride scout Moses E. "California Joe" Milner and Captain Louis M. Hamilton, who, mortally wounded, reels in the saddle.[9]

Taylor's other Washita image lionized the death of Sergeant Major Walter Kennedy (figure 2.4), who had been killed by the enemy after becoming separated from Custer's

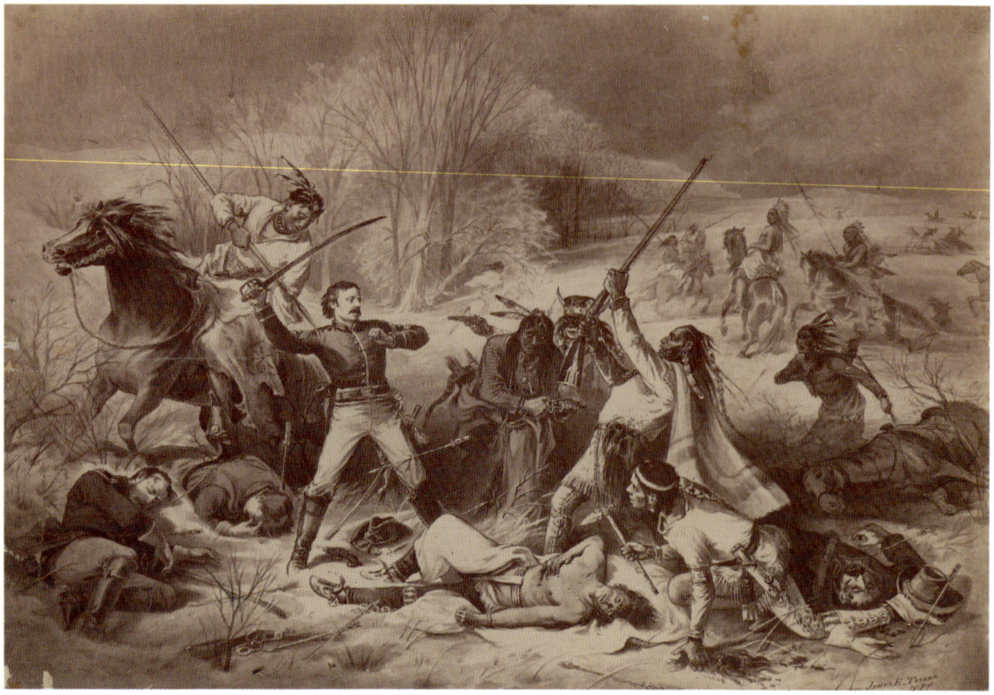

2.4. James E. Taylor, *Heroic Death of Walter Kennedy*, 1874. Engraving, 9 × 13 inches. National Anthropological Archives, Smithsonian Institution, Washington, D.C. (SPC BAE 4605 01602401)

main force. Although only Indians witnessed Kennedy's fate, and a doctor's subsequent examination of wounds on the noncom's body suggested otherwise, the artist chose to portray his subject, saber aloft, in a heroic stand against impossible odds.[10]

Visual interpretations of the battle continued to appear in schoolbooks, memoirs, and easel paintings into the twentieth century. Frederic Remington's 1889 rendition of Custer's charge in Edward Eggleston's *The Household History of the United States for Young Americans*, for example, placed the viewer at ground level, directly in front of the charging column of troops as it swept through Black Kettle's camp. The scene only hinted at the horrific slaughter under way but left no doubt as to the event's tragic outcome.[11]

On April 10, 1869, a little more than four months after the Battle of the Washita, President Ulysses S. Grant appointed a Board of Indian Commissioners to advise the government on Indian policy and to ensure the fulfillment of treaty obligations to Native nations. Among the men of "intelligence and philanthropy"[12] selected for this post was the New York artist and advocate Vincent Colyer (1825–1888), who, as a member of the United States Indian Commission of New York, was already in Indian Territory on an inspection tour of Native tribes of the southwestern United States.[13]

An associate member of the National Academy of Design, Colyer, was not the first easel painter to enter the region following the Civil War. That honor belonged to Worthington Whittredge (1820–1910), who in 1866 hurriedly traveled the Santa Fe

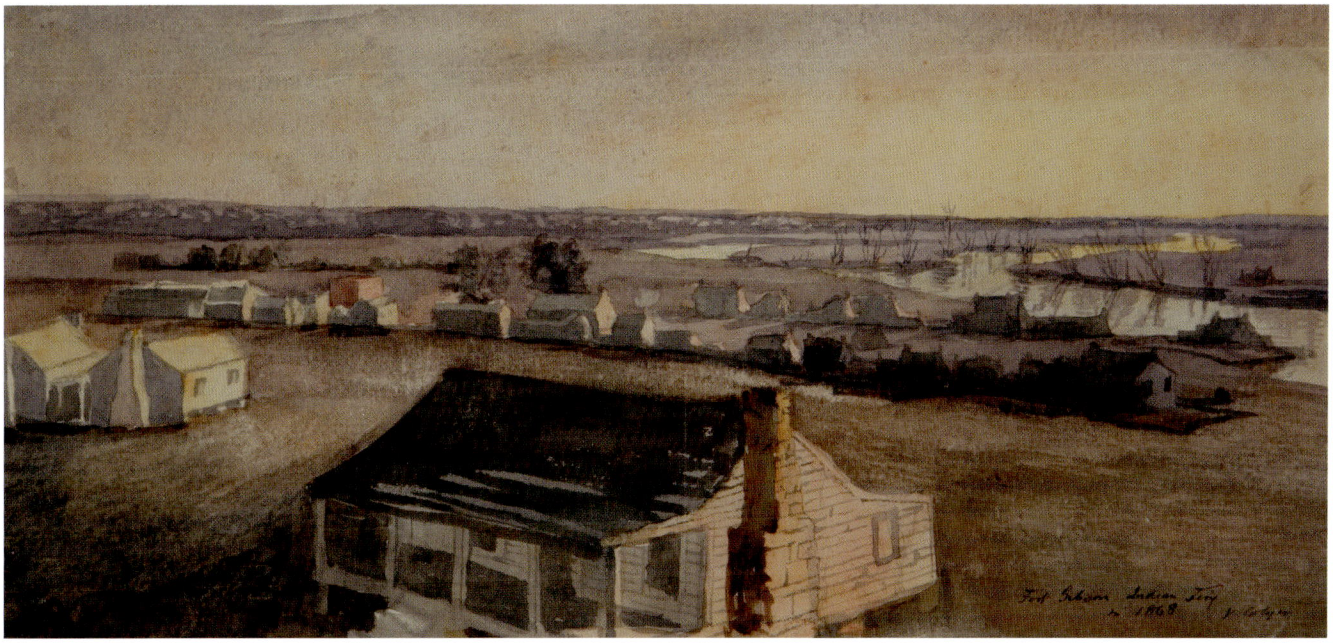

2.5. Vincent Colyer, *Fort Gibson Indian Territory in 1868*, 1868. Watercolor on paper, 5 × 10¼ inches. Gilcrease Museum, Tulsa, Oklahoma (0226.1378)

Trail's Cimarron Cuttoff, a sixty-mile stretch through what would become the Okahoma Panhandle. Whittredge, however, left no visual or written account of what he saw.[14]

Colyer arrived in eastern Indian Territory from Kansas in early March 1869. Delayed for several days at Fort Gibson by heavy rains, on March 11 he rendered a sketch of the old post (figure 2.5), one of many such small watercolor renderings he would complete during his tour, though his motive for doing so is unclear. The artist's published report of his journey, while replete with vivid and detailed observations, contains no illustrations, and he does not appear to have used any of the sketches as references for later easel paintings.[15]

Traveling southwestward through lands owned by the Five Tribes, Colyer arrived on March 29 at the Wichita Agency, where he found Cheyenne, Arapaho, Kiowa, Comanche, and Apache bands encamped. "How I wish," he later reported, "a Horace Vernet had been there to fix upon canvas the superb pictures of Indian life around us."[16] Although Colyer was no Vernet, he made numerous quick sketches of subjects of interest, and on the morning of April 9, he recorded more than one image of tribesmen arriving to parley with U.S. government officials (figure 2.6). As he later recalled, "They came in groups of two or three, and as most of them were attired in gay colors with shining ornaments, and all are superb riders, they made a most picturesque scene. I kept my pencil busily at work all morning, interrupted occasionally by the curiosity of the squaws and papooses, looking over my shoulder. They manifested great interest in what I was doing, and with mingled expressions of wonder and delight called each other's attention to it."[17]

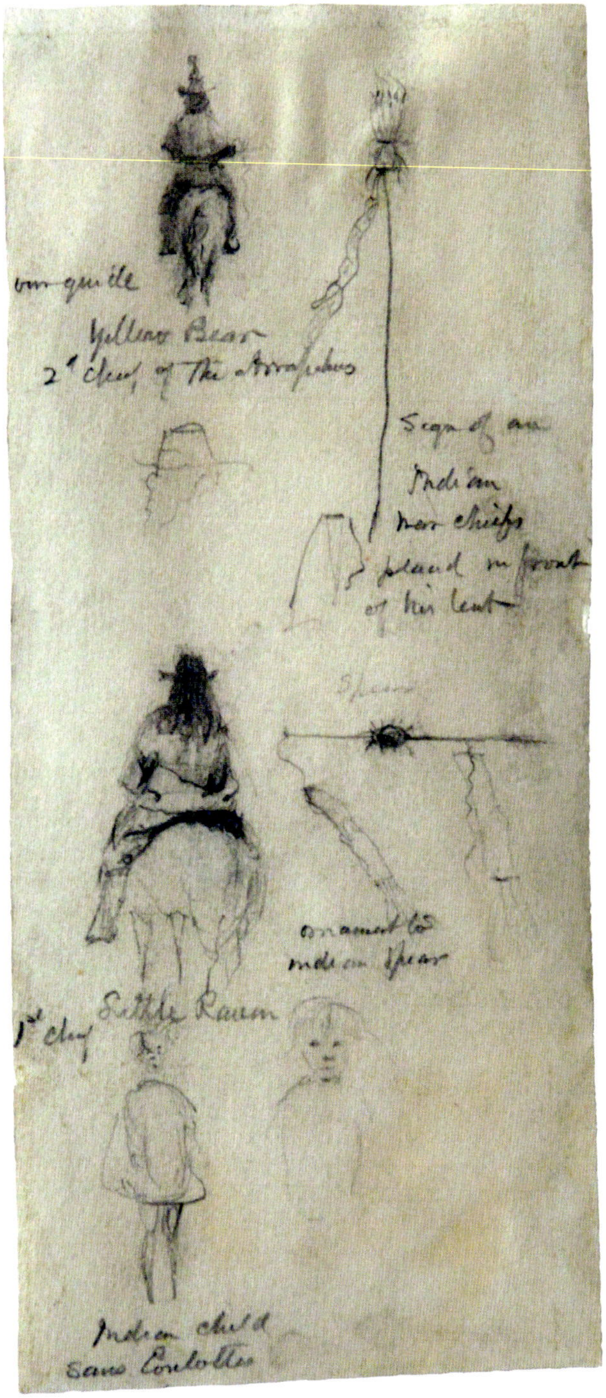

2.6. Vincent Colyer, *Yellow Bear and Little Raven*, 1869. Pencil on paper, 7⅞ × 3¼ inches. Panhandle-Plains Historical Museum, Canyon, Texas. Friends of Southwestern Art Purchase (2006-94-6). Photograph by Ralph Duke, 2015

Before leaving the area, Colyer also visited Camp Wichita (later known as Fort Sill), a fledgling military post staked out by General Philip Sheridan in the shadow of an impressive natural landform known as Medicine Bluff (figure 2.7). Remarkably, perhaps, the Indian commissioner's modest watercolor of the geological wonder was not the only landscape sketched by a white artist in that vicinity in 1869. Private Hermann Stieffel (1857–1886), a self-taught soldier-artist on escort duty from Kansas, also rendered a small view, titled *The Wichita Mountains from Medicine Bluff, Indian Territory* (figure 2.8). Stieffel's inclusion of an Indian family in his rudimentary composition gave the picture a sense of scale and acknowledged the continuing Native presence in the region.[18]

Colonel Benjamin Grierson, the commander at Camp Wichita, provided Commissioner Colyer with an infantry escort as far as Fort Bascom in New Mexico Territory, near present-day Tucumcari. The 430-mile journey took thirty-one days and presented plenty of potential subjects for Colyer's sketchbook, including a stirring buffalo hunt undertaken by a band of Kiowas under Lone Wolf. On the Canadian River, just before crossing the boundary between Indian Territory and the Texas Panhandle, the commissioner produced a watercolor sketch of the distinctive landform known as Antelope Hills.[19]

While the U.S. army attempted to cope with rebellious Southern Plains tribes, railroads were beginning to enter eastern Indian Territory. Between June 1870 and December 1872, the Missouri-Kansas-Texas (MKT) Railway Company extended its tracks from just south of Chetopa, Kansas, through Indian Territory to Denison, Texas. Building from Missouri during the same period, the Atlantic and Pacific (A&P) Railroad made considerably less headway, its line reaching only as far as the Cherokee community of Vinita.[20]

Railroad access made visiting Indian Territory easier and stimulated news coverage of the region. During the early 1870s, a number of writers and illustrators, some operating

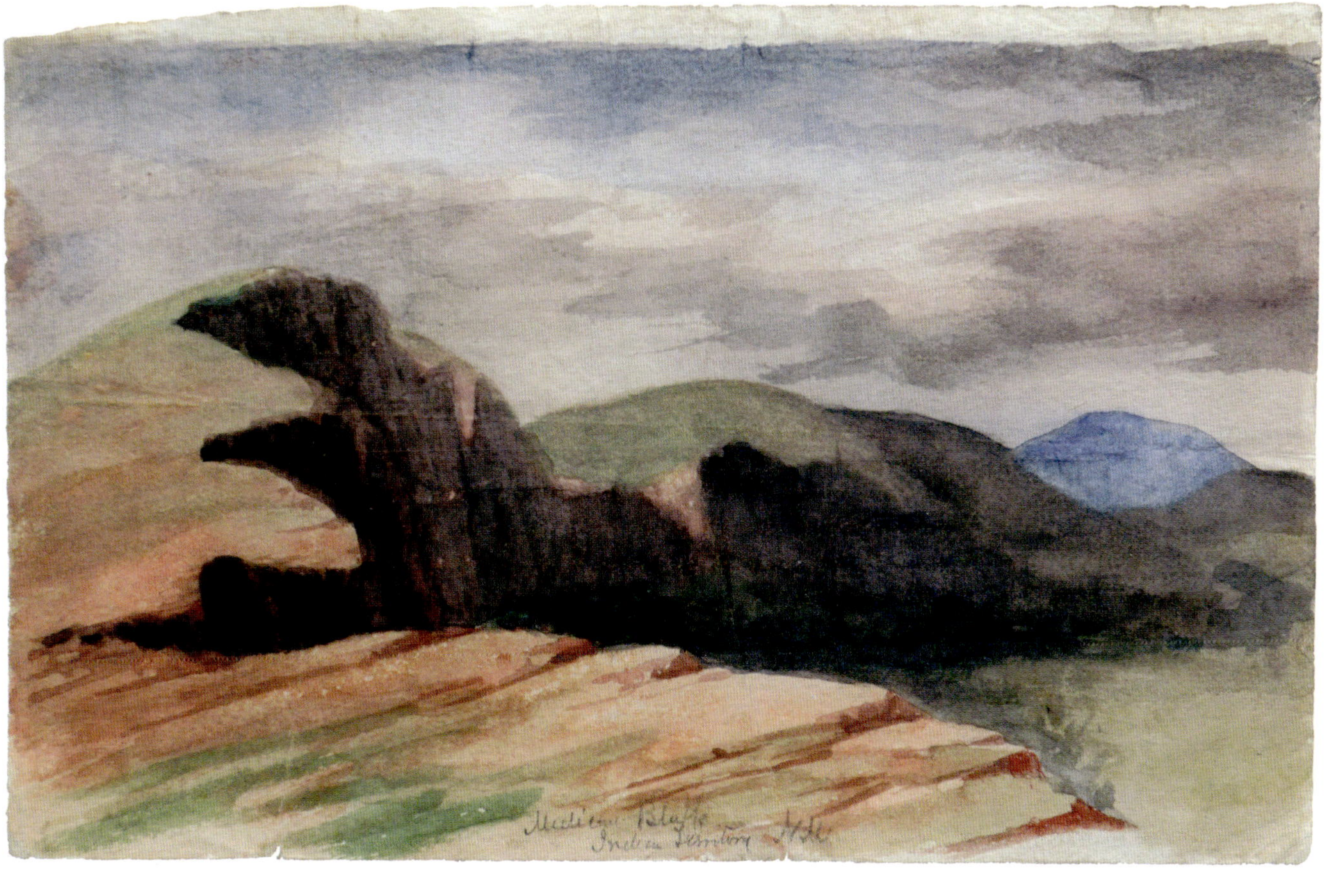

2.7. Vincent Colyer, *Medicine Bluff, Indian Territory,* 1869. Watercolor and pencil on paper, 5 ¼ × 8 inches. Panhandle-Plains Historical Museum, Canyon, Texas. Friends of Southwestern Art Purchase (2006-94-2). Photograph by Ralph Duke, 2015

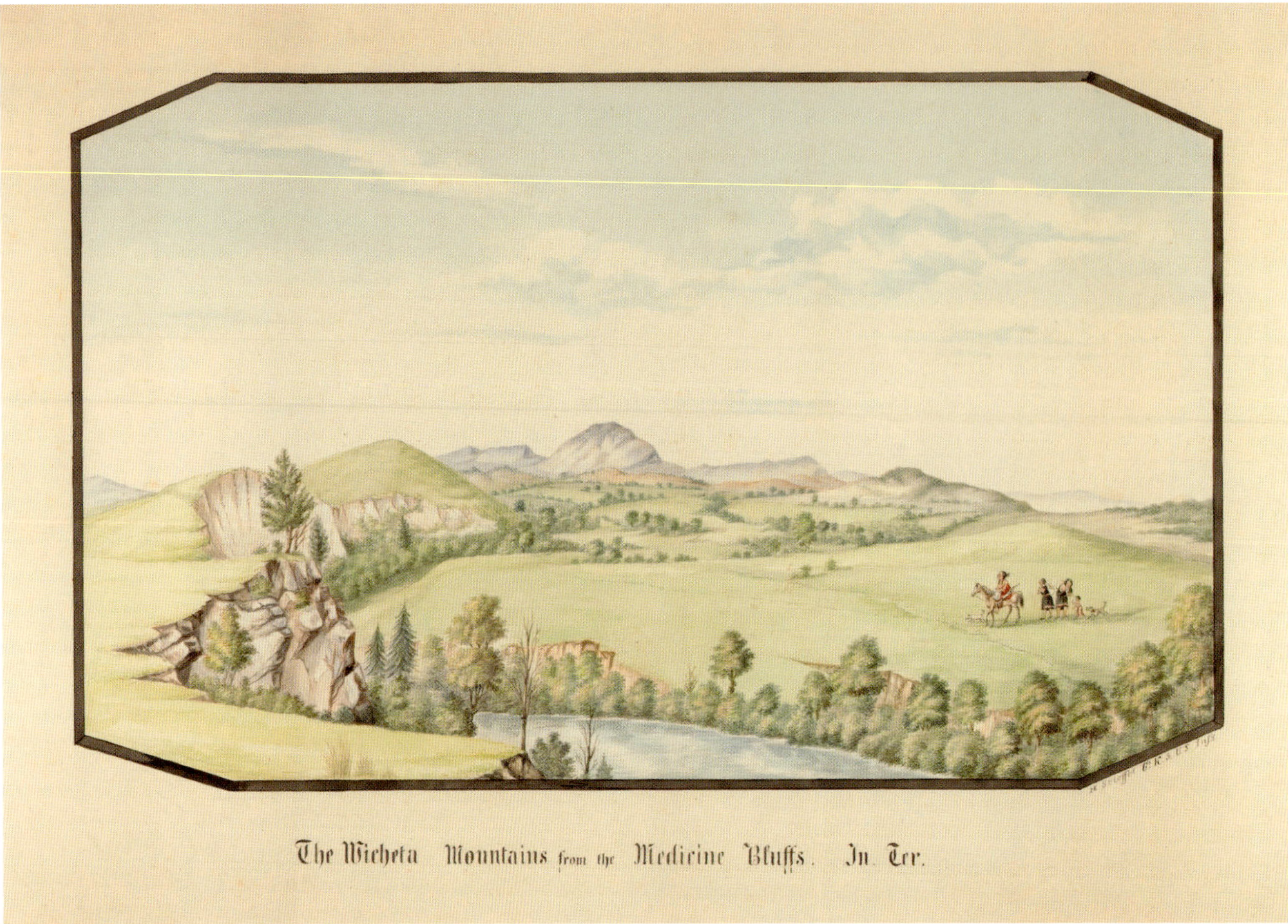

2.8. Hermann Stieffel, *The Wichita Mountains from Medicine Bluff, Indian Territory*, c. 1869. Watercolor, 11 ¾ × 18 ⅝ inches. Smithsonian American Art Museum, Washington, D.C. Gift of Mrs. T. T. Brown (1985.66.384,188)

independently and others commissioned by national newspapers and magazines, began reporting from the Five Tribes region. Indiana journalist John H. Beadle (1840–1897), the first on scene, spent a month in the territory in spring 1872 as part of a five-year journey through the Trans-Mississippi West. He spent most of his time in the Cherokee and Creek Nations visiting communities, farms, churches, and schools. Beadle devoted nearly two dozen woodcuts to Indian Territory in two chapters of his 1873 travelogue, *The Undeveloped West*. Most were derived from unattributed sketches and photographs and included representations of well-known historic events, such as the Trail of Tears, and more recent happenings, including the Going Snake Courthouse Massacre, an 1872 gun battle in the Cherokee Nation that claimed the lives of eight U.S. marshals and three civilians. Most of Beadle's illustrations, however, avoided sensationalism and reinforced the author's belief that through continued education and improvement, the Five Tribes possessed the "capacity and willingness for a perfect civilization."[21]

Meanwhile, writers and illustrators representing both *Scribner's* and *Harper's* had been dispatched to report on life in eastern Indian Territory as part of two larger travelogues—one related to the Trans-Mississippi West, and the other to the former slaveholding states of the South. In 1873 and the first half of 1874, writer Edward King reported on the political, economic, and social consequences of Southern Reconstruction for *Scribner's Monthly*.[22]

Illustrator James W. Champney (1843–1903), a Union army veteran recently returned from art study in Europe, accompanied King over much of his twenty-five-thousand-mile route, producing in the process more than five hundred sketches reflecting "Southern life, character, and scenery."[23] In late January, author and illustrator were spotted by a newspaper reporter in St. Louis "on their way to 'do' the Indian Territory for Scribner's."[24] They would make the trip in style aboard a special train with a car fitted out for their use. King recalled:

> As the Indian Territory boasts no towns worthy the name along either of the two lines of rail which penetrate its domain, the railroad company placed at the disposition of our party a superb hotel car, equipped with kitchen, drawing, and sleeping-room. The larder of the traveling-home was well stocked; engineer, fireman, and brakeman took their rifles, prepared for an encounter with deer, or to chase the cautious wild turkey; and a merry party, one frosty morning in January of 1873, rattled out of Sedalia. Both artist and writer were fascinated with this perfection of travel, this journeying so thoroughly at one's own will, with power to stop at every turn, and with no feeling of haste. Wherever it seemed to us good, we dismissed our train to a side track, and wandered off.[25]

King's account of his sojourn through Indian Territory appeared in the July 1873 issue of *Scribner's Monthly*, supported by more than three dozen wood engravings, most of them based on James Champney's sketches. Much of the text and more than half of the illustrations, however, related to the Kansas and Texas legs of the trip. About a quarter of the images devoted to Indian Territory were railroad related, which is not surprising, perhaps, given the splendid accommodations the author and illustrator enjoyed courtesy of the MKT (figure 2.9). Some of the railroad views were based on photographs taken by St. Louis–based Robert Benecke (1835–1903), who accompanied King and Champney through Indian Territory and as far as Denison, Texas, before departing to photograph on the Kansas Pacific Railroad.[26]

The first of Champney's illustrations to appear in King's article on Indian Territory portrays a distant train traveling through Limestone Gap in present-day Atoka County

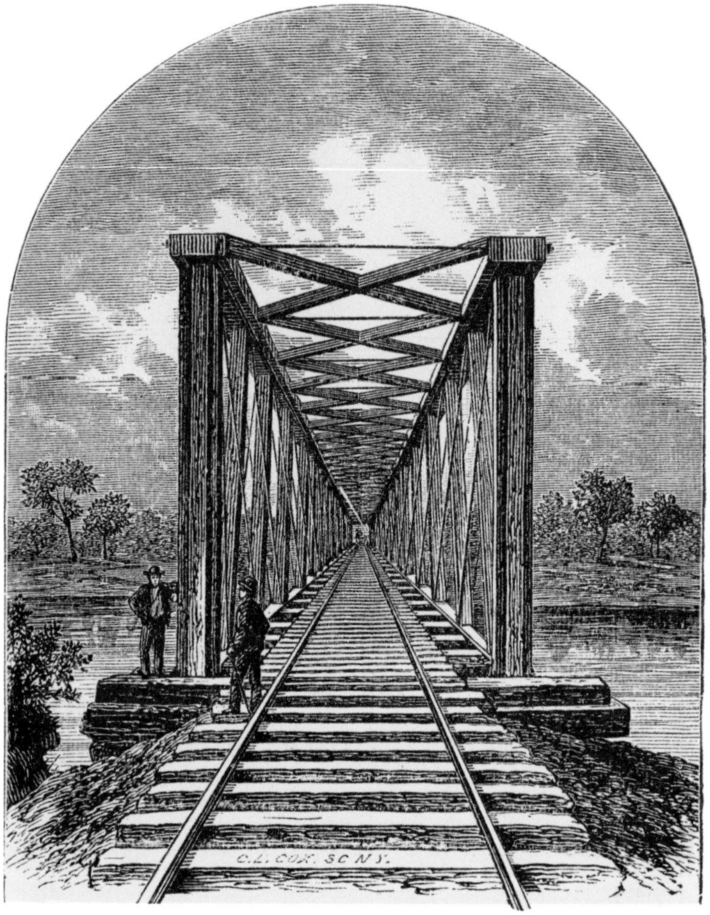

2.9. James Wells Champney, after a photograph by Robert Benecke, *Bridge across the North Fork of the Canadian River, Indian Territory (M., K. & T. Railway)*, in Edward King, *The Great South* (Hartford, Conn.: American Publishing, 1875), 199. Western History Collections, University of Oklahoma Libraries, Norman, Oklahoma

(figure 2.10). A horse skeleton and a decaying wagon, placed by the illustrator in the foreground of the image, symbolized and foreshadowed the deleterious effects of railroads on animal-powered transportation.[27]

In *"The Indian Consents,"* another railroad-related illustration infused with symbolism, a white businessman in bowler hat places his hand on the shoulder of a Native man, as a locomotive steams across a bridge in the distance. Facing the viewer, with his hands in his pockets, the Indian represents the Five Tribes, who had been forced to allow the railroad to cross their land.[28]

Champney produced more than a dozen character studies in pen and ink of people he met in the territory. Most were men, rendered either as standing figures or as portraits. Only two, a railroad employee and the postmaster at Fort Gibson, were identified by name. The rest were classified by occupation, location, or tribe, and not all of them were referenced in the text.[29]

Champney also sketched a number of genre scenes, a Creek school and the ferry at Fort Gibson among them. His drawing of a one-room log cabin, bearing the caption *An Indian Territorial Mansion*, poked fun at the region's rustic lifestyle. *Twilight on Pryor's Creek, Indian Territory*, the only pure landscape to adorn King's article, was redrawn, and probably enhanced, by engraver Thomas Moran, who in later years became a celebrated easel painter and interpreter of the American West in his own right.[30]

In 1875, Edward King's *Scribner's* articles were revised, rearranged, expanded, and compiled into a book also titled *The Great South*, which was published in both the United States and Great Britain.[31] The *New York Evening Post* noted that the forthcoming volume was to be "profusely illustrated from sketches by the celebrated *genre artist* CHAMPNEY, drawn on wood by Sheppard, Moran and others, and engraved and printed in the highest style of art."[32] Indian Territory was allotted its own chapter in

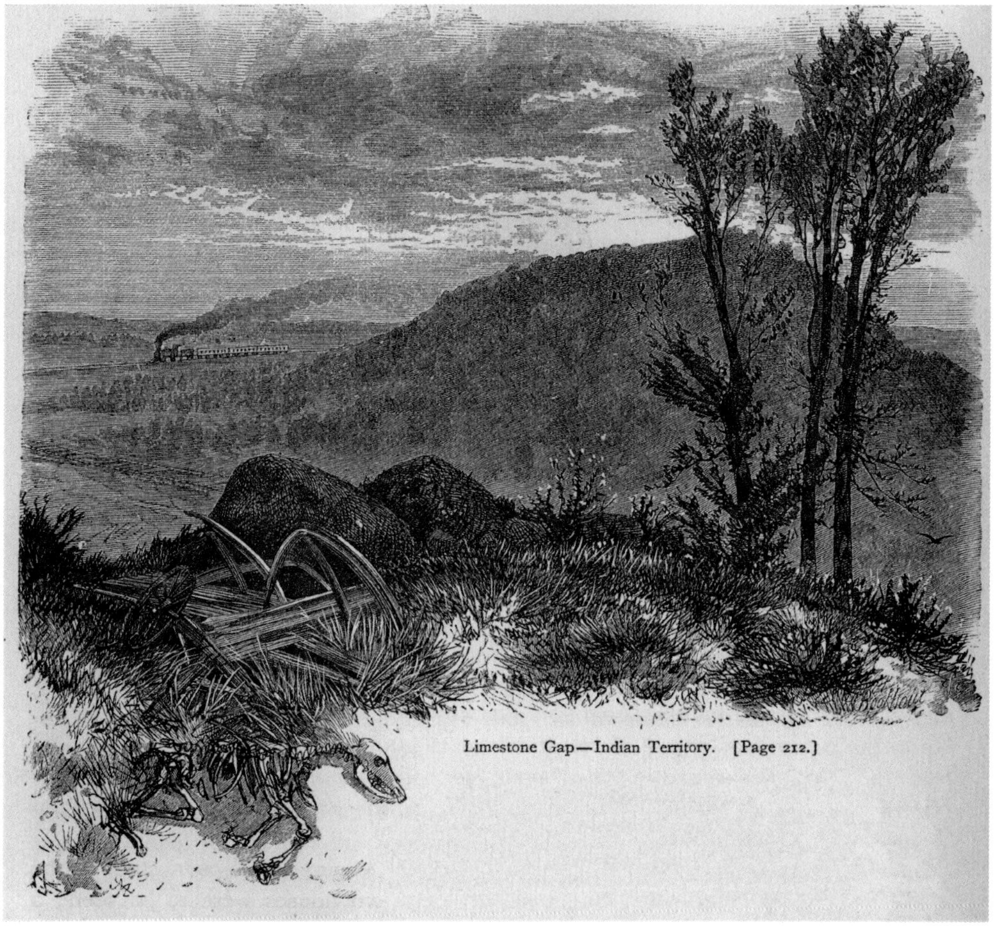

2.10. James Wells Champney, *Limestone Gap—Indian Territory*, in Edward King, *The Great South* (Hartford, Conn: American Publishing, 1875), 204. Western History Collections, University of Oklahoma Libraries, Norman, Oklahoma

the new volume, and some of Champney's illustrations were relocated and the captions altered to better reference the text.[33]

Following in the wake of King and Champney, *Harper's Weekly* artist-reporters Paul Frenzeny (1840–1902) and Jules Tavernier (1844–1889) visited Indian Territory in 1874 as part of a several-month transcontinental jaunt to the West Coast. Both men had recently immigrated to the United States from France. Frenzeny, a Hungarian by birth, had studied at the École Polytechnique in Paris and had served in the French army in Algeria and Italy and in Mexico under Emperor Maximilian. After arriving in New York, he studied drawing under John A. Hyde, and by 1868, he was illustrating American publications.[34]

Frenzeny's colleague Jules Tavernier, a product of the prestigious École des Beaux Arts, served as a field artist during the Franco-Prussian War and briefly as an illustrator with the *London Graphic* before making his way to the United States in 1872. His work had already decorated the pages of *Frank Leslie's Illustrated Newspaper*, *Harper's Weekly*, and the *New York Daily Graphic*.[35]

The two artists were acquainted and had collaborated on illustrations on at least two occasions before accepting the *Harper's Weekly* cross-country commission.[36] The magazine described the pair's upcoming trip for its readers:

> Our artists, Messrs. Frenzeny and Tavernier, will tell the story of an extensive tour, commencing at New York and intended to include the most interesting and picturesque regions of the Western and Southwestern portions of this country. These gentlemen will not restrict themselves to the ordinary routes of travel. They will make long excursions on horseback into regions where railroads have not yet penetrated, where even the hardy squatter, the pioneer of civilization, has not yet erected his rude log-cabin; and the pictorial record of their journeyings will be a most valuable and entertaining series of sketches.[37]

The artist-reporters reached Indian Territory in late 1873, not quite a year after King and Champney's departure. Frenzeny and Tavernier also came by way of the MKT line, carrying with them a sack of boxwood blocks and a mirror with which to reproduce their field drawings in reverse for subsequent engraving. The first of their Indian Territory subjects, *United States Signal Service—Watching the Storm* (figure 2.11), observed at Fort Gibson, appeared in *Harper's Weekly* on March 21, 1874. Given Oklahoma's prominence in the scientific prediction of volatile weather patterns in the twenty-first century, the image of two government spotters scanning the horizon for storms in the nineteenth seems both appropriate and prophetic.[38]

Frenzeny and Tavernier provided *Harper's Weekly* with more prosaic views of life in Indian Territory for issues published in April and May 1874. The pair witnessed most of the scenes they illustrated firsthand but reconstructed others from stories they heard or read. Such was the case with the image *Vigilance Court in Session*, which addressed the region's violent reputation and the extralegal means sometimes used to bring alleged criminals to justice. The illustration depicts the outdoor trial of a trio of alleged horse thieves. The accused plead their case in shadow and before a judge, who is armed with a rifle and bathed in righteous light. Nearby, a hangman rigs a rope to a nearby telegraph pole in anticipation of a guilty verdict and the fatal punishment to follow.[39]

At Denison, Texas, Frenzeny and Tavernier left the railroad and made their way back across Indian Territory to Wichita, Kansas. Although little is known of their route or other circumstances of their journey, historian Robert Taft, has speculated that the duo probably followed part of the Great Western Cattle Trail, and may even have accompanied drovers from Texas for a time.[40]

Though numerous artists and illustrators found the cattle trade of the late nineteenth-century American West a stimulating and picturesque subject, Frank

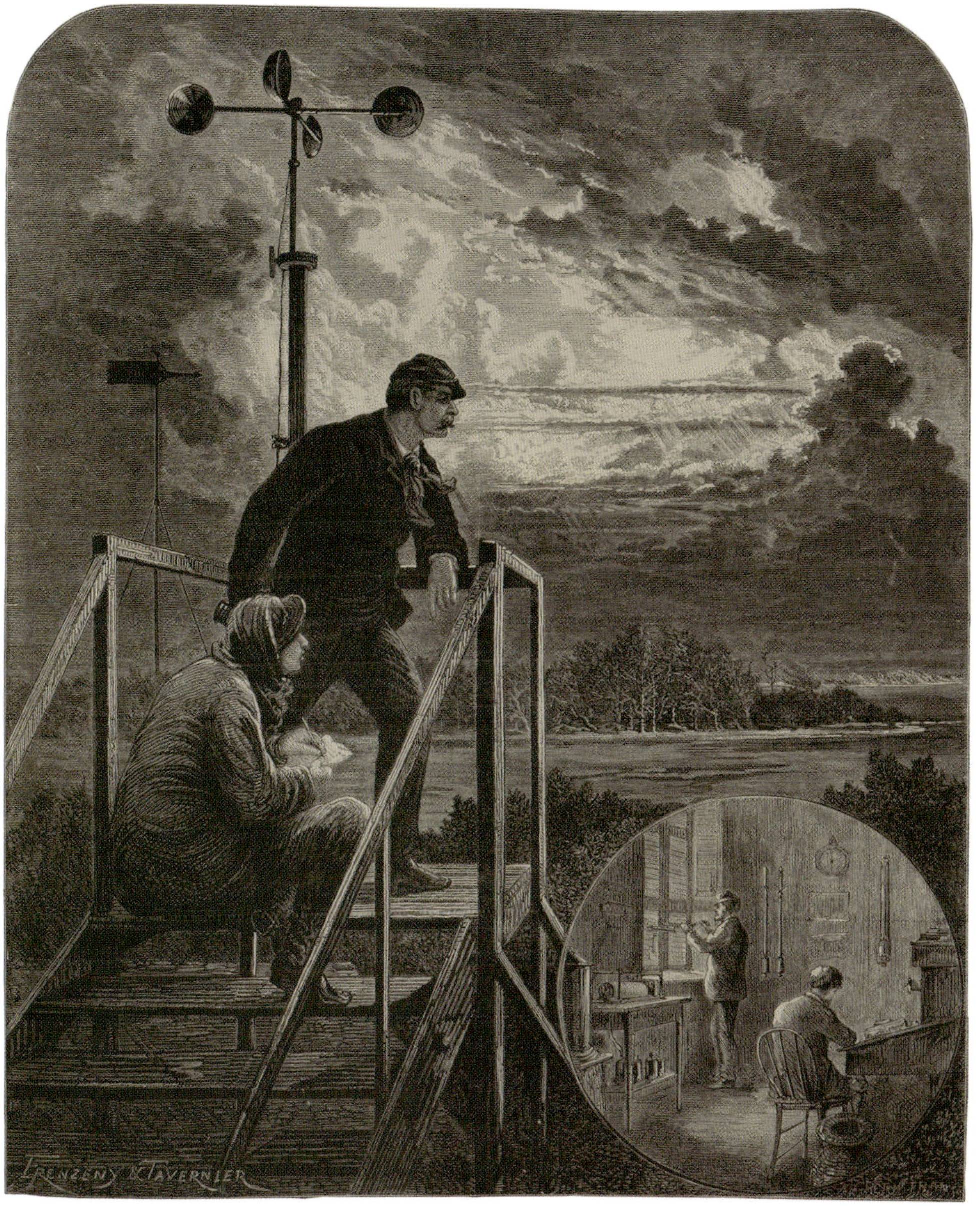

2.11. Paul Frenzeny and Jules Tavernier, *United States Signal Service—Watching the Storm*, *Harper's Weekly*, March 21, 1874, 267. University of Oklahoma Libraries, Norman, Oklahoma

Reaugh may have been the only professional easel painter to have produced scenes of late nineteenth-century ranching and trail driving in Indian Territory. Fascinated by longhorn cattle and open range, the Texas artist accompanied drives and attended roundups north of the Red River into the 1900s, translating what he saw into small but colorful pastels, rapidly rendered on the spot in an impressionistic style.[41]

Drovers and other travelers had largely avoided the western half of Indian Territory until the U.S. Army corralled the remaining nomadic Southern Plains Indian tribes on reservations after the Red River War of 1874. Exploration and mapping of the region resumed as well, and in 1876, Carl Julius Adolph Hunnius, a civilian cartographer and

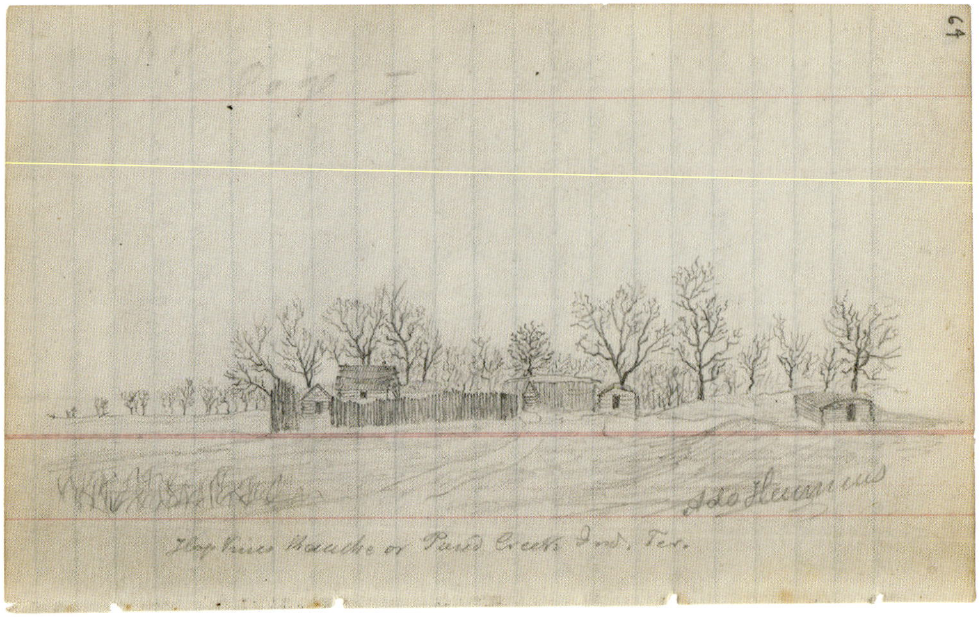

2.12. Carl Julius Adolph Hunnius, *Hopkins Ranch on Pond Creek, Indian Territory*, 1876. Pencil on paper, 3¾ × 6 inches. Carl "Ado" Hunnius diary entries, January 10–24, 1876, 64, folder Diary 1876, box 2, MS Collection No. 397, Carl Julius Adolph Hunnius Papers, Kansas State Historical Society, Topeka, Kansas (220118)

sketch artist stationed at Fort Leavenworth, Kansas, produced perhaps the first views of western Indian Territory since Vincent Colyer's visit in 1869. On January 10, 1876, Hunnius and civilian scout William "Billy" Dixon set out by wagon to measure the distance between Wichita, Kansas, and Darlington, the new Cheyenne Agency. Besides calculating mileage and keeping a detailed journal, Hunnius made rudimentary sketches of places of interest along the way. The second day on the road, for example, he produced a pencil drawing of Hopkins Ranch on Pond Creek, twenty-five miles south of Caldwell, Kansas, probably the first he rendered in Indian Territory (figure 2.12). The following day, near Hackberry Creek, he sketched the graves of settlers killed by Indians, and the next, a representation of Camp Supply, the largest military installation in the area.[42]

Established in 1868, on Wolf Creek, Camp Supply's log stockade and associated structures housed several companies of soldiers and had been the subject of a more elaborate bird's-eye view rendered by an anonymous artist and published in *Harper's Weekly*, February 27, 1869 (figure 2.13). The post and the prominent American flag that flew over it in the earlier image symbolized the U.S. government's authority over Indian country, and the long supply train appearing in the distance alluded to the post's primary function as a distribution point for Indian rations.[43]

Hunnius not only sketched interesting subjects during the trip but also collected several Indian artifacts for his hometown museum in Leipzig, Germany. After returning to Fort Leavenworth, he had scarcely completed a map of the route he and Dixon had followed when he was assigned, in late April, to a government topographical and scientific survey bound for the headwaters of the Red River. Hunnius again kept a detailed diary

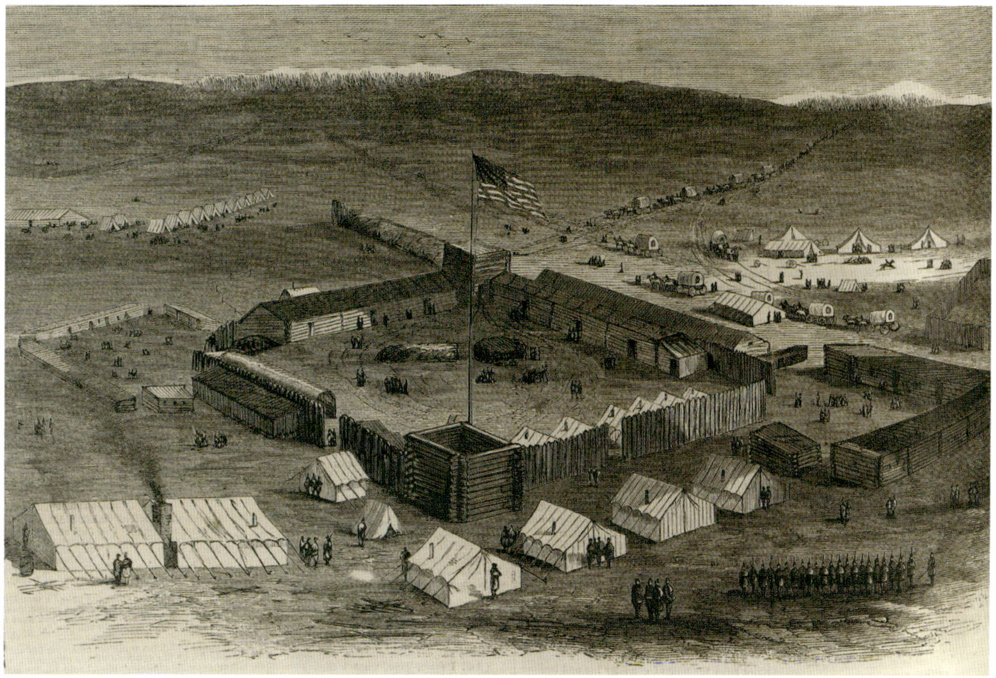

2.13. Unknown artist, *Camp Supply, Indian Territory*, in *Harper's Weekly*, February 27, 1869, 140. University of Oklahoma Libraries, Norman, Oklahoma

of events and created maps of the route, which proceeded from Fort Leavenworth to the Texas Panhandle by way of Camp Supply. Both Hunnius and the expedition commander, Lieutenant Ernest Howard Ruffner, rendered topographical sketches of landmarks along the route, with Ruffner producing watercolors as well as pencil and ink drawings. Never disseminated, these visual records of the expedition were soon lost or forgotten.[44]

Although the boomer movement to open the unassigned lands of Indian Territory to white settlement garnered the lion's share of attention from American newspaper and magazine illustrators in the 1880s, pictorial articles about the Native inhabitants of the region were not lacking. In 1888, George E. Foster (1849–1917), a journalist, an Indian advocate, and author of a biography of Cherokee linguist Sequoyah produced two such articles for Frank Leslie's publications. The first, titled "Among the Cherokees," appeared in *Frank Leslie's Popular Monthly* and was illustrated with a hodgepodge of engravings, based mostly on photographs, combined with illustrations recycled from Edward King's *The Great South* and Thomas McKinney and James Hall's classic multi-volume work *History of the Indian Tribes of North America, 1836–1844*.[45]

Foster claimed to have illustrated his second effort, published in *Frank Leslie's Illustrated Newspaper*, on August 11, 1888, under the intriguing title, "A Zig-Zag Journey through the Indian Territory," with "original lead pencil sketches" produced from firsthand observation. Most were drawings of substantial tribal council houses and schools in the Cherokee and Creek Nations, including the Indian University at Muskogee, which was described as an "elegant building," that welcomed children of eight tribes.[46] A typical Choctaw farm was also represented, as was a Pawnee teepee and brush arbor. "But few wigwams, like that of the early Pawnees[,] can be found today," Foster wrote in the accompanying text: "All over the territory the Indian has donned the garb of civilization and the fact is being proved that if the Government had spent half the money in educating the Indians that it has in fighting them, the Indian question would long ago have been settled."[47]

George Foster's trail through eastern Indian Territory was barely cold before famed special artists Frederic Remington and Rufus Zogbaum, on assignment for the *Century Magazine* and *Harper's Weekly*, respectively, arrived in the western reaches of the territory to measure the progress the tribes had made toward "civilization" after more than a decade of reservation life. Remington arrived first and spent nine days visiting Forts Sill and Reno as well as the Anadarko Agency in early July 1888, the last leg of a longer trip through the Southwest. Armed with a camera and sketchpad, both of which he used adeptly to record impressions of the region and its colorful inhabitants, the artist traveled from Henrietta, Texas, to Fort Sill by wagon, in the company of a loquacious Texas cowboy.[48]

A student of equestrian cultures, Remington paid uncommon attention to the Native horses and riders he encountered, observing the prevalence of cowboy-style tack and horsemanship among them and documenting their penchant for horse racing. He was effusive in his praise of Comanche horse breeders and traders and extolled the beauty of their "'painted' ponies." Along the way he collected traditional tribal horse gear and other artifacts that he could use later as props in his paintings (figure 2.14).[49]

During his four-day stay at Fort Reno, Remington visited local Cheyenne camps in the company of veteran guide and interpreter Ben Clark, who also provided the artist with historical and cultural background on the tribe. At the weekly government beef issue, an event the Cheyennes treated like an old-fashioned buffalo hunt, the artist wrangled a horse and rode along for a close-up view that he subsequently translated into an illustration.[50]

Remington recounted these and other experiences on the southern plains in a pair of articles published the following year in the *Century Magazine*.[51] Both were accompanied by considerable editorializing by the artist on the failures of government Indian policy as well as by uneven illustrations, some of which derived from sketches and others from photographs taken by the artist.

Cheyenne Scouts Patrolling the Big Timber of the North Canadian, the first of Remington's Indian Territory works to appear in print and more painterly than any of his illustrations in the *Century*, rated a double-page spread in the April 6, 1889, issue of *Harper's Weekly* (figure 2.15). In the black-and-white oil, a duo of uniformed and

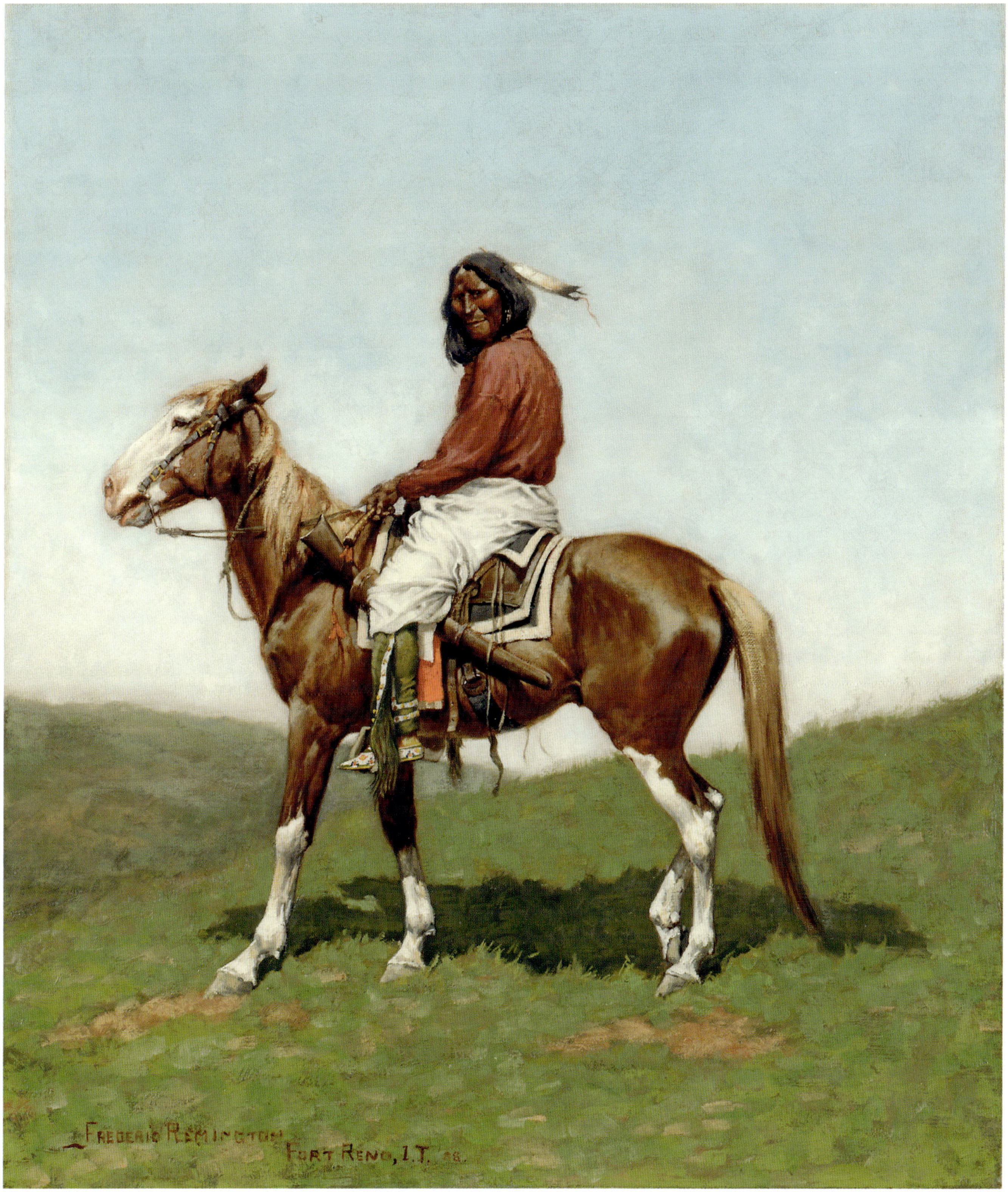

2.14. Frederic Remington, *Comanche Brave, Fort Reno, Indian Territory*, 1888. Oil on canvas, 24 × 20 inches. Private collection. © Christie's Images. Photograph courtesy Bridgeman Images

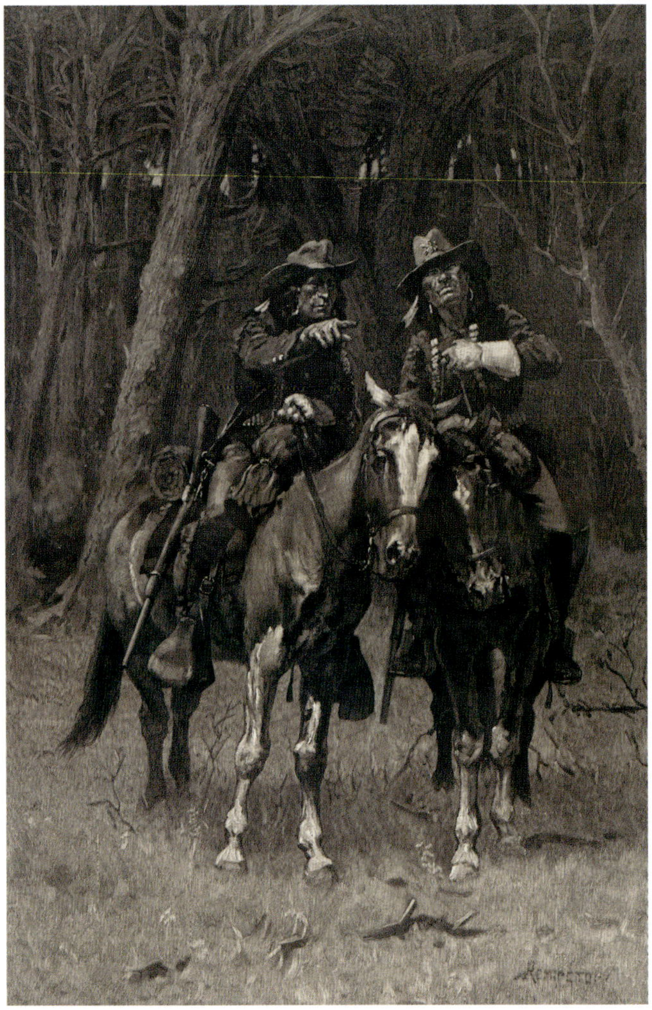

2.15. Frederic Remington, *Cheyenne Scouts Patrolling the Big Timber of the North Canadian, Oklahoma*, in *Harper's Weekly*, April 6, 1889, 264–65. University of Oklahoma Libraries, Norman, Oklahoma

mounted Indian scouts peer intently into the unknown, as one points at something beyond the picture plane. Framed by a pair of trees in the dense grove behind them, the horsemen and their mounts form a triangular composition that reinforces the drama of the scene. A brief accompanying article explained that boomer activity on the eve of the land rush accounted for the extraordinary vigilance of Indian scouts along the boundaries of the Cheyenne Reservation. In the following two decades, Remington would revisit the nocturnal theme explored in *Cheyenne Scouts* more than once as he slowly made the transition from hard-edged illustration to impressionist easel painting.[52]

In 1890, Remington produced his last, and undoubtedly his finest, painting associated with Indian Territory. An idealized equestrian portrait with a distinctly romantic palette, *Modern Comanche* (figure 2.16) expressed feelings of uncertainty for the once powerful tribe's future. Both horse and rider gaze wistfully at the uncertain destiny that awaits them beyond the far horizon. They no longer gallop in freedom across the open plains but travel at a walk along the narrow path called the "white man's road." While clearly transcending illustration, the work appeared in Colonel Theodore A. Dodge's series for *Harper's Monthly*, "Some American Riders," in 1891.[53]

On September 26, 1888, a little more than two months after Frederic Remington's whirlwind tour through Indian Country, popular military illustrator Rufus F. Zogbaum, arrived by railroad at Guthrie, on assignment for *Harper's Weekly*. His book *Horse, Foot and Dragoons*, an illustrated firsthand account of army life in Europe and in the United States, had just been published to complimentary reviews, and, for the moment at least, his stature as an illustrator rivaled that of Frederic Remington.

Zogbaum immediately joined cavalry troops from Fort Reno, drilling along the Cimarron River, on the lookout for " boomers" and illegal Indian traders. While in the field, he also hunted prairie chickens with officers of the command and got a look at a destructive range fire from a respectful distance.

Unlike Remington, Zogbaum was not carrying a camera when he arrived at Fort Reno. He telegraphed for one soon thereafter, but whether it arrived is uncertain.

FACING
2.16. Frederic Remington, *Modern Comanche*, 1890. Oil on canvas, 33 × 23 inches. Forsyth Galleries, Texas A&M University, College Station. Bill and Irma Runyon Art Collections (988.1.155)

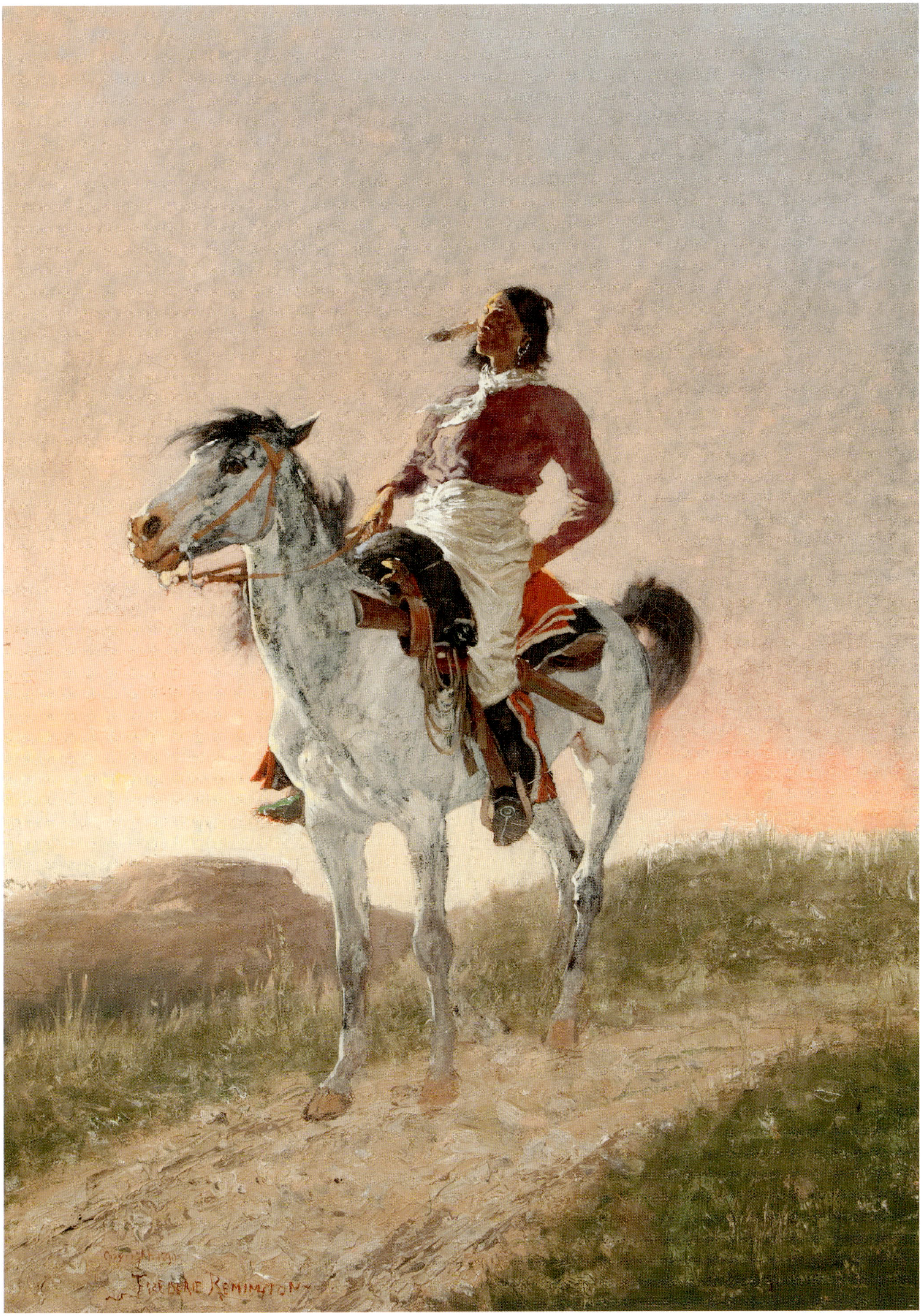
FREDERIC REMINGTON

Despite using photography for a painting reference, Zogbaum shared Remington's belief in the limitations of the medium in art, as he would later explain: "In common with all illustrators, I find that the work likely to pay best in the future is that which the camera cannot do. Scenes of human interest, filled with figures and action, are beyond the scope of any machine. A photograph is always more or less a failure in representing action; at the particular fraction of a second when light strikes the plate there really is no action."[54]

After spending a week in the field, Zogbaum accompanied the troops back to Fort Reno by way of the Cheyenne-Arapaho Agency at Darlington. The day after his arrival on post he visited the camp of the same Cheyenne scouts who had stimulated Frederic Remington's artistic imagination and, the day following, made the acquaintance of the venerable scout Ben Clark. For the next several weeks, Zogbaum traveled about the agency, learning what he could of reservation life, taking notes on what he saw and heard and sketching subjects of interest.

Zogbaum departed Fort Reno on October 22, after a visit lasting just under a month. Returning to the East Coast, he slowly began to convert his Indian Territory sketches into illustrations accompanied by text. The first such work, *A Court Martial in the Field*, did not find its way onto the pages of *Harper's Weekly* until March 1889. This and most of his other illustrations appeared individually in the publication, accompanied by short unattributed articles probably written by the artist himself. Because his images of military life were often generic and sometimes appeared in print months after the events they depicted, many were not identified with a specific locale, individual, or military unit in either the article or the caption.[55]

Fortunately, Zogbaum described in his diary some of the incidents that inspired his illustrations, making it possible to identify them with his 1888 stay on the southern plains. Such was the case with *Meeting with the Old Regiment*, a full page illustration published in *Harper's Weekly* on June 7, 1890.[56] Although the accompanying article did not identify the location of the scene or any of its participants, Zogbaum's diary entry for October 4, 1888, recording the arrival of General Wesley Merritt on an inspection tour of Indian Territory, accomplished both in a succinct word picture that his illustration mimicked:

> Ride out with all the officers of the command to meet Genl & Mrs. Merritt. After a brisk ride over the prairie & a halt of a few minutes we see the ambulance approaching & immediately mount & ride forward to meet it. A very pretty scene occurs where the Genl & his wife meet again with the officers of their old regiment. They crowd, dismtd around the vehicle & stand uncovered & exchanging greetings with their old commander. The meeting was most cordial on both sides.[57]

Harper's Weekly continued to publish Rufus Zogbaum's Indian Territory–based illustrations for almost a decade. "Life at an Indian Agency," the only article bearing the artist's byline as both author and illustrator, appeared in the news magazine in January 1890. Focusing on the changes reservation Arapahos and Southern Cheyennes faced with the coming of white settlement, the text of the piece covered some of the same ground as Remington's earlier article in *Century Magazine*, but it was more descriptive and less opinionated than its predecessor. Both men illustrated scenes of everyday Native life and Indian "types" with special emphasis on uniformed Indian soldiers and scouts.[58]

Like Remington, Zogbaum was smitten by the visceral "Wild West" feel of the government beef issue, which both artist-correspondents described and illustrated in similar terms. Denied Remington's horseback perspective of the proceedings, Zogbaum settled for the view from the seat of an army ambulance. His spirited, if sanitized, painting of the event, which he called "picturesque and exciting, if somewhat revolting," rated a double-page spread in print.[59] Although compositionally superior to Remington's painting of the beef issue, Zogbaum's effort (figure 2.17) paled when compared to his rival's ability to convey the action and frenzy that accompanied such occasions.

Throughout his career, Zogbaum produced at least a few easel paintings for exhibition and sale as well as marketing some of his commercial work. Two examples, *A Turkey Hunt, Indian Territory*, and *The Troop Guidon*, both inspired by the artist's only sojourn on the southern Great Plains, were offered for sale at the American Watercolor Society Annual Exhibition in New York in 1892.[60]

At least one other easel painting, a full-color oil titled *Troops Near Ft. Reno* (figure 2.18), is attributable to Zogbaum's only trip to Indian Territory. Set on a rainy day, undoubtedly one of the several that the artist noted in his diary during his stay at the post, the painting portrays two mounted cavalry troopers on a water-soaked trail that leads to a distant tree line. Though characteristic of its creator, the atmospheric effects and precise detail displayed in the work are also reminiscent of the well-known French military painters Alphonse-Marie-Adolphe de Neuville and Édouard Detaille, whose work Zogbaum had encountered in 1881, while studying art in Paris under noted figure painter Leon J. F. Bonnat.[61]

The departure of Frederic Remington and Rufus Zogbaum from Indian Territory in 1888 did not mark the end of artistic interest in the region and in its inhabitants. The decade of the 1890s would bring a covey of new artists, professional and amateur, to the southern plains, most of them still convinced that what was left of traditional Native lifeways would soon be swallowed up by the now-dominant white culture. It was perhaps appropriate, then, that Julian Scott, the first outside artist in the last decade of the nineteenth century to work among the Native inhabitants of the recently formed

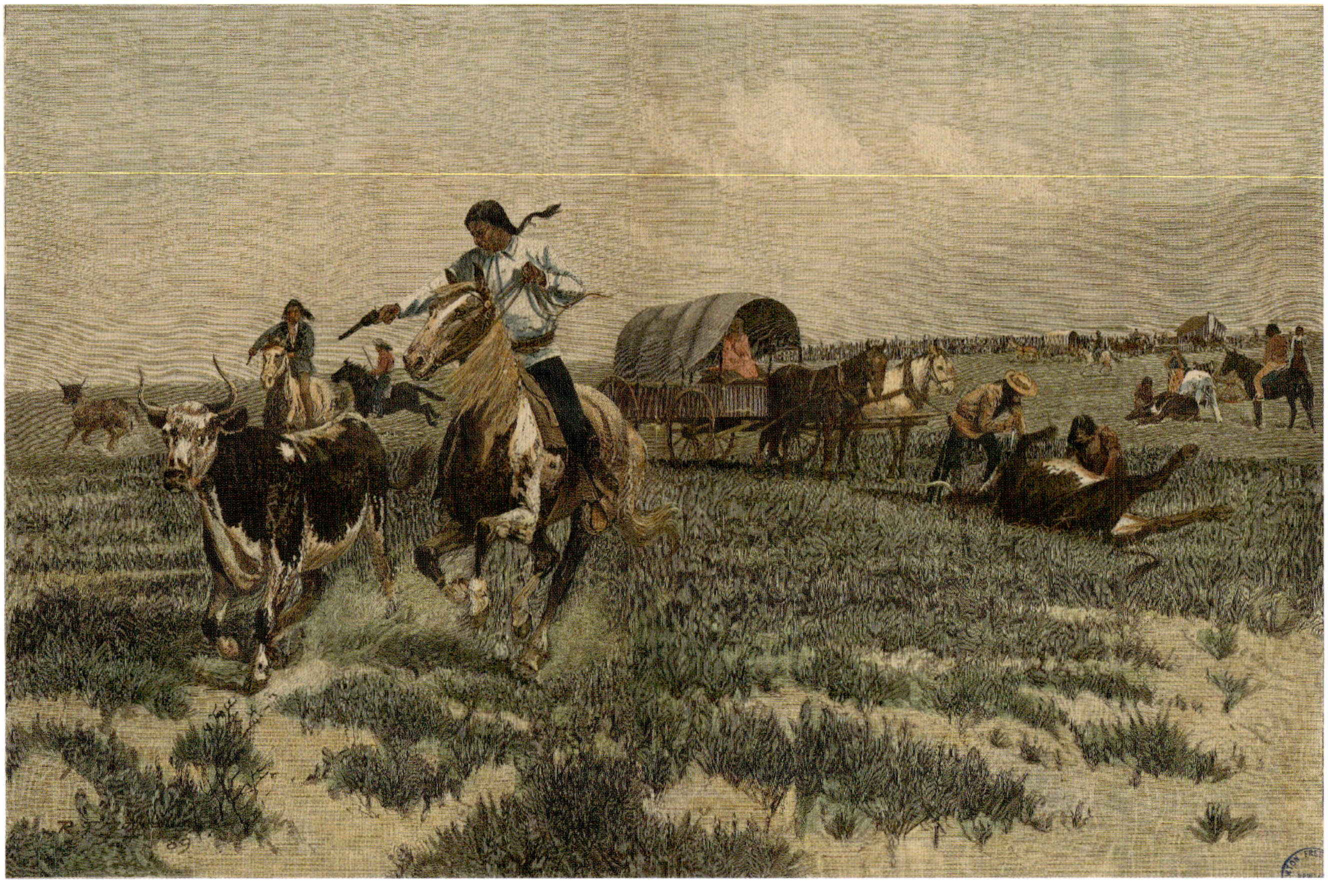

2.17. Rufus Zogbaum, *A Beef Issue in the Indian Territory*, in *Harper's Weekly*, January 4, 1890, 8–9. Color added. Oklahoma Historical Society, Oklahoma City, Oklahoma (21563.PE.HW.90.14)

Oklahoma Territory, also worked for the U.S. Census Office. Scott was one of five artists employed as "special agents" during the 1890 count, the first to provide a comprehensive report on tribal populations and conditions. The artists who accompanied census enumerators into the field were given the task of preparing written reports on various tribes and illustrating the final report with photographs, drawings, and paintings of typical Native life.[62]

A Union army veteran and recipient of the Congressional Medal of Honor, Julian Scott was best known for his history paintings of the Civil War. His tight compositions and strict academic style reflected his training at the National Academy of Design and under the eminent German-born history painter Emanuel Leutze. Over the years Scott had also embraced the medium of photography as a useful tool in the production of his paintings.[63]

Scott took a train as far as Pauls Valley, then hopped a stagecoach to Anadarko Agency, where he spent August and September 1890. While touring the Kiowa, Comanche, and Wichita Reservations he snapped scores of photographs with a No. 2 Kodak

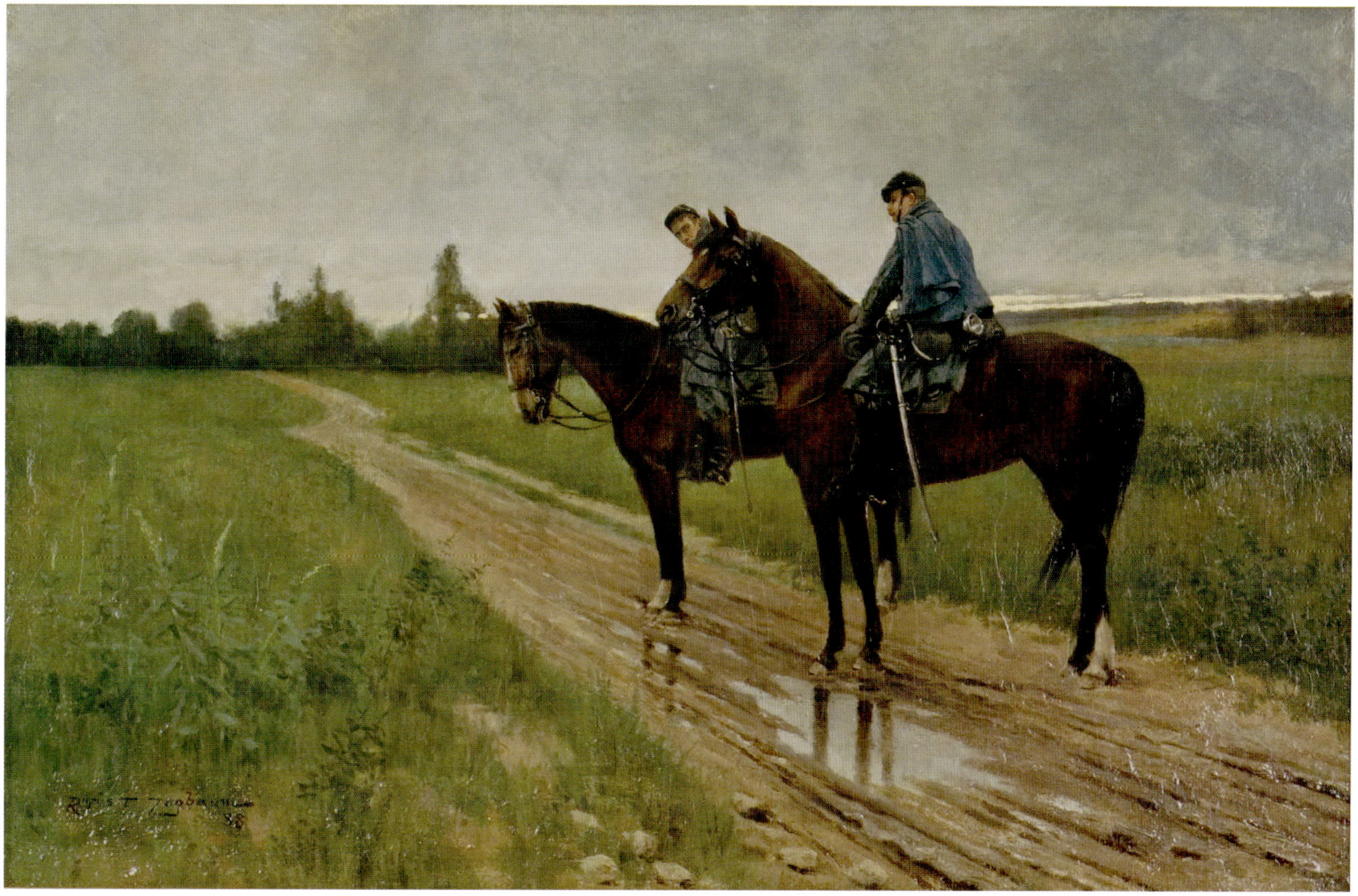

2.18. Rufus Zogbaum, *Troops Near Ft. Reno*, 1888. Oil on canvas, 16 × 24 inches. Private collection

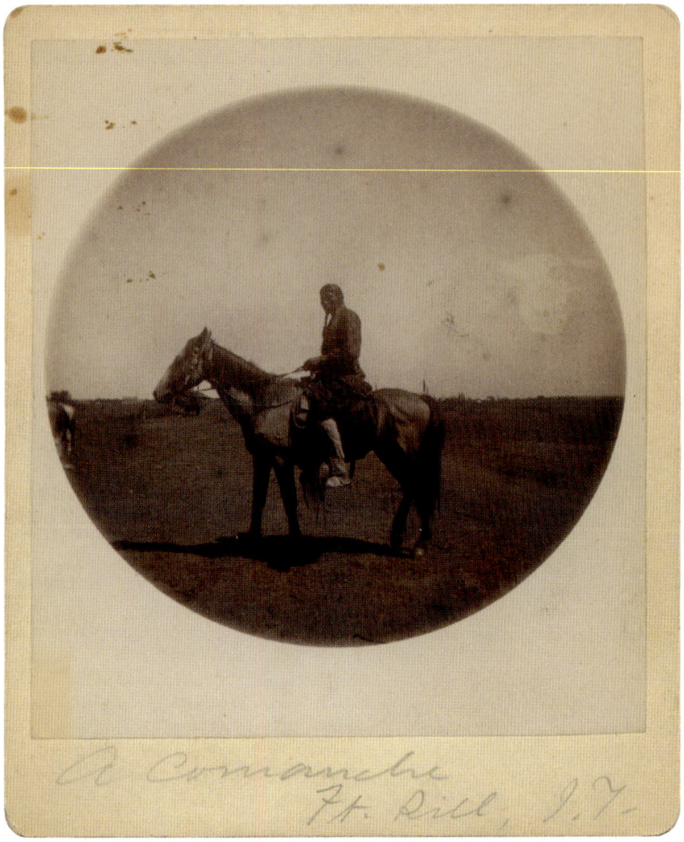

2.19. Julian Scott, *A Comanche, Ft. Sill, I.T.*, 1890. Julian Scott Photographs for the 11th Census, box 1, item 64, Manuscripts Division, Department of Rare Books and Special Collections, Princeton University Library, Princeton, New Jersey

camera, collected others from photographers Lenny and Sawyers, who operated a studio at Purcell, and made numerous sketches and detailed notes to include in his formal report (figure 2.19).[64]

At Fort Sill, on August 16, 1890, Scott photographed famed Comanche chief Quanah Parker and convinced him to pose seated for a quick three-quarter-length pencil sketch. The resulting image possessed a spontaneity and appeal largely absent in the artist's formal portraits of Parker, painted later at Scott's Plainfield, New Jersey, studio (figure 2.20). He produced more than one such work, having orders for the chief's likeness from an Anadarko Indian trader and another from the sitter himself.[65]

Rendered in the tradition of Indian portraits produced by George Catlin, Charles Bird King, and other early American artists, the conventional three-quarter head-and-shoulders view of Quanah that appeared in the published census report highlighted the subject's mixed-blood heritage. Although clad in white man's clothes and accoutrements—a soft-collared white shirt, brown vest, black tie, and plaited red watch fob—Parker's dark skin, braided hair, red-painted cheeks and ears, as well as the star-shaped silver ornament at his throat, all spoke to his Native roots. Pictured against a solid background, Scott's artistic interpretation of Quanah was straightforward and, despite its ethnographic detail, void of the tired trope of the "noble savage." Given Quanah's prominence and reputation and Scott's mixed personal opinions of the Native leader, especially regarding Parker's involvement in the Peyote Religion, it is surprising that the census agent referred to Quanah only once in his official report, noting only that Parker had been active in discouraging gambling among members of his tribe.[66]

In all, Julian Scott executed more than three-quarters of the twenty-one paintings converted into chromolithographs for the census volume devoted to Indians, as well as numerous other paintings and drawings reproduced in black and white. Most were of Indian subjects in New Mexico and Arizona. Besides his portrait of Quanah Parker, Scott contributed only two other illustrations with connections to Indian Territory, both chromolithographs.

FACING
2.20. Julian Scott, *Quanah Parker*, 1890. Oil on board, 12 × 10 inches. National Cowboy and Western Heritage Museum, Oklahoma City, Oklahoma (1976.033). Photograph © Dickinson Research Center

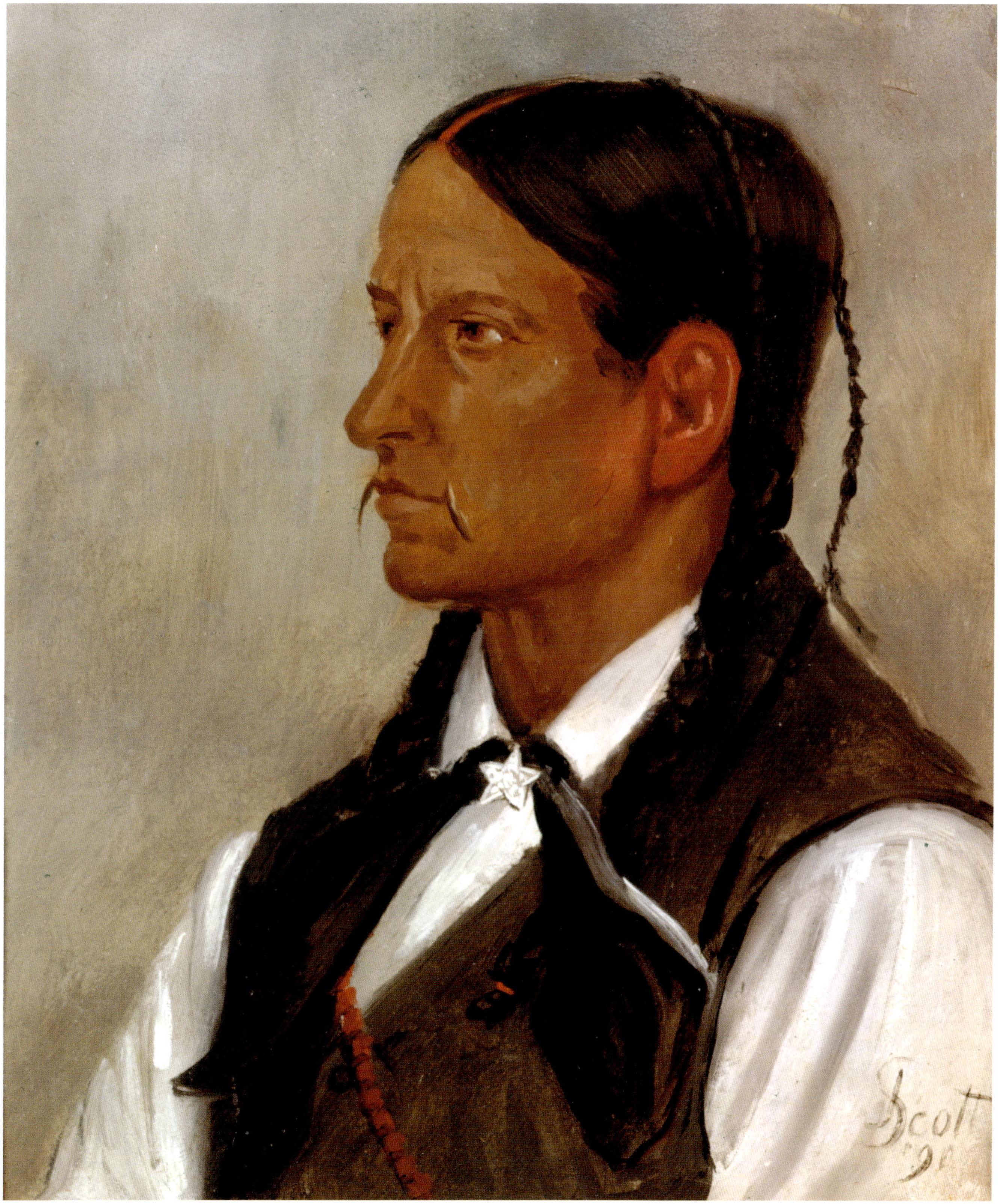

One was a standing portrait of Scar-Faced Charley, a famed Modoc warrior and chief, who had been exiled with other tribal members to the Quapaw Reservation in northeastern Indian Territory after waging war with the United States in Northern California in 1873. Faithfully copied from a studio photograph taken in 1877 by C. M. Bell, Scott's image presents Charley in non-Native garb, complete with a polka-dot bow tie. Thick black hair, cut short in the style of a white man, tops the old Indian's head, while his firm, if disfigured, countenance expresses a mixture of pride, resignation, and hope.[67]

The last of Scott's Oklahoma-based illustrations to appear in *Report on Indians Taxed and Indians Not Taxed in the United States (Except Alaska) at the Eleventh Census: 1890* was yet another portrayal of the government beef issue, this time on the Comanche Reservation. Rendered in color and derived both from personal observation and from some of the several photographs he took at the scene on August 10, 1890, Scott's watercolor of the Indians' horseback chase after longhorn steers failed to communicate the unrestrained excitement and deep emotions of those involved. The former soldier found the carnage involved in killing and butchering beeves in this manner repellant, and his written account of the proceedings, far superior to his painting in description and detail, concluded with the comment, "This exhibition of savage cruelty, permitted as it is by a kind and indulgent government, is no credit to our civilization."[68]

Scott's brief stay on the southern plains inspired several more sketches and paintings, some no doubt created for his own amusement, and some for trade to obtain Indian artifacts. Outside R. A. Sneed's Red Store at Fort Sill, for example, he captured a moving pen-and-ink likeness of a sad-faced elderly Indian man, who sits barefooted, with a bow and arrows in hand, perhaps recalling the free roaming of his youth, when his tribe hunted buffalo for its subsistence. *Horseman Anadarco* [*sic*], *I.T.* (figure 2.21), an equally vibrant and more unusual subject, portrayed a mounted tribesman shaded by a bright red umbrella. After returning to Plainfield, Scott produced a full-length oil-on-canvas portrait of a colorfully dressed Native woman holding a butcher knife in one hand, titled *At Adda-ka-pap's Camp, Cache Creek, I.T.* (figure 2.22).[69]

After leaving the Anadarko Agency in early October 1890, Scott moved on to Santa Fe and his next assignment among the Pueblos of New Mexico and Arizona. The following fall, he returned to Indian Territory, again in connection with the census. Although his exact itinerary is uncertain, and the trip does not seem to have inspired any art, notations on some of his photographs indicate visits to such locales as Tahlequah, Atoka, Okmulgee, Muskogee, Wagoner, and Ardmore.[70]

Five land rushes between 1889 and 1895, the subsequent settlement of former Indian lands by lottery, crime and violence, as well as the quest for statehood, kept both Indian

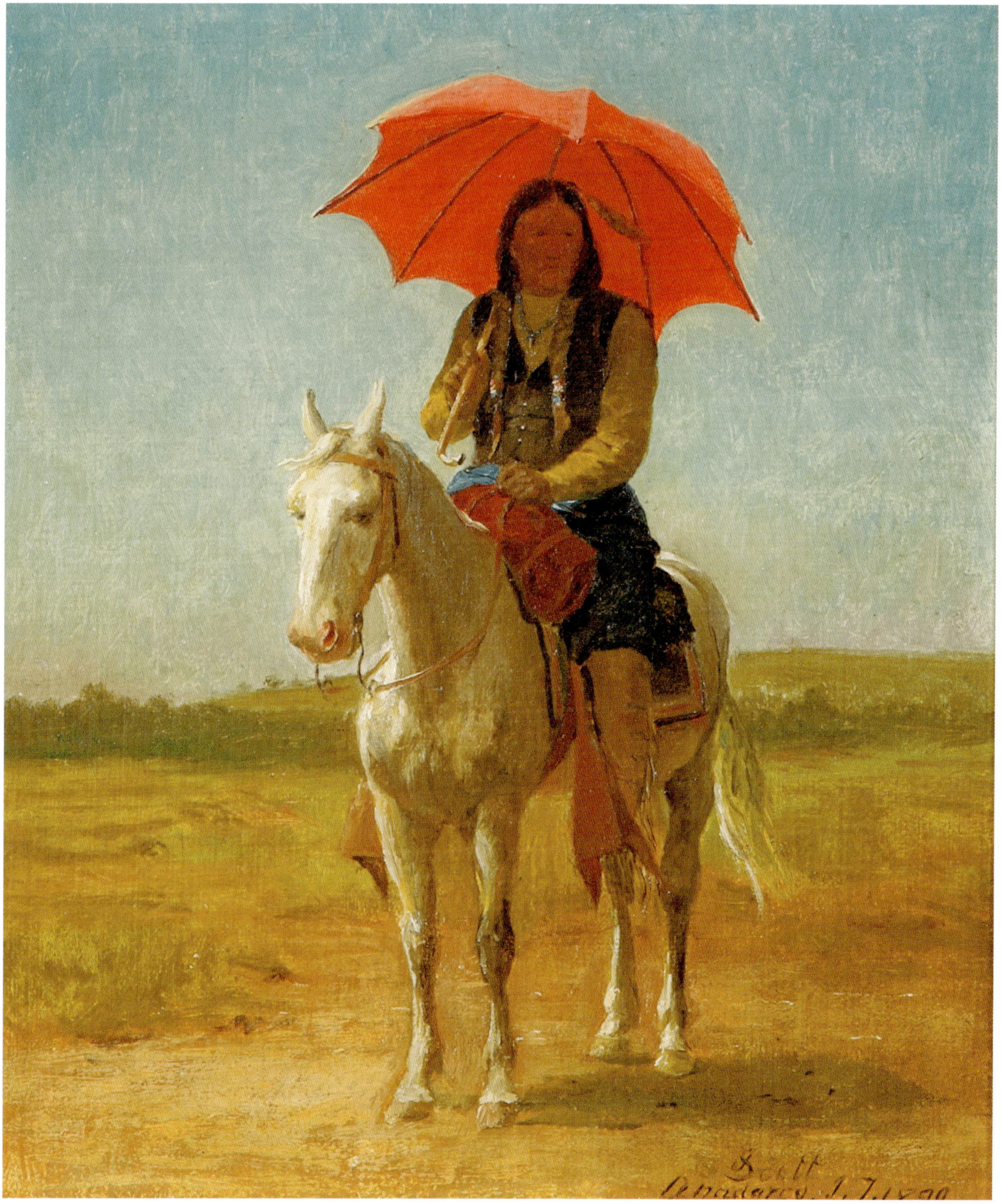

2.21. Julian Scott, *Horseman, Anadarco* [*sic*], *I.T.*, 1890. Oil on canvas, 12.5 × 10.5 inches. Private collection. © Christie's Images. Photograph courtesy Bridgeman Images

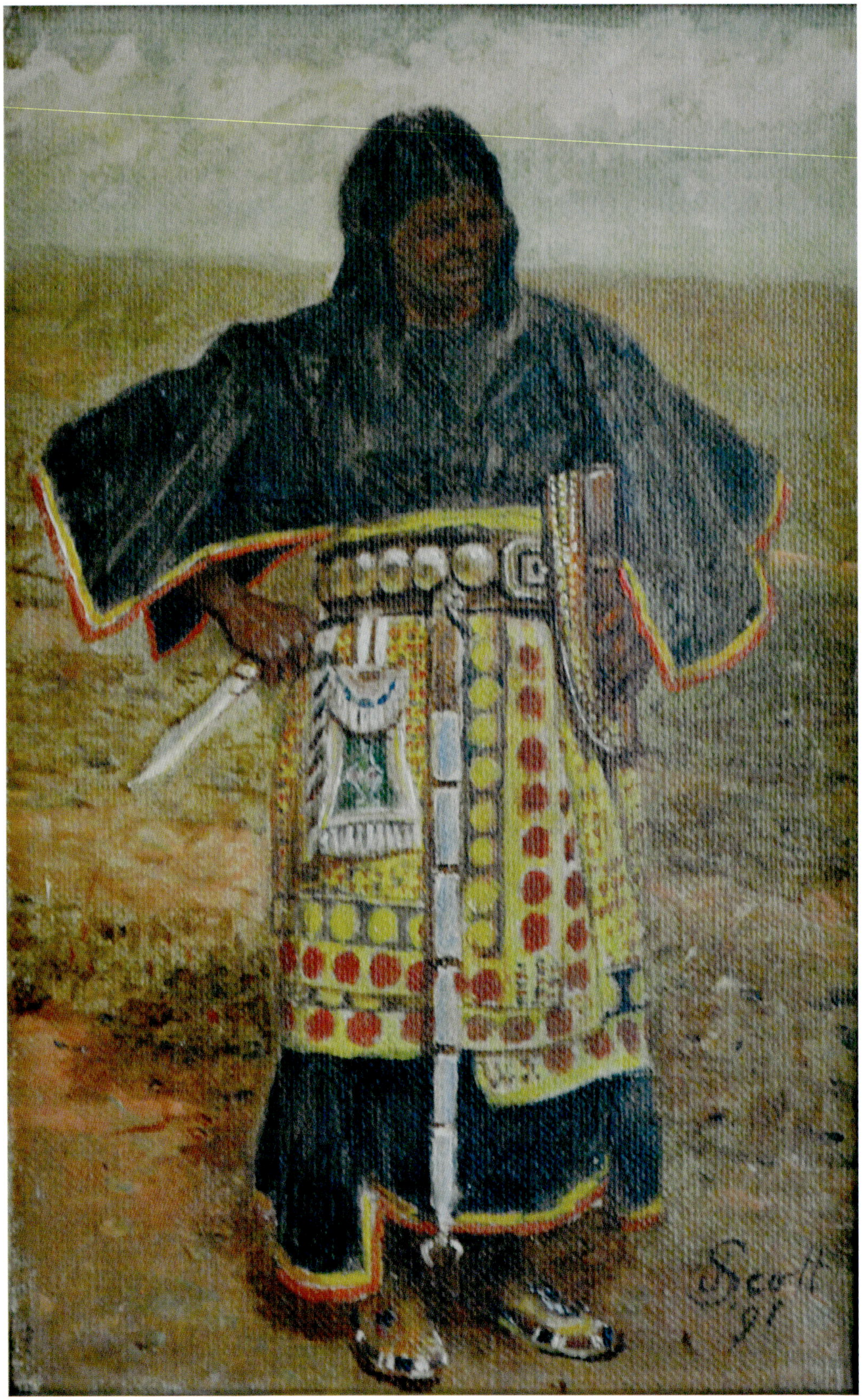

2.22. Julian Scott, *At Adda-ka-pap's Camp, Cache Creek, I.T.*, 1891. Oil on canvas, 9 ¾ × 6 ⅛ inches. Private collection

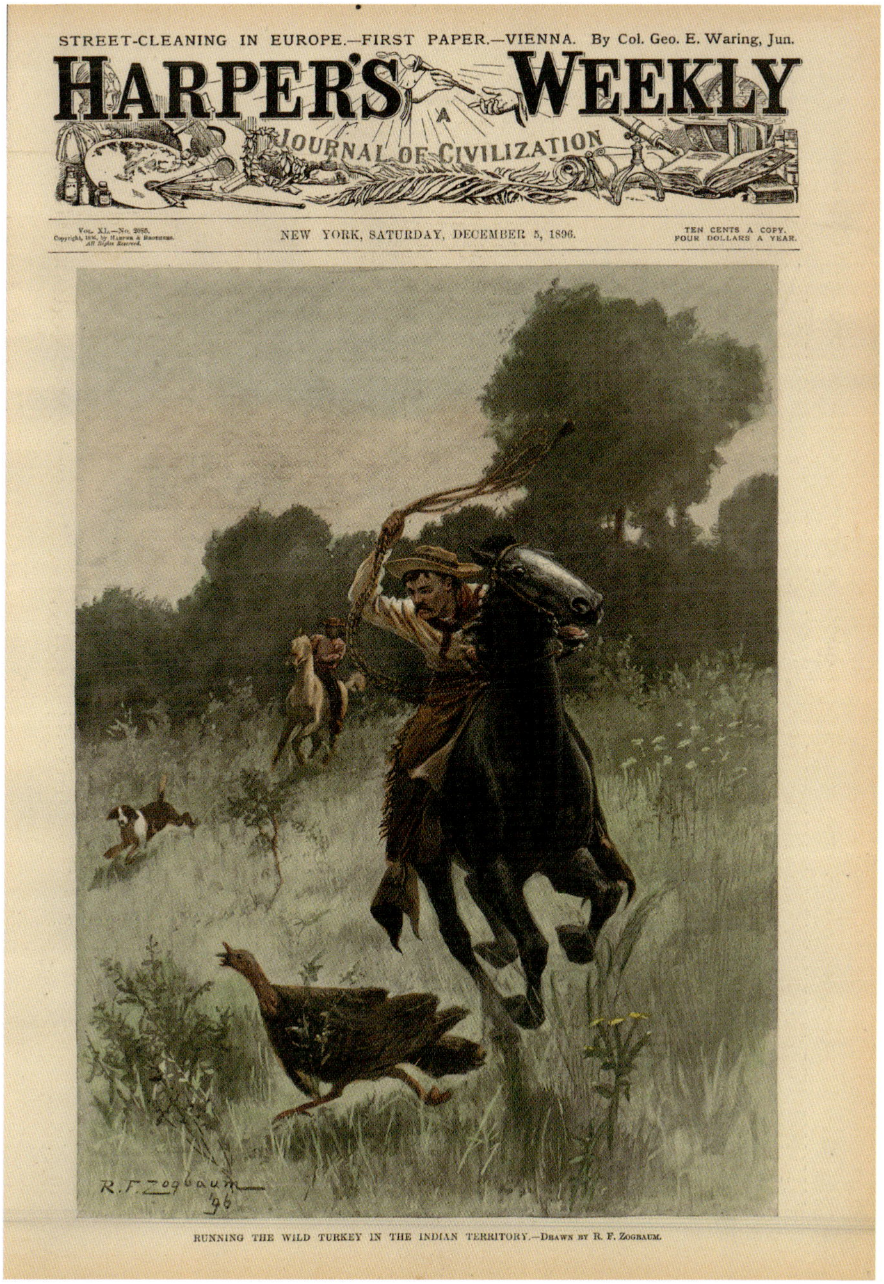

2.23. Rufus Zogbaum, *Running the Wild Turkey in the Indian Territory*, cover of *Harper's Weekly*, December 5, 1896. Color added. Oklahoma Historical Society, Oklahoma City, Oklahoma (21563.PE.HW.96.12.5)

and Oklahoma Territories in the news and continued to stimulate their visual representation into the twentieth century. Although bison had been all but exterminated on the southern plains by the 1880s, other populations of wild game were relatively plentiful. They were hunted for food and sport and were occasionally the subject of national attention. Rufus Zogbaum delivered at least two hunting scenes connected to Indian Territory as a result of his 1888 visit to Fort Reno, although neither of them was visually noteworthy. Both appeared in *Harper's Weekly*: *Hunting Wild Turkey by Moonlight* in

1889, and *Running the Wild Turkey in the Indian Territory* on the cover of the December 5, 1896, issue (figure 2.23).[71]

In 1891 the sporting magazine *Outing* published an illustrated first-person account of deer hunting in Oklahoma Territory. Responding to the "gravitating power of sport and good fellowship," author Francis J. Hagan and several friends, including Charles Smith, a mixed-blood Choctaw, descended with their pack of hunting dogs on the town of Purcell, ready for action.[72] Although the party found "plentiful" deer and "vast quantities of small game," the accompanying illustrations failed to portray either the quantity or the quality of the hunters' quarry, and the scenes of alternating forest and verdant open range were more reminiscent of Yellowstone National Park than the Cross Timbers of central Oklahoma.[73]

Not surprisingly, most of the artists and illustrators attracted to Indian and Oklahoma Territories between 1890 and statehood in 1907 focused their work on the Native nations residing there. In the three decades since the Civil War, U.S. political and military leaders came to appreciate the power of illustrators in shaping public opinion and government policy, particularly when it came to Indians. At the same time, the relationships that prominent illustrators and publications enjoyed and cultivated with key officers paid off through access to military posts, Indian reservations, and inside information. Thus, on October 2, 1894, when General Nelson Miles issued a spur-of-the-moment invitation to Cincinnati artist Henry François Farny (1847–1916) to join him on his inspection tour of Oklahoma Territory, the artist dropped what he was doing, gathered his sketchbook and camera, and departed the same day.[74]

This was not Henry Farny's first trip west. In 1881 the artist had spent several weeks at the Standing Rock Reservation, in Dakota Territory, sketching and photographing among the resident tribes and hoping, in vain, to capture a likeness of the famous Lakota leader Sitting Bull. Farny completed his first painting of an Indian the following year and, during the decade that followed, began to specialize in Indian subjects. Illustrations of Northern Plains and Southwest tribes for *Century*, *Harper's Weekly*, and other prominent publications sustained him while he honed his skills and dreamed of someday painting for himself. Although some criticized his mixing of cultural artifacts from more than one tribe as well as other perceived inaccuracies in his illustrations, Farny's portrayals of cultural conflict between Indians and whites gained a following nevertheless. In 1885 his painting *The Captive*, of a partially naked white man staked out in an Indian camp, won a medal at an American Art Association exhibition, and four years later, a suspenseful canvas titled *Danger* carried off a bronze medal at the Exposition Universelle in Paris. By the time he reached Oklahoma, Farny was accepting fewer illustration assignments and executing more easel paintings, most of them small, detailed, and tightly composed works, rendered in a somber palette of gouache and watercolor, indicative of his German training.[75]

On his 1894 trip, Farny reached the hamlet of Duncan in Oklahoma Territory by rail, then boarded an army ambulance sent to convey him to Fort Sill. The thirty-mile journey carried him over rolling plains, endowed here and there with stands of wildflowers, running streams, groves of trees, and red clay barrens. The lonely beauty of the scene, which he compared to English meadows, impressed the artist. Apart from a few ox-drawn freighting outfits, however, people and animals were scarce. By the time he reached the post, Farny was convinced that, despite its picturesque qualities, the mostly Indian land through which he traveled would always remain pastoral and sparsely populated, for it "lacked flattering inducements to the pioneer settlers, even though it be a gift from the Government."[76]

At Fort Sill, the artist delightedly discovered plenty of compelling and colorful subject matter close at hand. Geronimo and about two hundred other Apache prisoners of war, originally from Arizona and under guard at the post since the previous October, were the most accessible, and the reservations of the Comanches, Kiowas, Wichitas, and other tribes also lay nearby. Working primarily in pencil or pen and ink, the artist also completed an occasional plein-air sketch in gouache (figure 2.24). He made full use of his camera as well, although some of his intended subjects were reluctant to pose for the device. The artist later recalled one Indian girl who fled "like a frightened partridge" when he pointed his lens toward her while she was picking pecans.[77]

During his brief stay on the southern plains, Farny observed Native dances, watched an Apache nine soundly defeat a team of soldiers in a game of baseball, and got along well with the Apache soldier detailed to take care of him during his stay on post. The Indian corporal later named his new baby Farny in honor of the artist.[78]

Although Farny was generally supportive of the army's experiment of enlisting all-Indian infantry and cavalry units, he recognized some of the cultural problems involved. The regulation requiring Native troopers to cut their long hair was one stumbling block, and the artist also believed that a concession to "native taste in toilet," in the form of a looser-fitting military uniform for Indian troops, might be adopted to good effect.[79]

Within a few days of Farny's return from Oklahoma, an article describing his experiences appeared in the *Cincinnati Commercial Gazette*, accompanied by a quartet of illustrations. Three were pen and ink drawings: a Kiowa camp, two Indian boys on horseback, and the head of a Tawakoni tribesman. The other was a small gouache portrait Farny had rendered of Geronimo, who, afterward, had autographed it (figure 2.25).[80]

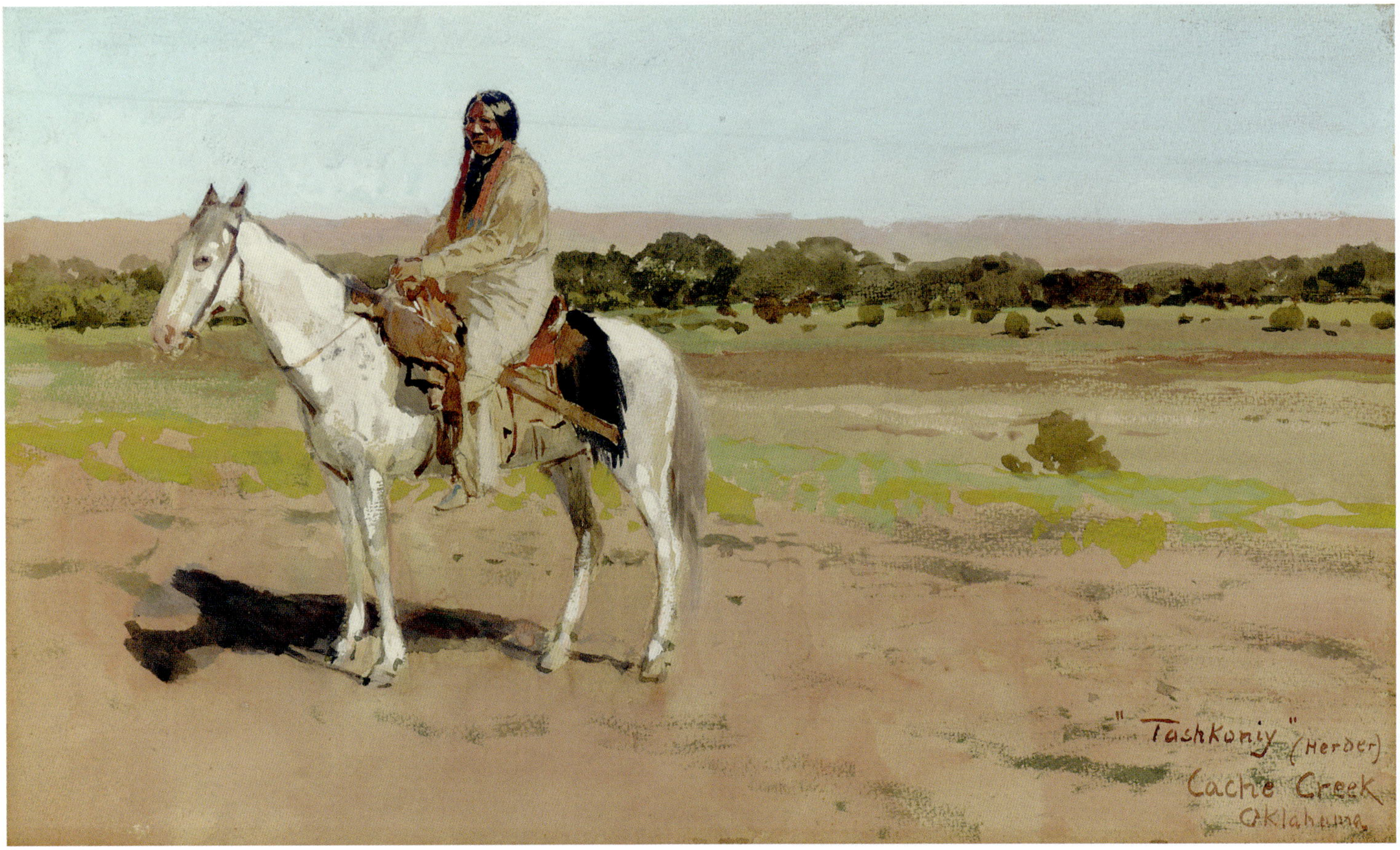

2.24. Henry François Farny, *Tashkoniy (Herder), Cache Creek, Oklahoma*, n.d. Gouache on paper, 9 ¾ × 16 inches. Private collection. © Christie's Images. Photograph courtesy Bridgeman Images

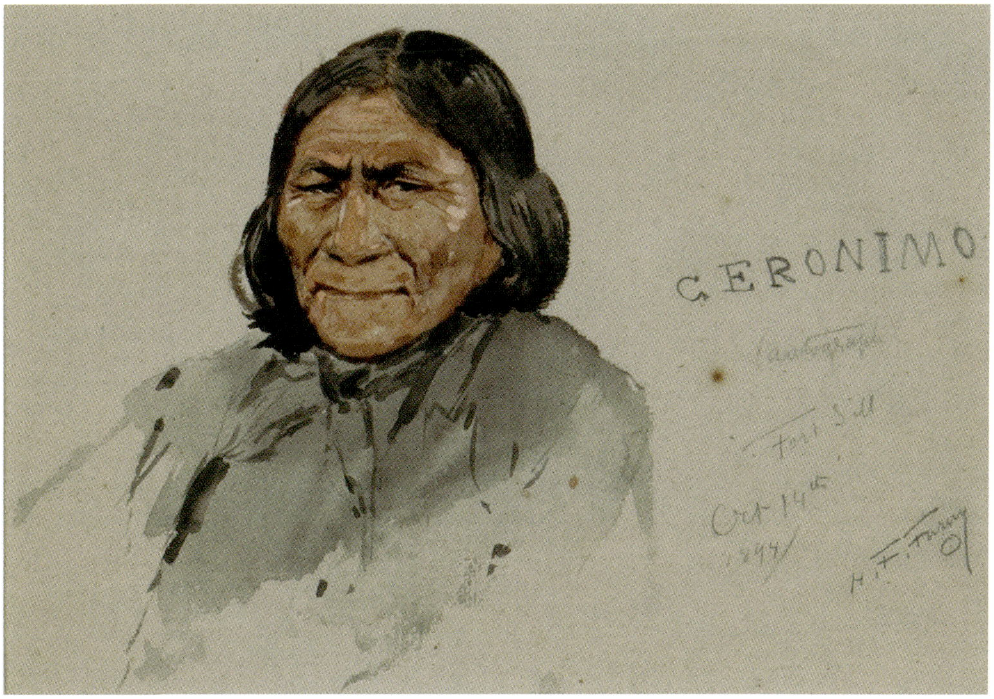

2.25. Henry François Farny, *Geronimo*, 1894. Gouache on paper, 7 ½ × 9 ¾ inches. Desert Caballeros Western Museum Collection, Wickenburg, Arizona. Gift of Mr. and Mrs. Aiken Fisher. Photograph © Terrence Moore

In 1894 the artist produced such paintings as *Southern Plains Indian Warrior*, *Indian with Tomahawk*, *Evening Camp*, and perhaps others rooted in his recent trip west. Farny's experiences around Fort Sill informed his paintings for the rest of his life. Although he considered the persistence of Native customs and lore in the face of modernization quaint, romantic, and ultimately doomed, the art market for traditional scenes of Indian life remained strong. By 1900 the topic of cultural conflict between Indians and whites that had played such an important role in Farny's early work had largely given way to themes of loss and decline in Native culture. The artist maintained his preference for the medium of gouache and transparent watercolor, in works that were increasingly idealized and symbolic.[81]

On March 12, 1897, Fort Sill welcomed Chicago portraitist Elbridge Ayer Burbank, who arrived at the post intent on securing a likeness of Geronimo for his uncle Edward Everett Ayer, a prominent collector of American Indian artifacts and president of the Field Museum of Natural History.[82]

Within three days Burbank was at work on the Chiricahua Apache leader's portrait, and by March 21 he had completed both full and profile views. He had also begun a portrait of Giaume Honemetah (Gi-aum-e Hon-o-me-tah), "a pretty, mischievous girl who talked like a magpie to her companions" and, according to Burbank, was "known as the 'belle of the Kiowas'" (figure 2.26). To accentuate the natural exoticism of his model, the artist draped the girl's shoulders with a colorful Navajo blanket borrowed from an army officer.[83]

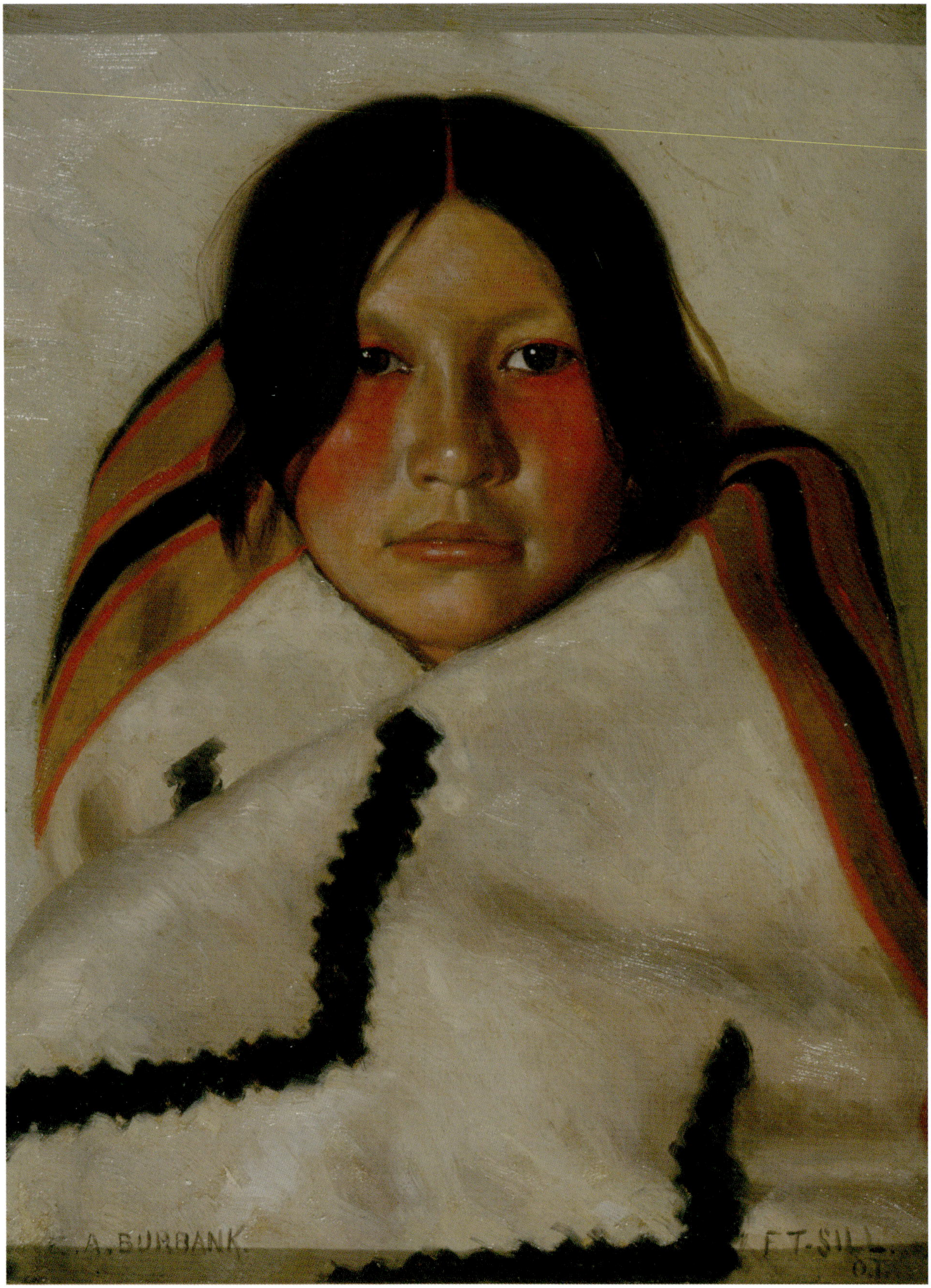
A. BURBANK.
FT-SIL
O.T.

Showing remarkable diligence and endurance, as well as a winning way with his sitters, Burbank had completed fourteen oil portraits by mid-April and was hard at work depicting a bonneted Comanche named Bon-e-ta.[84] Shortly after, he expressed satisfaction with his Indian works, "as they make beautiful pictures so rich in color and the costume so artistic and then they have a historical value."[85]

Although portraiture was the focus of his trip to Oklahoma Territory, Burbank apparently captured other subjects of interest. Early in his visit, for example, he reported sketching an "interesting" fence and gate built by the Apaches. Given the tribe's incarceration, perhaps the artist appreciated the irony as well as the design of the barrier.[86]

Back in Chicago by June, Burbank had framed and delivered the artwork due his uncle and arranged for an exhibition of nineteen other paintings at the Thurber Art Galleries shortly thereafter.[87] All but two soon quickly sold, launching Burbank's career as one of the preeminent American Indian portraitists of the late nineteenth and early twentieth centuries.[88]

Displaying a Catlin-like obsession for Indian portraiture, the indefatigable artist crisscrossed the West in search of fresh subject matter. He returned to Oklahoma Territory in 1899 and again in 1900, completing likenesses of many other Native sitters and five additional portraits of Geronimo. Artist and model became friends, and along with painting Geronimo's likeness (figure 2.27), Burbank also recorded parts of the Apache leader's life story. He found Geronimo to be a loving husband and father, generous to the poor, and an inveterate gambler. The old warrior also exhibited a fine sense of humor, and on visits to Burbank's studio, Geronimo sometimes exchanged good-humored barbs with the artist's sitters and with bystanders from other tribes, who had gathered to watch Burbank paint.[89]

Burbank initially offered his models two or three silver dollars to pose for him. When some of his sitters demanded more, he created a pay scale that varied depending on the subject's clothing, accoutrements, and overall visual impact. The artist claimed that Geronimo routinely demanded half a dollar more than any of his other models, and that after returning from the Indian Congress in Omaha in 1898, with a newfound appreciation of the worth of his likeness, Geronimo demanded a whopping twenty-five dollars to sit for the artist in March 1899. Around the same time, the artist sold one of his portraits of the famous Apache to a patron for three hundred dollars.[90]

Burbank's third visit to Oklahoma in the fall of 1900 was his longest, lasting nearly a year. Although he did most of his painting in a makeshift studio he established in a hotel in Darlington, near Fort Reno, a newspaper article in May 1901 reported him planning trips to Fort Sill and the upper Washita to paint Red Moon's band of Cheyennes. He also paid visits to the Cherokees, Kickapoos, Shawnees, Modocs, Ottawas, Sacs and Foxes, and other tribes in eastern Indian Territory (figure 2.28).[91]

FACING
2.26. Elbridge Ayer Burbank, *Gi-aum-e Hon-o-me-tah (Young Woman), Kiowa, Fort Sill, Oklahoma Territory*, 1899. Oil on panel, 8 × 6 inches. Newberry Library, Chicago, Illinois (Ayer Art Burbank, No. 77)

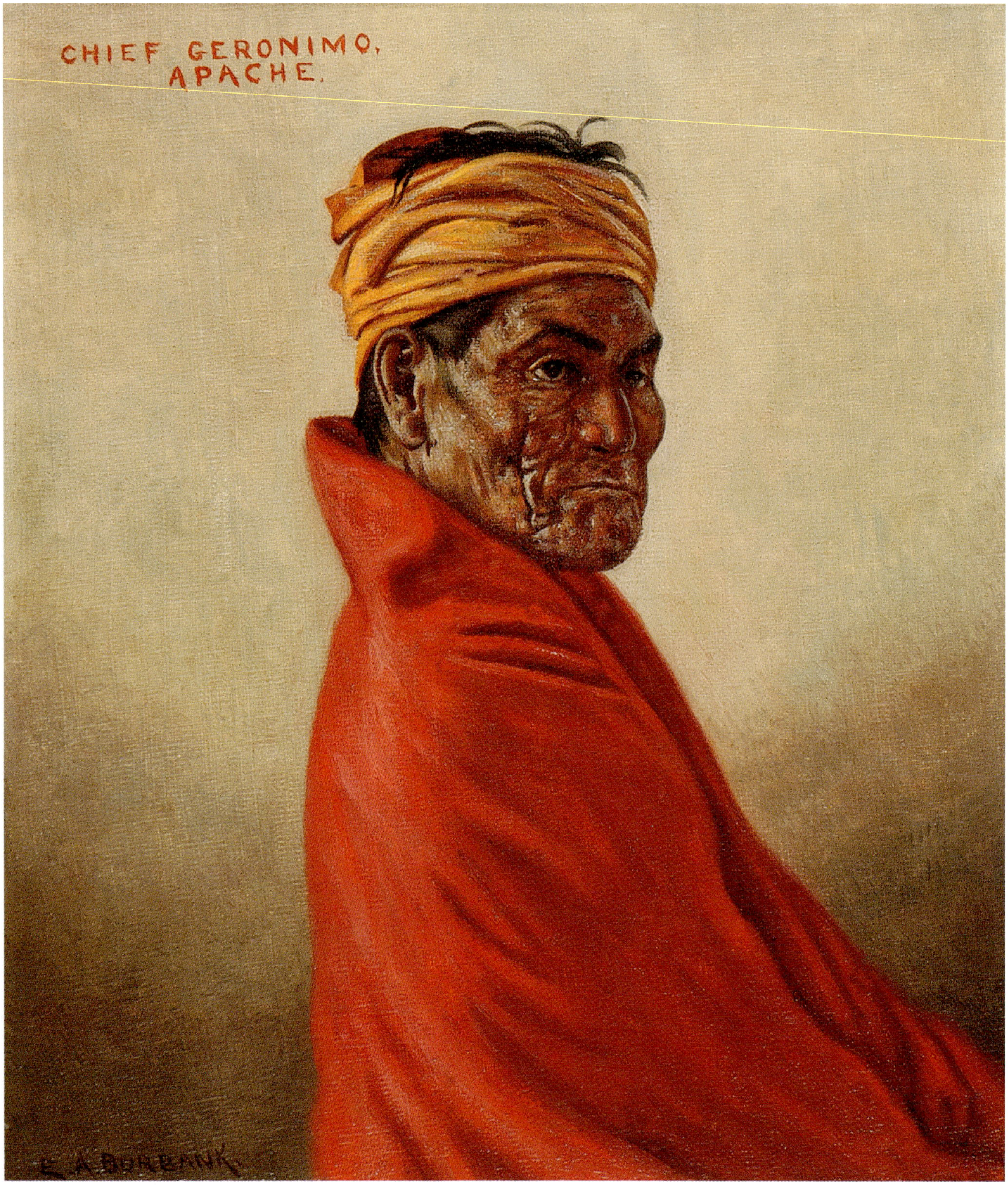

2.27. Elbridge Ayer Burbank, *Chief Geronimo, Apache*, c. 1899. Oil on canvas, 12 × 10 inches. Eiteljorg Museum of American Indians and Western Art, Indianapolis, Indiana (1989.2.27)

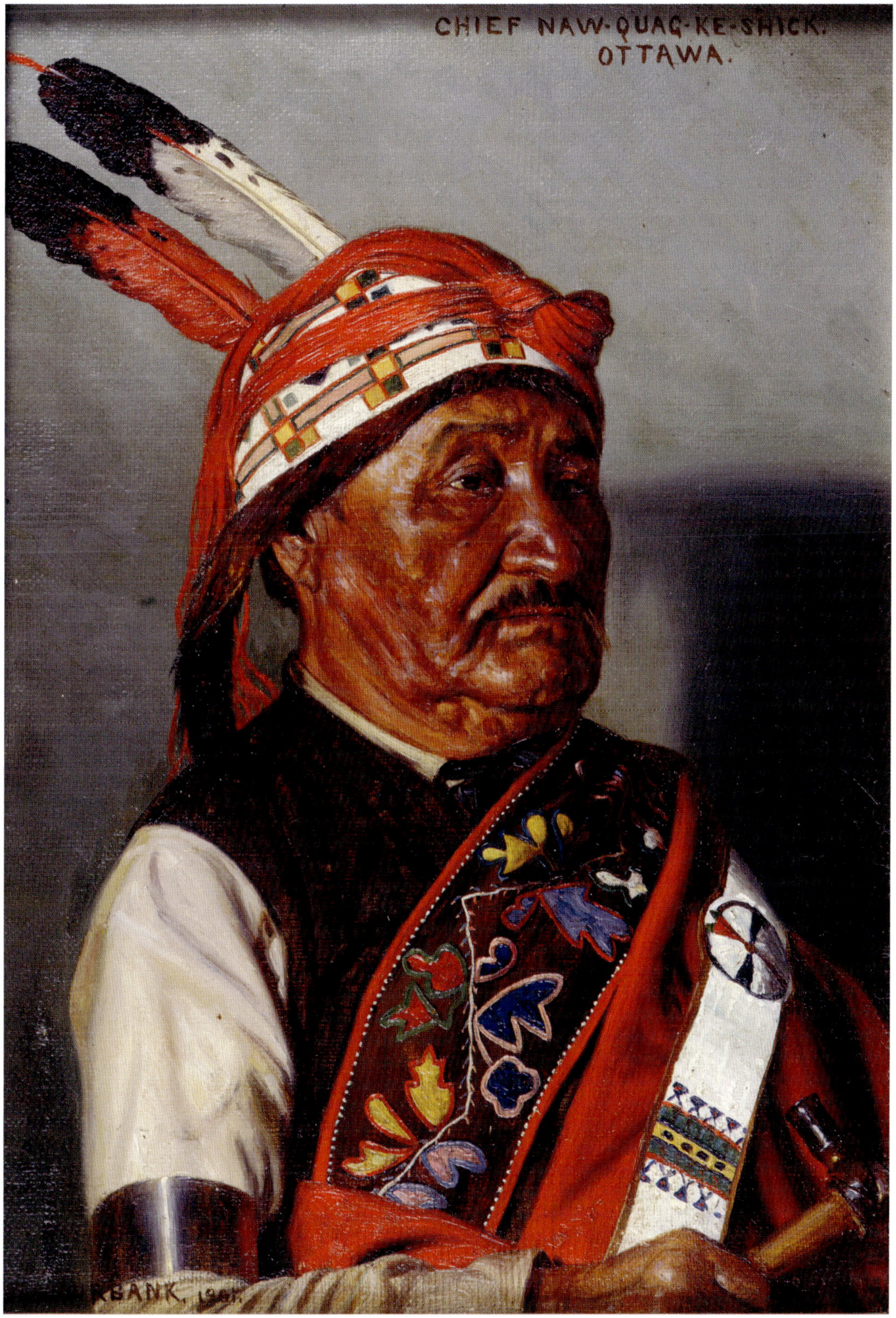

2.28. Elbridge Ayer Burbank, *Chief Naw-quag-ke-shick; Ottawa, Half-Male*, 1901. Oil on canvas, 13 × 9 inches. The Butler Institute of American Art, Youngstown, Ohio (912-O-553)

Having studied a half-dozen years in Munich, Burbank shared Henry Farny's training, palette, texture, and eye for detail but favored oil and Conté crayon over watercolor as mediums. After blocking out a rough silhouette of his model in crayon, Burbank added the eyes, nose, mouth, and cheeks in quick succession, with firm draftsmanship and deft brushwork. The instinctive application of light, shadow, and color followed. He avoided toning his canvases in advance as many portraitists did, believing that it resulted in abnormally heavy shadows.[92]

Influenced by posing conventions employed by photographers, such as those of John K. Hillers in his contributions to Bureau of American Ethnology reports, Burbank typically painted his models in frontal, profile, or three-quarters views as they sat in a chair in front of a white canvas background. He found Indians to be exceptionally patient models. "They don't know what nerves are," he told one reporter. "They sit as if petrified."[93] To preserve his own energy and that of his sitters, Burbank worked only four hours a day and, when painting, took breaks every half hour so his models could relax. During one break, the artist grabbed a rifle and took potshots at a jackrabbit from his studio window.[94]

Burbank found some of his models taciturn and haughty, but others friendly and engaging. He enjoyed the company of most of his subjects and made every effort to gather cultural information as well as likenesses from them. One old Cherokee warrior described in graphic detail how to scalp an enemy.[95]

When he finished a portrait, Burbank inscribed the sitter's name phonetically on the surface of the image along with his or her tribe and location. Back in Chicago, the artist marketed his work to individuals, both privately and through annual exhibitions at the Thurber Art Galleries. Youngstown, Ohio, art collector Joseph G. Butler, Jr., made the largest single purchase of Burbank's work: 118 paintings in 1902. The Smithsonian Institution and the Field Museum bought many others for exhibition and study.[96] "Ethnologically considered," a newspaper reporter wrote in 1901, "these portraits are of priceless value, for another generation and the American Indian—the artistic American Indian—will be but a memory. In his place will be the half-breed, with store clothes and the educated Indian from Carlisle."[97]

Corporate customers included the Santa Fe Railway, which bought several southwestern subjects for use on advertising calendars over the years. The Chicago Colortype Company is said to have profited handsomely from the sale of 11 million lithographs made from Burbank's fetching portrait of Giaume Honemetah, which the company had purchased for a mere two hundred dollars.[98]

Oklahoma had achieved statehood by the time Burbank made his final visit there in 1908 and had begun producing artists of its own, although mostly amateur. As early

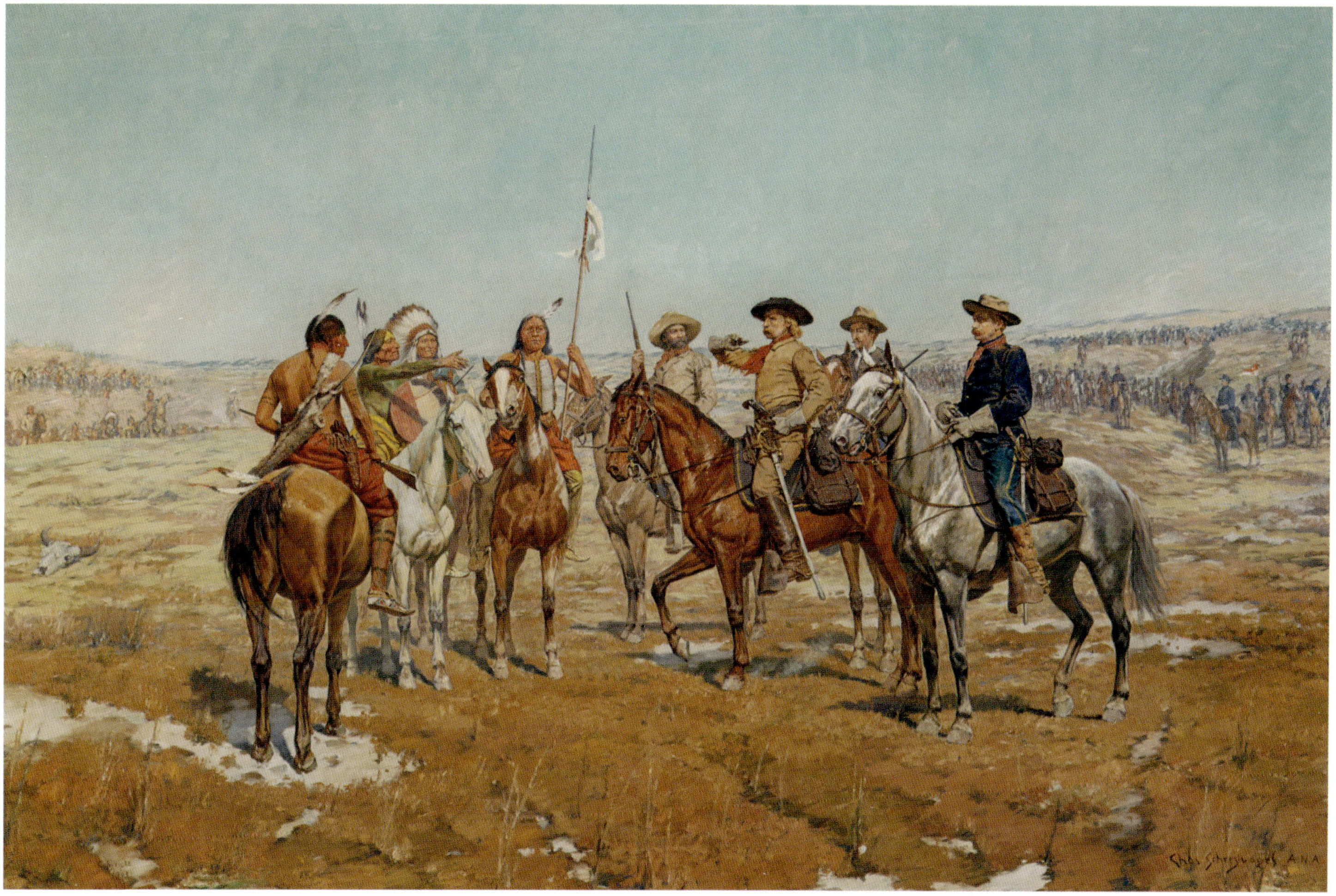

2.29. Charles C. Schreyvogel, *Sheridan's Campaign, Custer's Demand*, 1903. Oil on canvas, 61 × 86 inches. Gilcrease Museum, Tulsa, Oklahoma (0127.1254)

as 1894, an annual territorial fair promoted the fine arts and provided premiums in the catchall category of "Paintings and Fancywork," which also included photography, such crafts as china painting, sewing, embroidery, rag carpets, yarn rugs, and doilies, among others. Fifteen artists entered that year, at least two-thirds of them women. Exhibiting an Oklahoma landscape, a head portrait, and an unspecified subject rendered on bolting cloth, Pauline Ashton claimed the award for the best collection of paintings. Martha Avey entered the largest group by a single artist, nine works in all, including landscape, still life, floral, portrait, figure, and animal subjects. In 1905 she would be appointed the first supervisor of art for Oklahoma City public schools, and later, art director for Oklahoma City University.[99]

By the early 1900s, Kansas-born Nellie Shepherd (1877–1920), who had settled with her parents and siblings on a homestead near Oklahoma City after the Land Run of 1889, was already displaying a talent for painting that would make her perhaps the

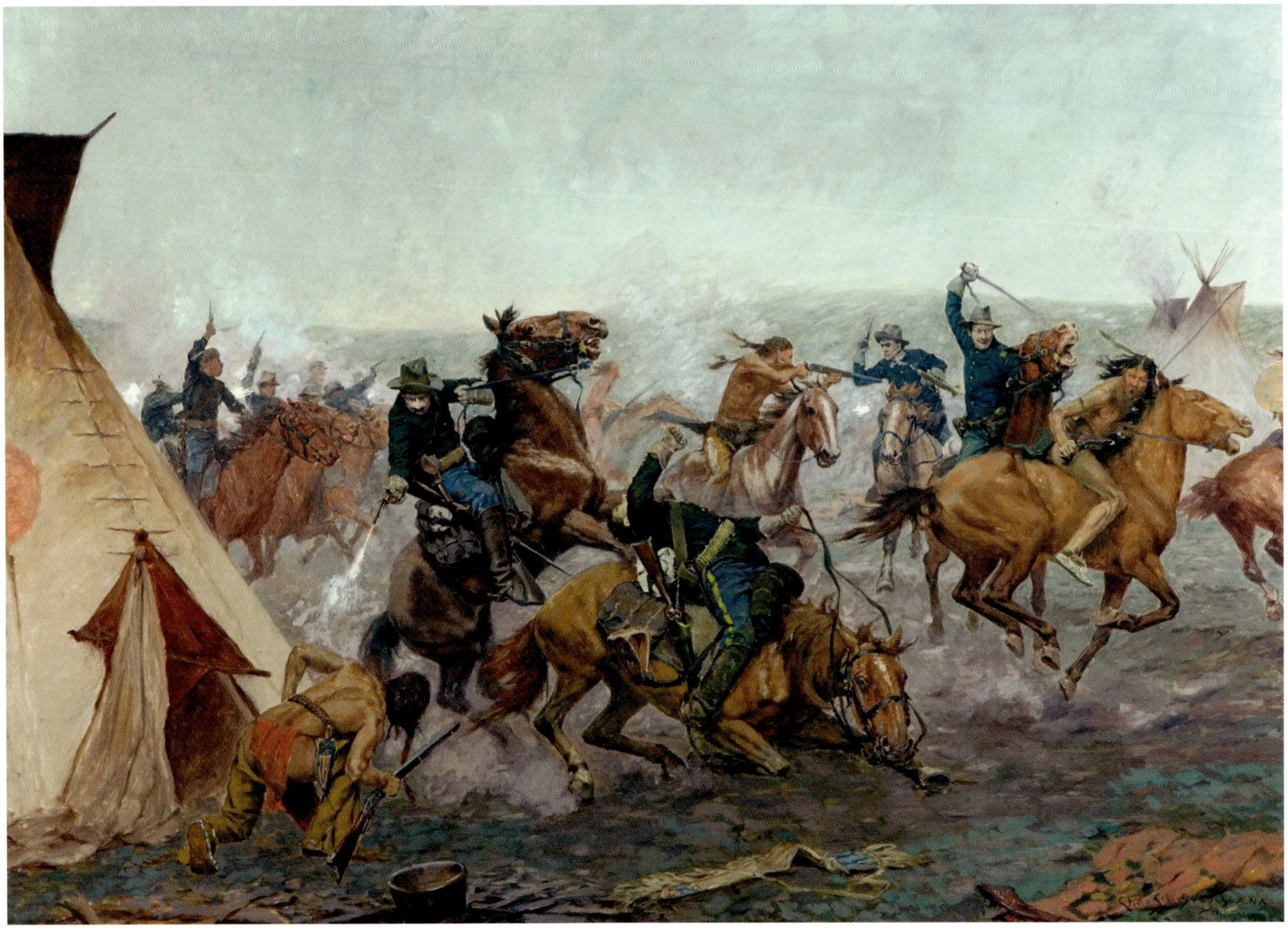

2.30. Charles C. Schreyvogel, *Early Dawn Attack*, 1904. Oil on canvas, 33⅜ × 45⅛ inches. Gilcrease Museum, Tulsa, Oklahoma (0127.1255)

first homegrown professional artist to reside in the new state. In 1904 some of her work decorated the Oklahoma building of the St. Louis World's Fair to positive reviews, and the Scott Drug Store mounted the first public exhibition of her paintings in Oklahoma City. "There is a striking individuality about all of Miss Shepherd's work," the *Oklahoman* noted, "which lifts it quite beyond and above the plane of commonplace, and makes it very worthy of study."[100]

Despite the efforts of Nellie Shepherd and the fledgling art community she represented, when it came to professional artists, Indian and Oklahoma Territories, on the eve of statehood, were still largely dependent on the talent and interest of outsiders. Just after the turn of the twentieth century, the academically trained easel painter Charles Schreyvogel drew on the region's colorful past in two works, *Custer's Demand* (1903; figure 2.29) and *Early Dawn Attack* (1904; figure 2.30). The former drew the ire of artist Frederic Remington, who publicly scorned its inaccuracy as a history painting. The latter, said to have been inspired by the attack on Black Kettle's village at the Battle of the Washita, symbolized the conquest of the West. The artist completed both works at his Hoboken, New Jersey, studio and, rather than seek models on the reservations of Oklahoma, used local talent and cast members from Buffalo Bill's Wild West instead.[101]

In 1906, a well-known Oklahoma City businessman brought Alfred Montgomery, the famed "farmer painter" of Kansas, to town to lecture on art at the local Chautauqua and to produce an oil rendering of an Oklahoma wheat field.[102] Known for his realistic style, Montgomery was said to paint "corn that the rats will try to gnaw."[103] Before departing for his home state, the gregarious artist displayed his work in Tulsa, where he presented visiting Kansas governor Edward W. Hoch with a picture of an ear of corn—painted on a cigar box lid.[104]

Between the outbreak of the Civil War in 1861 and advent of Oklahoma statehood in 1907, the visual representation of the people, places, and events making up life in Indian Territory was largely the province of a relative few newspaper and magazine illustrators, whose work was the product not only of observation and imagination, but also of political and economic motives and social and cultural bias. Almost without exception, the trope of "vanishing race" and artists' desire to capture traditional Native culture through their work motivated the handful of easel painters drawn to the region in the 1890s and early 1900s. Although Indian Territory was a far different place at the dawn of the twentieth century than it had been at the beginning of the Civil War, the art that it had inspired was still deeply rooted in the past and would remain so for years to come.

Notes

1. Honey Springs, a well-known rest stop along the Texas Road, was also the location of a Confederate commissary depot. See Ralph Jones, "Honey Springs, Battle of," *Encyclopedia of Oklahoma History and Culture*, accessed December 12, 2015, www.okhistory.org/publications/enc/entry.php?entry=HO025; *The War in Arkansas—The Battle of Honey Springs, July 17.—Defeat of the Rebels under General Cooper by the U.S. Troops under Major-General James G. Blunt.*—From a sketch by James R. O'Neill, *Frank Leslie's Illustrated Newspaper*, August 29, 1863, 364; Don Jensen, "O'Neill and the Band: The Baxter Springs Massacre, Part 1," Kansas Genealogy Trails, March 2011, http://genealogytrails.com/kan/cherokee/oneillandtheband.html; Don Jensen, "O'Neill and the Band: The Baxter Springs Massacre, Part 2," Civil War Wisconsin, April 2011, http://civilwarwisconsin.com/campfire-stories/43-oneill-and-the-band-part-two.html.
2. Jones, "Honey Springs."
3. W. David Baird and Danney Goble, *Oklahoma, a History* (Norman: University of Oklahoma Press, 2008), 113–29.
4. For an overview of Davis's career, see John M. Coward, "Making Images on the Indian Frontier: The Adventures of Special Artist Theodore Davis," *Journalism History* 36, no. 3 (Fall 2010): 150–59.
5. Ibid., 152.
6. "Indian Prisoners Taken by Custer," *Harper's Weekly*, December 26, 1868, 825–26; "The Indian War," *Harper's Weekly*, January 16, 1869, 41–42; "Issuing Beef to the Indians at Medicine Bluff Creek," *Harper's Weekly*, March 27, 1869, 204–205.
7. "The Battle of the Washita—General Custar's [*sic*] Report to General Sheridan," *Frank Leslie's Illustrated Newspaper*, December, 26, 1868, 235; "The Battle of Washita—The Attack on Black Kettle's Cheyenne Camp, Washita River, Indian Territory, by the Seventh Regiment Cavalry Under Major-General George A. Custer, Nov. 27th," *Frank Leslie's Illustrated Newspaper*, December, 26, 1868, 233.
8. George A. Custer, *My Life on the Plains; or, Personal Experiences with Indians* (New York: Sheldon, 1874; repr., Norman: University of Oklahoma Press, 1962), 242, page citations refer to the 1962 edition; Kappes's career is discussed in John Davis, "Alfred Kappes," *Paintings and Sculpture in the Collection of the National Academy of Design*, vol. 1, *1826–1925*, ed. David Dearinger (New York: Hudson Hills Press, 2004), 329.
9. An overview of Taylor's life and career can be found in Charles G. Markantes, "James E. Taylor, Artist and Correspondent," *Research Review: The Journal of the Little Big Horn Associates* 12, no. 1 (Winter 1998): 2–13. See also Paula Fleming, "Drawing the Western Frontier: The James E. Taylor Album," Smithsonian National Museum of Natural History, Department of Anthropology, accessed July 1, 2015, http://anthropology.si.edu/naa/exhibits/taylor/taylor.htm.
10. Fleming, "Drawing the Western Frontier."
11. For an informed scholar's commentary on Remington's illustration in Eggleston's *Household History*, see Brian W. Dippie, "Drawn to the West," *Western Historical Quarterly* 35, no. 1 (Spring 2004): 10.
12. U.S. Congress, *The Statutes at Large and Proclamations of the United States of America from December 1869–March 1871*, vol. 26, ed. George P. Sanger (Boston: Little, Brown, 1871), 40.
13. Colyer was appointed to his post as

commissioner of the United States Indian Commission of New York in October 1868 and began his inspection tour among tribes in southern Kansas in mid-February 1869. He entered eastern Indian Territory in early March 1869. See Vincent Colyer, "Report of the Hon. Vincent Colyer, United States Special Indian Commissioner, on the Indian tribes and reservations of Eastern Kansas, Indian Territory, Northern Texas, New Mexico, Northeastern Arizona, and Southeastern Colorado, obtained by personal observation and inspection among these tribes during the year 1869," *Report on the Commissioner of Indian Affairs Made to the Secretary of the Interior for the Year 1869* (Washington, D.C.: Government Printing Office, 1870), 70–75.

14. Robert R. White, "Artists of Territorial New Mexico, 1846–1912" (PhD diss., University of New Mexico, Albuquerque, 1993), 321.
15. Colyer, "Report," 70–75. Art historian Robert R. White has suggested that the works Colyer completed while Indian commissioner were "done for his own amusement and relaxation and almost certainly were never exhibited." See White, "Artists of Territorial New Mexico," 7.
16. Colyer, "Report," 81.
17. Ibid., 83.
18. Stieffel's brief sojourn to Fort Sill is discussed in Edgar M. Howell, *Hermann Stieffel: Soldier Artist of the West*, Contributions from the Museum of History and Technology, Paper 12, U.S. National Museum Bulletin 225 (Washington, D.C.: Smithsonian Institution, 1960), 8, 14.
19. Colyer, "Report," 87. Colyer's party arrived at Bascom on May 11, 1869. The commander of Colyer's military escort was often at odds with the Indian commissioner and disputed parts of his account of the journey to New Mexico. See Richard T. Jacob, "Military Reminiscences of Captain Richard T. Jacob," *Chronicles of Oklahoma* 2, no. 1 (March 1924): 9–36. The Antelope Hills are located in present-day Roger Mills County, Oklahoma. See Vincent Colyer, *Antelope Hills*, 1869, watercolor on paper, Panhandle-Plains Historical Museum, Canyon, Texas, Friends of Southwestern Art Purchase (2006-94-7).
20. Baird and Goble, *Oklahoma*, 122.
21. John H. Beadle, *The Undeveloped West: Or, Five Years in the Territories. . . .* (Philadelphia, Pa.: National Publishing, 1873), 420, and illustrations on 410 and 416.
22. See Claudine Chalmers, *Chronicling the West for Harper's: Coast to Coast with Frenzeny and Tavernier in 1873–1874* (Norman: University of Oklahoma Press, 2013); Edward King, *The Great South* (Hartford, Conn.: American Publishing, 1875), i.
23. King, *The Great South*, ii.
24. "Personal Items," *San Francisco Daily Evening Bulletin*, February 1, 1873, 1.
25. King, *The Great South*, 188.
26. Edward King, "The Great South: The New Route to the Gulf," *Scribner's Magazine* 6, no. 3 (July 1873): 257–88; Peter E. Palmquist and Thomas R Kailbourn, *Pioneer Photographers from the Mississippi to the Continental Divide: A Biographical Dictionary, 1839–1865* (Stanford, Calif.: Stanford University Press, 2005), 103.
27. See [James Champney], *Limestone Gap*, in King, "The Great South," 257.
28. See [James Champney], *"The Indian Consents,"* in ibid., 283.
29. Champney's character studies in King, "The Great South," include *Jeff. Davis* (p. 258); *The Pet Conductor* (p. 258); *Charlie* (p. 260); *Warming Himself* (p. 265); *A Creek Indian* (p. 272); *"I'm From Alabama"* (p. 272); *A Creek Indian Woman* (p. 272); *At the Ferry* (p. 273); *"Has the Arkansaw Riz?"* (p. 273);

Uncle John Cunningham (p. 274); *An Adopted Indian Citizen* (p. 274); *An Indian Mule-Driver* (p. 275); *Indian Ball-Player* (p. 279); *A Terminus Type* (p. 281); and *A Southwestern Land-Owner* (p. 287).

30. For Champney's genre and landscape works, see ibid., including *Fort Gibson, Indian Territory* (p. 270); *A South-Western Ferry* (p. 271); *An Indian Territorial Mansion* (p. 277); *A School Among the Creeks* (p. 279); *Toll Bridge—Limestone Gap, Indian Territory* (p. 281); and *Twilight on Pryor's Creek, Indian Territory* (p. 269).
31. See King, *The Great South*, ii.
32. "Book Notices," *New York Evening Post*, June 20, 1873, 2.
33. Champney signed his work "Champ" to avoid confusion with the work of other Boston artists. Some of his work was redrawn by *Scribner's* staff artists, such as Thomas Moran, to better fit the magazine. King, *The Great South*, ii, 269.
34. The pair's visit to Indian Territory and the stories and illustrations they prepared for *Harper's* is covered in detail in Chalmers, *Chronicling the West*, 52–65; "New York Letters," *Sunday Oregonian* (Portland), May 22, 1887, 1.
35. Robert Taft, "The Pictorial Record of the Old West: I. Frenzeny and Tavernier," *Kansas Historical Quarterly* 14, no. 1 (February 1946): 6.
36. Ibid., 7.
37. "Leaf from a Sketch-Book," *Harper's Weekly*, November 8, 1873, 994.
38. Chalmers, *Chronicling the West*, 4; "Watching the Storm," *Harper's Weekly*, March 21, 1874, 267.
39. *Harper's Weekly*, April 11, 1874, 326; Chalmers, *Chronicling the West*, 63–64.
40. Taft, "Pictorial Record," 9.
41. Michael R. Grauer, "Charles Franklin 'Frank' Reaugh," in *Windows on the West: The Art of Frank Reaugh*," ed. Peter F. Mears (Austin, Tex.: Harry Ransom Center, 2015), 6; Music and Art Page, *Dallas Morning News*, March 3, 1901, 19; Roy C. Ledbetter, "Frank Reaugh: Painter of Longhorn Cattle," *Southwestern Historical Quarterly* 54 (July 1950): 15, www.jstor.org/stable/30241842.
42. Robert L. Knecht, "Ado Hunnius, Great Plains Cartographer" (Master's thesis, Emporia State University, Emporia, Kansas, 1987), 133–37.
43. *Camp Supply, Indian Territory*, in *Harper's Weekly*, February 27, 1869, 140.
44. Knecht, "Ado Hunnius," 138, 150. The Ruffner survey is covered in depth in T. Lindsay Baker, comp. and ed., "The Survey of the Headwaters of the Red River, 1876," *Panhandle-Plains Historical Review* 58 (1985): 1–121.
45. George E. Foster, "Among the Cherokees," *Frank Leslie's Popular Monthly*, February 1888, 231–38. For a brief biography of Foster and a bibliography of his work, see "Notes and Documents: Bibliography of George E. Foster's Published Works on the Cherokee, In the J. B. Milam Historical Collection," *Chronicles of Oklahoma* 26, no. 2 (1948): 245–46.
46. George E. Foster, "A Zig-Zag Journey through the Indian Territory," *Frank Leslie's Illustrated Newspaper*, August 11, 1888, 417, 410.
47. Ibid., 410.
48. Frederic Remington, "Artist Wanderings Among the Cheyennes," *Century Magazine* 38, no. 4 (August 1889): 536–44.
49. Ibid., 538.
50. Ibid., 544.
51. Frederic Remington, "On the Indian Reservations," *Century Magazine* 38, no. 3 (July 1889): 394–404; Remington, "Artist Wanderings," 536–44.
52. "Cheyenne Scouts in Oklahoma," *Harper's Weekly*, April 6, 1889, 267, and illustration,

Cheyenne Scouts Patrolling the Big Timber of the North Canadian, 264–65; Nancy K. Anderson, "Dark Disquiet: Remington's Late Nocturnes," in *Frederic Remington: The Color of Night*, ed. Nancy K. Anderson (Washington, D.C.: National Gallery of Art in association with Princeton University Press, 2003), 61, and figs. 5–6.

53. Col. Theodore Ayrault Dodge, "Some American Riders," First Paper, *Harper's Monthly* 82, no. 492 (May 1891): 859.

54. P. G. H., Jr. [Philip G. Herbert, Jr.], "Rufus S. Zogbaum," *Book Buyer* 12 (April 1895): 134.

55. For examples, see *A Court Martial in the Field*, in *Harper's Weekly*, March 2, 1889, 168–69; *The Arrival of the Mail in Camp*, in *Harper's Weekly*, October 5, 1889, 792.

56. "The Old Regiment," *Harper's Weekly*, June 7, 1890, 443, and illustration, *Meeting with the Old Regiment*, 449; Rufus Zogbaum, diary entry, October 4, 1888, diary of September 25, 1888, to October 20, 1888, Rufus F. Zogbaum Papers, 1883–1908, American Heritage Center, University of Wyoming, Laramie.

57. Zogbaum diary, October 4, 1888.

58. For an example of the delayed publication of Zogbaum's Indian Territory images, see Rufus Zogbaum, *Running the Wild Turkey in Indian Territory*, in *Harper's Weekly*, December 5, 1896, cover; Rufus F. Zogbaum, "Life at an Indian Agency," *Harper's Weekly*, January 4, 1890, 11–12.

59. Zogbaum, "Life at an Indian Agency," 11, quotation describing *A Beef Issue in the Indian Territory*, which appeared on pages 8 and 9 in the same issue of *Harper's Weekly*.

60. Zogbaum, who had shown his work at the annual exhibitions of the society since 1882 and been elected a member of the group in 1888, offered *A Turkey Hunt, Indian Territory*, for $200 and priced *The Troop Guidon* at $450. See *Illustrated Catalogue of the Twenty-Third Annual Exhibition of the American Watercolor Society* (New York: American Watercolor Society, 1892), n.p.

61. Zogbaum diary, October 4, 20, and 21, 1888; B. Byron Price, "Rufus Fairchild Zogbaum: A Champion of the West," *Persimmon Hill* 20 (Summer 1992): 38–41.

62. In March 1890 the western half of Indian Territory was designated as Oklahoma Territory. The other artists appointed to visually document the census effort were Gilbert Gaul, Peter Moran, Henry R. Poore, and Walter Shirlaw. See Robert J. Titterton, *Julian Scott: Artist of the Civil War and Native America* (Jefferson, N.C.: McFarland, 1997), 185–86.

63. Ibid.

64. Scott arrived at Anadarko, Oklahoma Territory, on August 1, 1890. See Titterton, *Julian Scott*, 190; Julian Scott, "Kiowa and Comanche and Wichita Reservations," in Department of the Interior, Census Office, *Report on Indians Taxed and Indians Not Taxed in the United States (except Alaska) at the Eleventh Census: 1890* (Washington D.C.: Government Printing Office, 1894), 538–42. The Firestone Library at the Princeton University Library, Princeton, New Jersey, owns a collection of 170 albumen prints taken by Julian Scott in connection with the eleventh U.S. census.

65. Titterton, *Julian Scott*, 201–202, 209nn80–82.

66. Department of the Interior, *Report on Indians Taxed and Indians Not Taxed*, 540.

67. The final report consisted of nearly seven hundred pages of text, numerous maps, and 205 plates, containing mostly black-and-white photographs, all arranged by state. Sackett and Wilhelms Lithographing Company of New York produced the twenty-one (9 × 7 inches) lithographs. For the lithographs of Scott's portraits of *Quanah Parker* and *Scar-faced Charley*,

see Department of the Interior, *Report on Indians Taxed and Indians Not Taxed*, illustrations between 540 and 541, and between 246 and 247. For the photographic image, see C. M. Bell, *Scar-Faced Charley, Modoc*, 1877, photograph a, leaf 27, album 2, (WA) WC054, Department of Rare Books and Special Collections, Princeton University Library, Princeton, New Jersey, http://arks.princeton.edu/ark:/88435/xk81jk826.

68. Department of the Interior, *Report on Indians Taxed and Indians Not Taxed*, 541.
69. Titterton, *Julian Scott*, 192–93.
70. The 1890 date placed by Scott on the photographs taken in the Five Tribes region is incorrect. His second trip occurred in 1891. See the Julian Scott photograph collection at the Firestone Library.
71. See Zogbaum, *Hunting Wild Turkey by Moonlight*, in *Harper's Weekly*, April 6, 1889, 267; Zogbaum, *Running the Wild Turkey in Indian Territory*, in *Harper's Weekly*, December 5, 1896, cover.
72. Francis J. Hagan, "Deer Stalking in the Indian Territory," *Outing Magazine*, October 1891, 21.
73. Ibid., 21, 23, 26, 28.
74. "A Painter on the Plains," *Cincinnati Commercial Gazette*, October 28, 1894, 22.
75. Mary Sayre Haverstock, Jeannette Mahone Vance, and Brian Meggitt, comps. and eds., *Artists in Ohio, 1787–1900: A Biographical Dictionary* (Kent, Ohio: Kent State University Press, 2000), 280–82; Graydon R. Sikes, "Henry Farny's Paintings of American Indians, 1894–1916: Images of Conflict Between Indians and Whites Evolve into Symbolic Representations of the Demise of the Western Frontier" (Master's thesis, University of Cincinnati, Ohio, 2005), 24.
76. "A Painter on the Plains," 22.
77. Ibid.
78. Ibid.
79. Ibid; B. Byron Price, "The Utopian Experiment: The Army and the Indian, 1890–1897," *By Valor and Arms* 3 (1977): 15–35.
80. "A Painter on the Plains," 22.
81. For a discussion of the evolution of Farny's style and thematic approach, see Sikes, "Henry Farny's Paintings of American Indians."
82. "Burbank's Real American Reds," *Decatur (Ill.) Daily Review*, October 27, 1901, available within the *Elbridge Ayer Burbank Timeline*, Harvard-Diggens Library, www.harvard-diggins.org/Burbank/index2.htm; Martin Padget, *Indian Country: Travels in the American Southwest, 1840–1935* (Albuquerque: University of New Mexico Press, 2004), 137; E. A. Burbank to Edward Ayer, March 12, 1897, Edward E. Ayer Collection, Newberry Library, Chicago, Illinois.
83. E. A. Burbank to Edward Ayer, March 14 and 21, 1897, Ayer Collection.
84. E. A. Burbank to Edward Ayer, April 18, 1897, Ayer Collection.
85. Padget, *Indian Country*, 138.
86. E. A. Burbank to Edward Ayer, March 14, 1897, Ayer Collection.
87. E. A. Burbank to Edward Ayer, June 2, 1897, Ayer Collection.
88. Padget, *Indian Country*, 138.
89. William H. Gerdts, *Art Across America*, 3 vols. (New York: Abbeville Press, 1990), 2:127, 129; "The Indians His Models," *Kansas City Star*, May 26, 1901, 2; "Elbridge Ayer Burbank—1858–1949," *Pony Express*, 1966, available within the *Elbridge Ayer Burbank Timeline*, Harvard-Diggens Library, www.harvard-diggins.org/Burbank/index2.htm.
90. "Indians Make Fine Models," *Reno (Nev.) Evening Gazette*, February 18, 1899, available within the *Elbridge Ayer Burbank Timeline*, Harvard-Diggens Library, www.harvard-diggins.org/Burbank/index2.htm.

91. “Burbank’s Real American Reds.”
92. Gerdts, *Art Across America*, 2:127, 129; “The Indians His Models.”
93. “The Indians His Models.”
94. Ibid.
95. Ibid.; “Indians Make Fine Models.”
96. *Chicago Post*, October 19, 1901, cited in *Elbridge Ayer Burbank: A Chronology*, Harvard-Diggens Library, www.harvard-diggins.org/Burbank/chronology.htm; Padget, *Indian Country*, 138.
97. “Burbank’s Real American Reds.”
98. Padget, *Indian Country*, 138; “Elbridge Ayer Burbank—1858–1949.”
99. “Personal Mention,” *Harvard (Ill.) Herald*, February 6, 1908, 5; “Personal Mention,” *Harvard (Ill.) Herald*, March 12, 1908, 5; “Territorial Fair” *Oklahoma Times Journal* (Oklahoma City), October 2, 1894, 4.
100. “An Art Display,” *Oklahoman* (Oklahoma City), December 4, 1904, 22. By the time of Shepherd’s death from tuberculosis in 1920, one of her paintings had received an award at the Paris Grand Salon, and she had headed both the art department of the Oklahoma College for Women and the Oklahoma Art Association. See Dianna Everett, “Shepherd, Nellie Ellen,” *Encyclopedia of Oklahoma History and Culture*, accessed November 23, 2015, www.okhistory.org/publications/enc/entry.php?entry=SH024.
101. Brian Dippie, *Custer’s Last Stand: The Anatomy of an American Myth.* (Lincoln: University of Nebraska Press, 1976), 38; Rebecca S. Wingo, “Charles Schreyvogel (1861–1912),” *The Artistic Legacy of Buffalo Bill Cody*, accessed September 29, 2015, http://rebeccawingo.com/bonner/schreyvogel.php; Sarah J. Blackstone, *The Business of Being Buffalo Bill: Selected Letters of William F. Cody, 1879–1917* (New York: Greenwood, 1988), 52; “Buffalo Bill’s Nephew Hurt,” *New York Times*, May 1, 1909, 9.
102. “Farmer Painter to Address Chautauqua,” *Oklahoman* (Oklahoma City), July 26, 1906, 6.
103. “The Whitcomb Riley of Art in Topeka,” *Topeka (Kans.) Daily Capital*, July 30, 1906, 8.
104. Ibid.

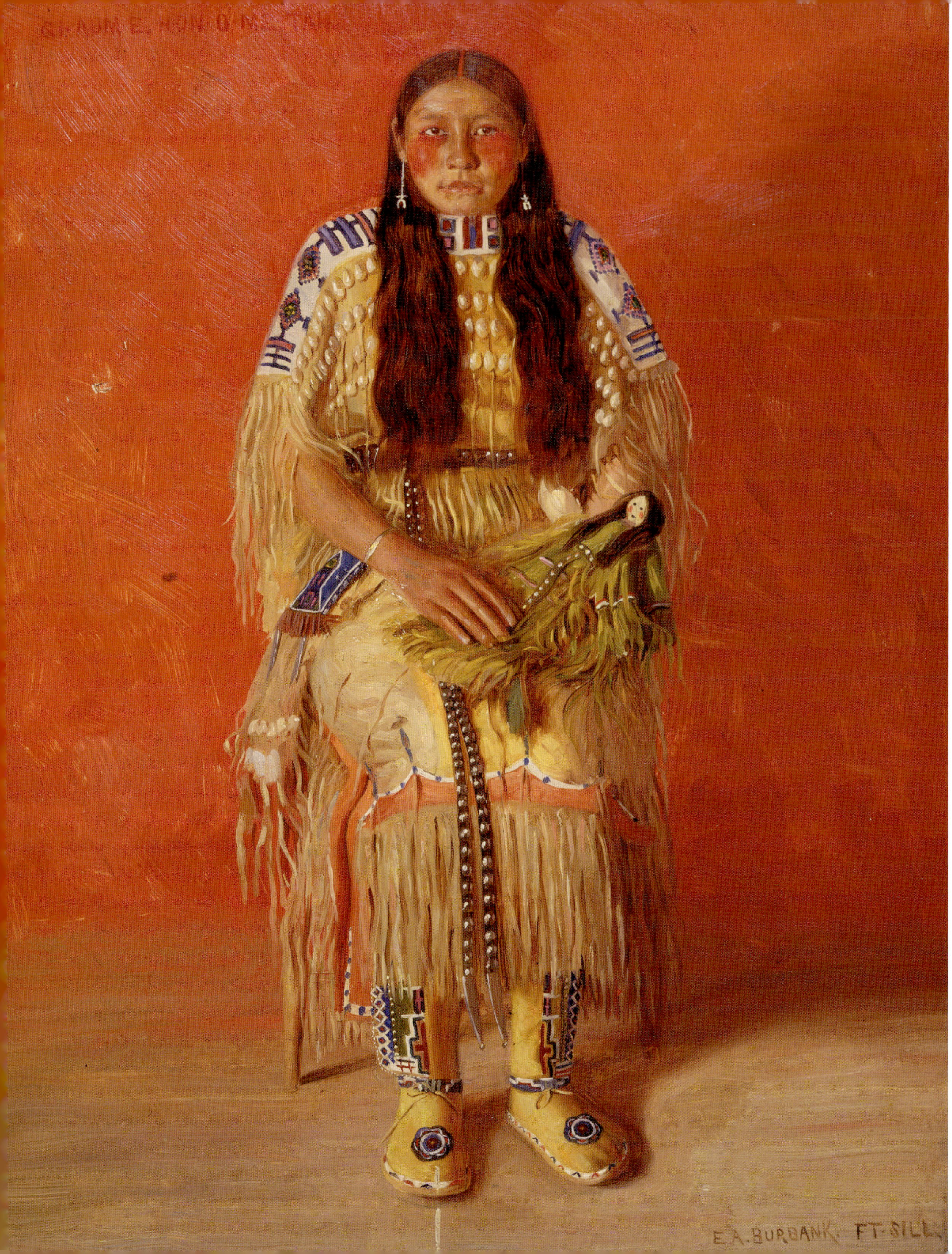
E.A.BURBANK. FT-SILL.

3 ON TO OKLAHOMA

Reportage, Spectacle, and Statehood

MARK ANDREW WHITE

The founding of Oklahoma Territory is a singular event in American history. It was established in 1890 within Indian Territory, which was a diaspora that had been created by the Indian Removal Act of 1830 for Plains tribes native to the region and tribes displaced or forcibly removed from their lands in the east. The 1889 Indian Appropriations Act opened for settlement all lands within Indian Territory that were unassigned to a particular tribe. On April 22, 1889, less than two months after Pres. Grover Cleveland signed the bill on March 2, the first Oklahoma Land Run began. Hopeful settlers amassed at a starting line, and when the signal was given at high noon, they raced forward into the Unassigned Lands, by whatever means of transport they had at their disposal, to claim a parcel. In essence, the 1889 run, as well as the four that followed, was a federally sponsored Darwinian contest, in which those with the fastest transportation, the greatest endurance, and perhaps some foreknowledge of the lay of the land succeeded in securing a location.[1] Guile sometimes proved an effective tool, and many unfortunates arrived at an ideal location only to find a "sooner" had entered the Unassigned Lands early and already staked a claim.

Journalists on both sides of the Atlantic hailed the 1889 run as a momentous event in history, using illustrative prose to describe the unique scenes before them. William Willard Howard, who chronicled the event for *Harper's Weekly*, opined that "in its picturesque aspects the rush across the border at noon on the opening day must go down in history as one of the most noteworthy events in Western civilization. At the time fixed, thousands of hungry home-seekers, who had gathered from all parts of the country, and particularly from Kansas and Missouri, were arranged in line along the border, ready

FACING
(Detail) Elbridge Ayer Burbank, *Gi-aum-e-hon-o-me-tah; Kiowa; full-female*, n.d. Oil on canvas, 12 × 9 inches. The Butler Institute of American Art, Youngstown, Ohio (912-O-577)

to lash their horses into furious speed in the race for fertile spots in the beautiful land before them."[2] Howard not only recognized the historical import of the event, but he also gave it a decidedly pictorial cast, as though the run deserved immortalization in paint and ink.

Within hours of the run, Guthrie, Oklahoma City, and Kingfisher, each of which had boasted little more than a train station and a land office the day before, became settlements of thousands and, within a few months, thriving cities and towns. Artists and illustrators joined writers like Howard in capturing the spectacular details of the 1889 run, but none of their reports would be as iconic as those published of the Cherokee Outlet Land Run of September 16, 1893. The largest of the five land runs and a significant expansion of the territory, the occupation of the Cherokee Outlet impressed witnesses with its singularity; a correspondent from the British journal the *Graphic* speculated that "probably such a race has never been seen before, and will never be again, and no one who took part in it will forget September 16, 1893."[3] As proof of this assertion, the journal illustrated one of the iconic photographs that William S. Prettyman or a colleague had shot from the starting line, depicting the furious rush for homesteads (figure 3.1).

For the press, the marvel of the masses racing for land, the manufacture of new communities, and even the treachery of the sooners made for great copy, and numerous artists, journalists, and photographers sought to record the remarkable details of the founding of Oklahoma Territory. Differences in style and detail notwithstanding, most approached the story of Oklahoma Territory as a grand spectacle, fully conscious that they were not only observing history in the making but also shaping its representation for a mass of readers and viewers. An editorial appearing in the *St. Louis Post-Dispatch* the day before the 1889 run portrayed the event as a pivotal moment in the development of civilization, precisely because of its spectacular nature: "The spirit which animates these people, good and evil, is the spirit which has made this continent a garden. Within an incredible time what was a barren waste and wilderness will be turned into thriving cities, farms and homes. . . . The inspiration of human progress is the spectacle."[4]

Sensationalism and theatricality infused many of the reports, and numerous journalists, whether writers or artists, perceived Oklahoma Territory as the climax of the lengthy drama of westward expansion, in which the struggle between barbarity and civilization played out over a matter of days. American progress achieved its perfect form in the spirit of the land runs and in the overnight fabrication of entire cities, and the artful reportage of these events provided audiences with affirmation of American exceptionalism. An examination of the visual record that accompanied the articles, pamphlets, and books chronicling Oklahoma's founding and development demonstrates that

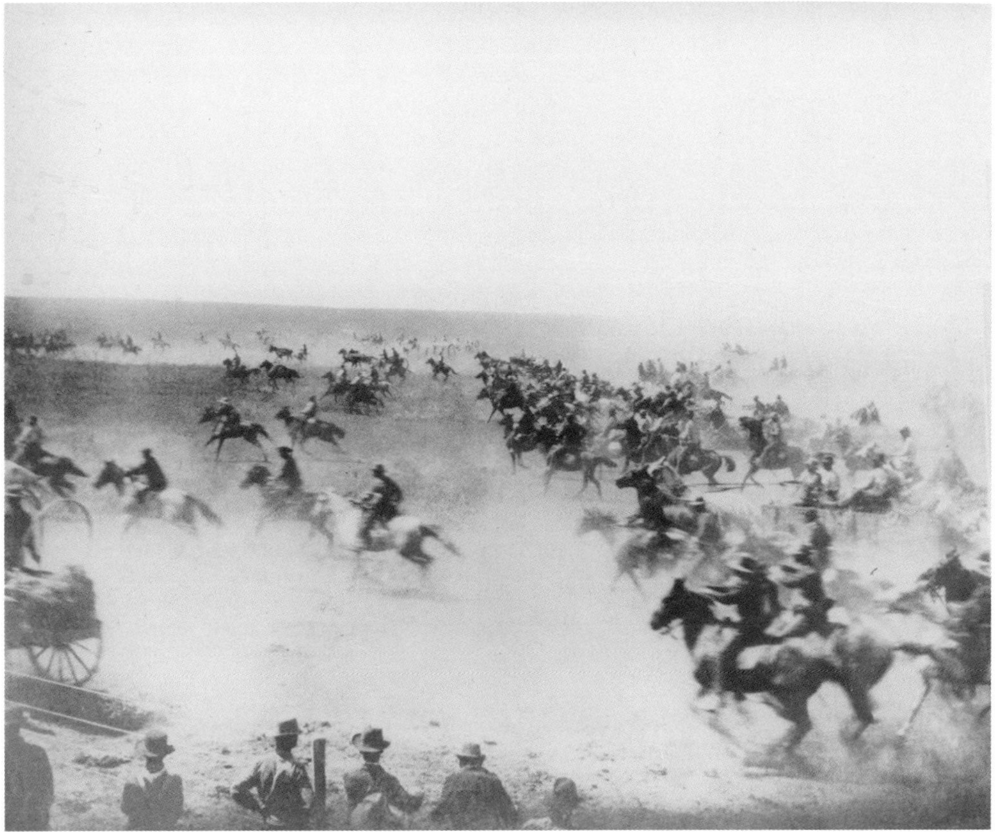

3.1. Thomas Croft and P. A. Miller, associates of William S. Prettyman, Cherokee Outlet, *At the Starting Signal at High Noon*, September 16, 1893. Photographic copy print. National Cowboy and Western Heritage Museum (2000.005.9.1873). Photograph © Dickinson Research Center

pictorial representation informed and reinforced these perceptions. Moreover, images of Oklahoma Territory from 1889 to the eve of statehood in 1907 relied consciously on the established vocabulary of westward expansion to celebrate its culmination in the founding of Oklahoma at the end of the nineteenth century. Most commentators admired the speed and efficiency with which American civilization settled one of the last remaining frontiers, though some lamented the accompanying criminality, greed, and base capitalism, which they perceived as a debasement of the founding ideals of the United States. That dichotomy accompanied reports of Euro-Americans' first furtive attempts to settle Oklahoma.

Questions regarding the merit of Oklahoma settlement first captured national attention in 1880, when Captain David L. Payne and the boomers began entering Indian Territory with the hope of establishing permanent homes.[5] Payne was a veteran of the Kansas Infantry during the Civil War, a scout under General Philip Sheridan during the Indian campaigns in the late 1860s, and a member of the Kansas legislature in 1871. He had also guided hunting parties and pioneer trains at various times in his life, but it was his leadership of the Oklahoma boomers that brought him to national attention. Payne believed that nearly 2 million acres in the center of Indian Territory known as the

“Unassigned Lands” were not allotted to any particular tribe and cited as proof an 1866 treaty in which these lands were surrendered by the Seminole and Creek as a concession to the U.S. government for the tribes’ support of the Confederacy during the Civil War. As intended, the majority of the confiscated lands were given to other tribes, but the Unassigned Lands and large portions of the Cherokee Outlet remained vacant.

Settlement of the Unassigned Lands had become a prickly issue in February 1879, following the publication of an article in the *Chicago Times* by Elias Cornelius Boudinot, a Cherokee citizen, a clerk for the House of Representatives Committee on Private Land Claims, and a lobbyist for the Missouri, Kansas, and Texas Railroad.[6] Boudinot encouraged settlement of the Unassigned Lands and proposed legislation that would make the area an official territory of the United States under the name Oklahoma. His appeal was joined by Morrison Munford, owner and editor of the *Kansas City Times*, who reprinted Boudinot’s thesis.[7] Munford used the volatile term “boomers” to describe a movement still in its infancy yet ready to explode, and the articles in his paper established a common rhetoric for the undertaking. The boomer movement would advocate the settlement of Oklahoma for the ensuing decade. Oklahoma teemed with natural resources, from virgin timber to delightful fruits and mineral resources that appeared ready for the taking, despite government opposition. It was, wrote *Kansas City Times* correspondent John Forbes, “a land not flowing with milk and honey, but affluent with natural products as the original paradise.”[8] Proponents of westward expansion had used such biblical metaphors for much of the nineteenth century, and Munford’s editorial flair made Oklahoma both a prelapsarian Eden and the Promised Land of Moses and the Israelites. The *Times* chose Charles C. Carpenter as its equivalent to the biblical patriarch and a figurehead for the boomer movement. Carpenter had scouted for Major General John C. Frémont during the Civil War and later led the campaign to settle the Black Hills in 1876, despite government prohibitions. Clad in buckskin and sporting long hair in the style of Wild Bill Hickok and George Armstrong Custer, Carpenter cultivated a frontier persona that proved useful as a proponent of westward expansion.

In April 1879, settlers under Carpenter’s direction, but without the man himself, prepared to cross the territorial boundary from Coffeyville, Kansas. President Rutherford B. Hayes, mindful of the protests of Cherokee and Creek delegations to Washington, quickly issued a proclamation on April 26 barring unlawful entry.

The *Kansas City Times* responded with a new campaign of support for the boomer movement that depicted Carpenter as the new Moses, encouraging would-be settlers with the single commandment: “On to Oklahoma” (figure 3.2).[9] This rallying cry was hoped to incite fervor for settlement of U.S. government-owned lands, while strategically disassociating the movement from illegal incursions into Indian Territory, lands

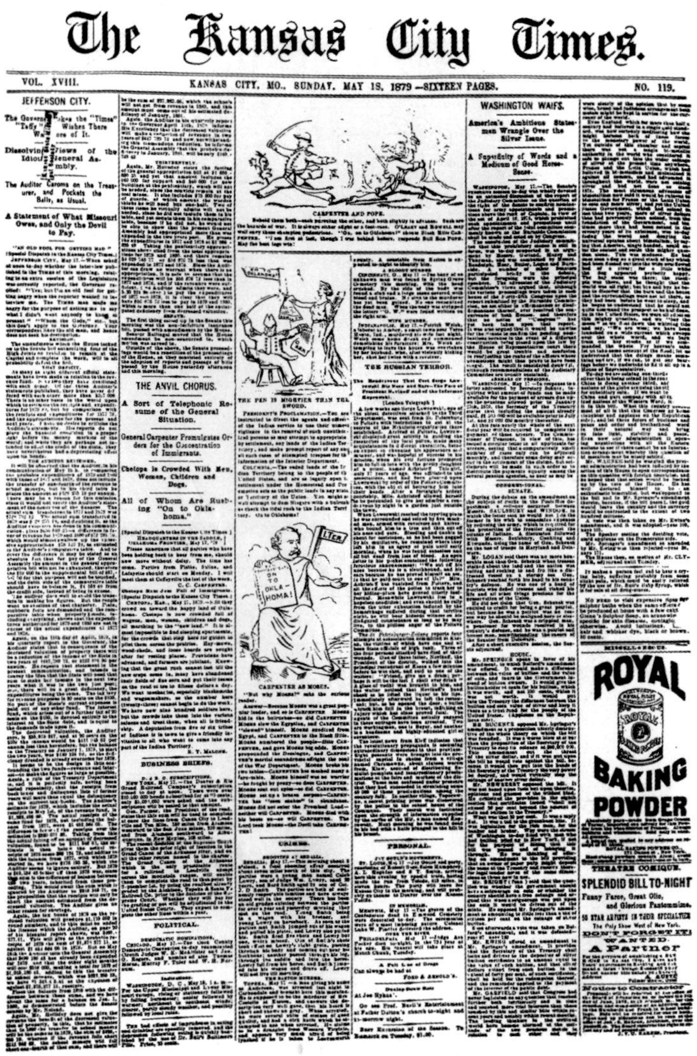
The Kansas City Times.

VOL. XVIII. KANSAS CITY, MO., SUNDAY, MAY 18, 1879—SIXTEEN PAGES. NO. 119.

JEFFERSON CITY.

WASHINGTON WAIFS.

THE ANVIL CHORUS.

CARPENTER AS MOSES.

ROYAL BAKING POWDER

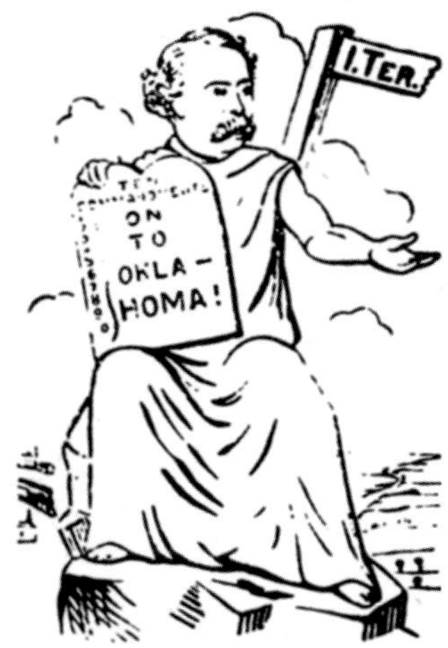

3.2. Unknown artist, *Carpenter as Moses*, in *Kansas City Times*, May 18, 1879, 1, and in Carl Coke Rister, *Land Hunger: David L. Payne and the Oklahoma Boomers* (Norman: University of Oklahoma Press, 1942).

belonging to various Native nations.[10] When boomers from Kansas crossed the border in May, the U.S. Army ejected them with little fanfare, and soon thereafter Carpenter receded from the public eye.

The rhetoric of westward expansion the *Times* used to characterize the movement reappeared when David Payne picked up the cause of Oklahoma settlement in 1880, and he was just as adept at using the press to his advantage. Payne made his first incursion with a small band of would-be settlers in April 1880, founding the settlement Ewing on the site of present-day Oklahoma City. Lieutenant George H. G. Gale and troops of the Fourth Cavalry promptly arrested the group and escorted them back to Kansas. Payne returned to Ewing in July with similar results, although this time, Judge Isaac Parker

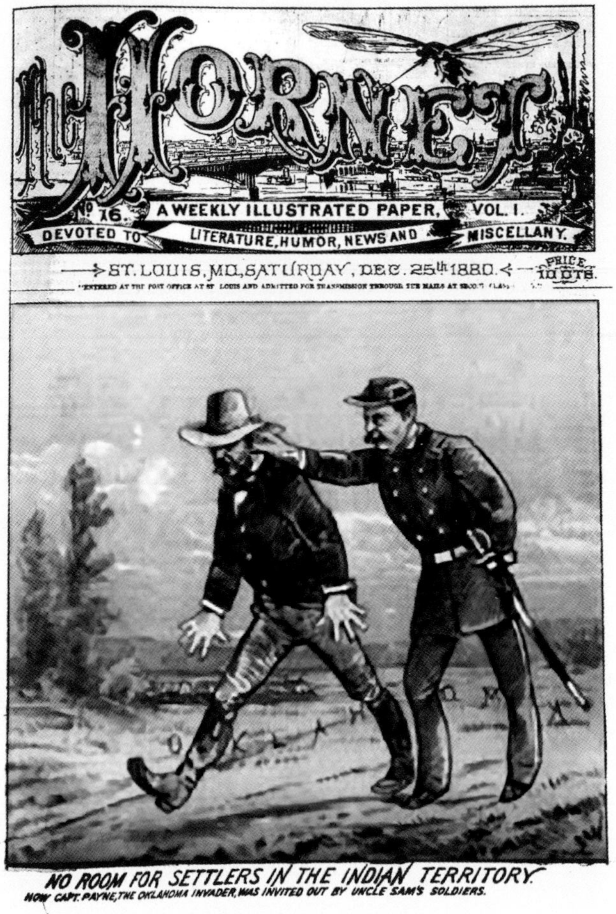

3.3. Unknown artist, front cover of *The Hornet: A Weekly Illustrated Paper*, December 25, 1880. St. Louis Public Library, St. Louis, Missouri

fined Payne the maximum penalty of one thousand dollars for violation of the Indian Intercourse Act.

With two unsuccessful entries in less than a year and a third try planned for late in 1880, the national press took notice. *The Hornet*, an illustrated St. Louis weekly, represented Payne as a disobedient child pulled out of Oklahoma by his ear (figure 3.3). For *The Hornet*, Payne was the "Oklahoma Invader" who had to be forcibly removed by "Uncle Sam's Soldiers," suggesting that the entry into Oklahoma violated not only the law but also the will of the American people. *Frank Leslie's Illustrated Newspaper*, a popular periodical with a national readership, followed suit in January 1881 with an article titled "Invading Indian Territory." *Leslie's* sent an unnamed reporter to Payne's Kansas camp in December of that year to report on preparations for the next incursion. Payne and the boomers, again characterized as lawless invaders, were reported adopting a military-style organization in preparation to cross into the territory from Hunnewell, Kansas. The suite of illustrations artist Charles Silverton created to accompany the article depicts the militarization of the boomer camp. In the illustration *Drilling in Camp*, for example, a company of armed men stand at attention receiving instruction from Payne, or more likely from Hill Maidt, who had been named the military commander because of his past army service (figure 3.4).[11] Against a backdrop of covered wagons, with families in attendance and the American flag flying high, they evoke the stalwart pioneers of the Oregon and California Trails. But as Silverton makes clear, these settlers are prepared to seize territory and violate American law by force of arms.

Emboldened by phrases such as "No Turning Back" and "On to Oklahoma" emblazoned on their covered wagons, Payne's boomers consciously adopted the rhetoric and trappings of Manifest Destiny to support their mission. On one particular Sunday, the boomers engaged in a dress parade, then held a church service, which Silverton depicted in *Sunday Service in Camp* (figure 3.5). A chaplain named Cary preached from Exodus, with particular emphasis on Moses's appeal to Pharaoh to "let my people go," so that they might claim the modern-day Canaan. The American flag and the various slogans of the boomers were displayed prominently, and religious hymns and a rendition of the

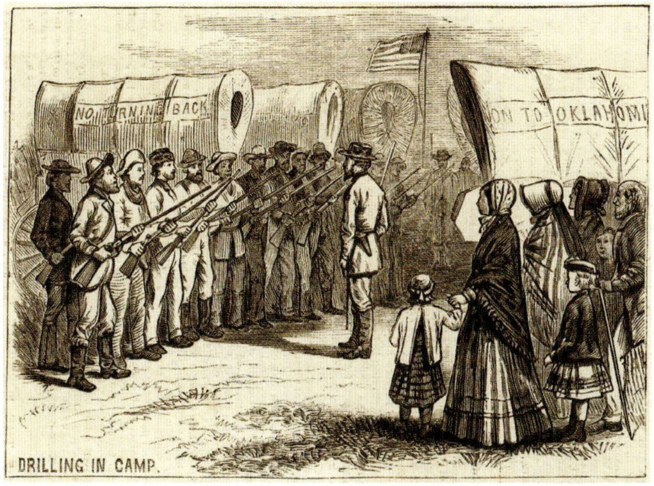

3.4. Sketch by unknown artist, after Charles Silverton, *Drilling in Camp*, 1881, in *Frank Leslie's Illustrated Newspaper*, January 1, 1881, 300. Ann Cowan Dixon Archives and Special Collections, Harding University, Searcy, Arkansas

3.5. Sketch by unknown artist, after Charles Silverton, *Sunday Service in Camp*, 1881, in *Frank Leslie's Illustrated Newspaper*, January 1, 1881, 300. Ann Cowan Dixon Archives and Special Collections, Harding University, Searcy, Arkansas

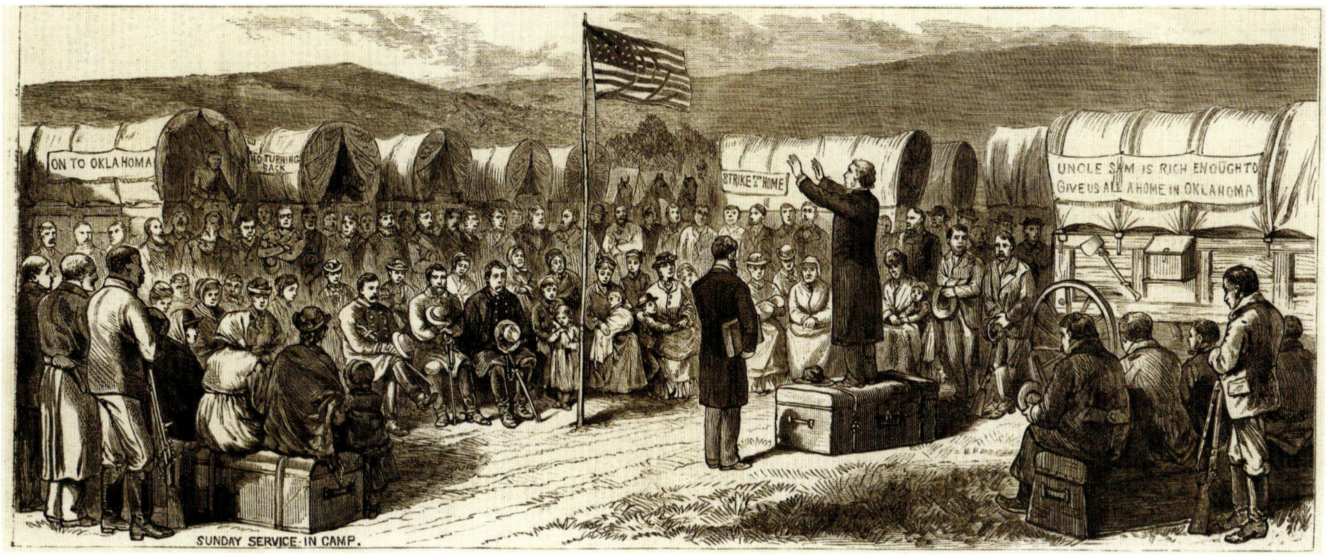

"Star-Spangled Banner" added to the pomp of the service.[12] Payne and his boomers not only positioned themselves as patriotic Americans committed to the core values of freedom and liberty, but they also invoked the blessings of an altruistic God, who, they hoped, would loosen the restrictions imposed by a hegemonic government. The boomers hoped to realize through divine providence their manifest destiny to expand American civilization and its democratic ideals into unsettled Oklahoma, just as pioneers of a generation earlier had hoped for the country as a whole. The readership of *Frank Leslie's*, whether or not they supported the settlement of the territory, would have recognized the ideology propelling the boomers as the same that had justified American expansion across North America. The boomers, who knew the importance the press played in the endeavor, heightened the spectacle for *Frank Leslie's* audience in hopes this would engender sympathy for their cause. This was no mere reportage, but an attempt

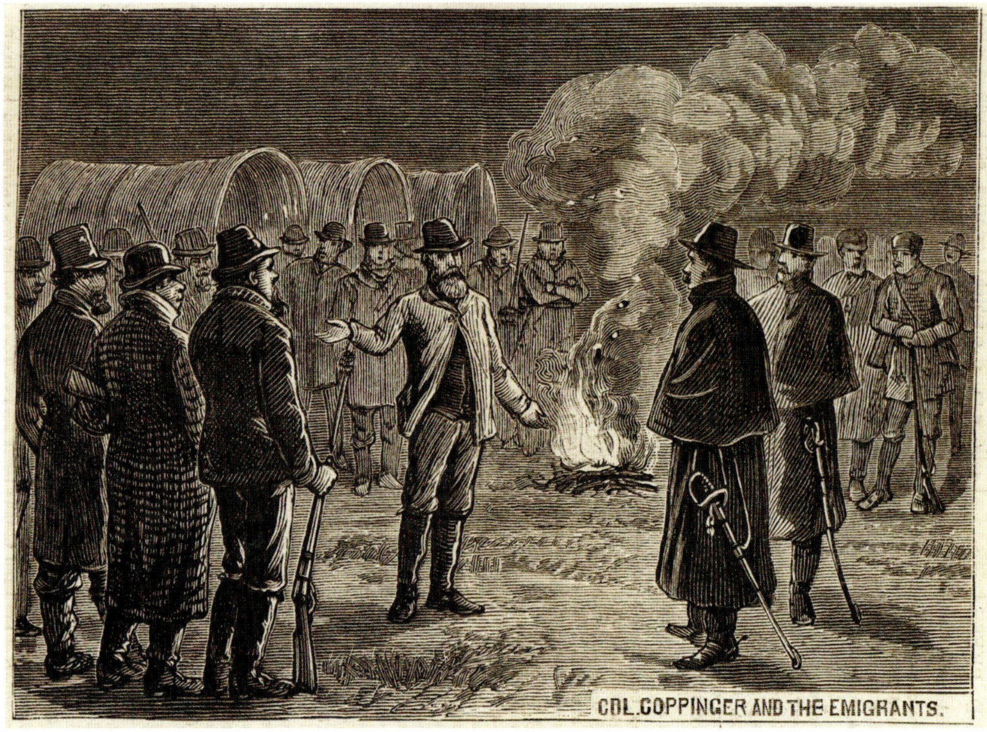

3.6. Sketch by unknown artist, after Charles Silverton, *Col. Coppinger and the Emigrants*, 1881, in *Frank Leslie's Illustrated Newspaper*, January 1, 1881, 300. Ann Cowan Dixon Archives and Special Collections, Harding University, Searcy, Arkansas

to shape public opinion and political policy through a strategic performance of core American values.

Despite their provocative rhetoric and actions, the boomers engaged in friendly relations with the Tenth U. S. Cavalry under Major John Joseph Coppinger, who had been sent to escort the boomers back into Kansas if they crossed the border into Indian Territory. Coppinger and the cavalry were invited to attend Sunday services and given preferential seating in the front row, as pictured in the *Frank Leslie's* illustration, *Sunday Service in Camp*. Coppinger had previously warned the boomers of his duty, illustrated in Silverton's *Col. Coppinger and the Emigrants* (figure 3.6), and the military followed the camp closely from the rear. Military intervention and inclement weather ultimately stalled the planned incursion that year, but Payne persisted and continued to publicize the efforts of what was now called the Oklahoma Colony, using his growing celebrity as a promotional tool. The former "Oklahoma Invader" became a frontier hero by the mid-1880s, as his supporters advertised his military background and his western persona. This fanfare clearly annoyed the editor of the *Cherokee Advocate*, a staunch opponent of the boomers, who characterized Payne as "a Dime Novel Reader."[13]

In truth, Payne's friendship with William F. "Buffalo Bill" Cody, one of the mainstays of dime novels, enhanced his western celebrity. In October 1880, prior to the failed invasion in late 1880, Payne visited St. Louis, where he engaged in a friendly debate with Buffalo Bill over marksmanship. They tried to best each other at Sportsman's Park, until Cody finally announced that he could produce sparks from the end of Payne's cigar with successive shots from his pistol. Of the five shots Cody took, four had the desired effect, but the fifth missed the mark and took off part of Payne's mustache. The novelty of the incident reportedly impelled Buffalo Bill to make a lithograph of the event, although prints have yet to surface.[14]

Whether Payne actually lost part of his mustache to Buffalo Bill's errant shot remains questionable, but the event apparently left no ill will between the two. Payne would make an appearance in the program of the 1884 season of the Buffalo Bill's Wild West (figure 3.7), where he was billed as "'Oklahoma' Payne, the Progressive Pioneer" and "The Distinguished Cimarron Scout and 'Oklahoma' Raider." The program valorized him as both a martyr to the ideal of frontier settlement and a figure of unfailing principles, who struggled against the corruption of unidentified moneyed interests: "To continue this fight against the greed of remorseless capitalists, Capt. Payne has endured hardships few men have been forced to suffer, proving himself true to principle, and a frontier hero of just renown—a man who cannot be intimidated nor swerved by hardships from his purpose and duty." In all likelihood, Payne never appeared in the show because of other commitments, but Cody must have recognized the promotional value of "Oklahoma Payne."[15]

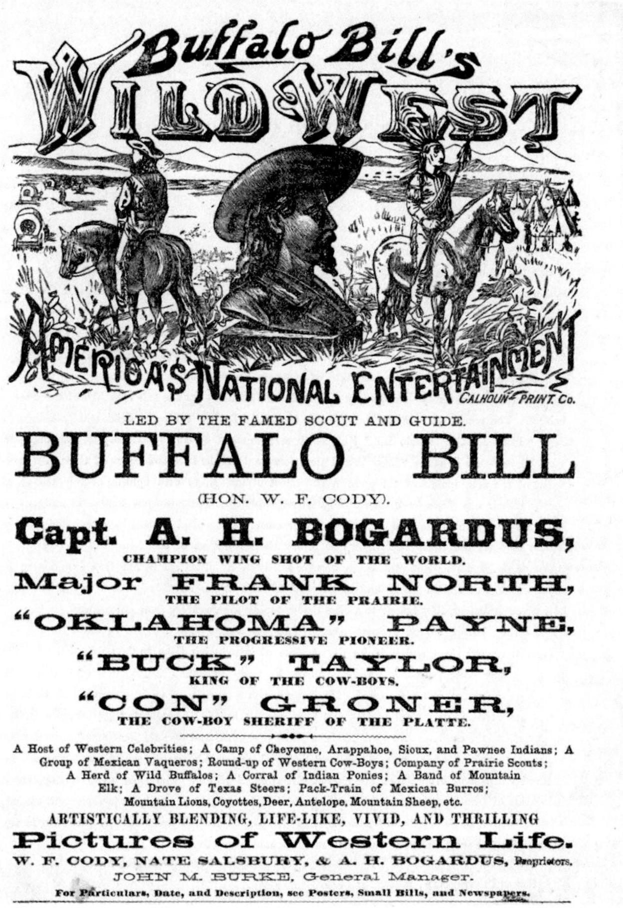

3.7. Unknown artist, program cover, *Buffalo Bill's Wild West: America's National Entertainment, Led by the Famed Scout and Guide Buffalo Bill (Hon. W. F. Cody)*. . . . (Hartford, Conn.: Calhoun, 1884). Western History Collections, University of Oklahoma Libraries, Norman, Oklahoma

Payne's celebrity as a western hero of stalwart character was not restricted to the hyperbole of Buffalo Bill's Wild West. In the previous year, the sensational tabloid *National Police Gazette* had also remarked that Payne was "doubtless one of the principal figures of the great West" and "an intelligent, active, faithful worker in any cause he espouses, but given to severe hardship and frontier life, in which he has become famous as scout, guide, and soldier."[16] The *London Daily News*, echoing the sentiments of the Wild West program, explained that Payne and his followers had "found themselves heroes, for the West looked upon them as sufferers from the despotic power of the Government."[17] For the propagandists of the boomer movement, Payne's attempt to settle the last frontier in the West placed him in a pantheon of scouts and trailblazers that included Kit Carson, Wild Bill, and Buffalo Bill. His mother was said to be a cousin

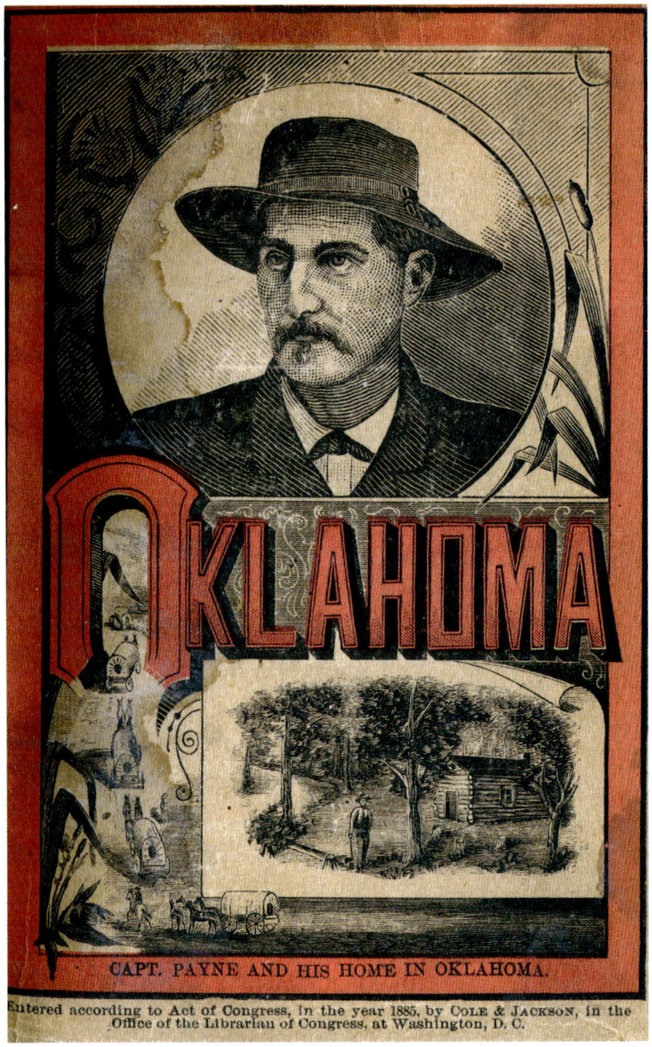

3.8. Unknown artist, front cover of A. P. Jackson and E. C. Cole, *Oklahoma! Politically and Topographically Described. History and Guide to the Indian Territory. Biographical Sketches of Capt. David L. Payne, W. L. Couch, Wm. H. Osborn, and Others* (Kansas City, Mo.: Ramsey, Millet, and Hudson, 1885). Western History Collections, University of Oklahoma Libraries, Norman, Oklahoma

to Davy Crockett.[18] Payne's redoubtable constitution and frontier pedigree, when paired with the boomer's skillful appropriation of the rhetoric of Manifest Destiny, added to his perceived legitimacy and that of his cause.

The boomer leader's reputation ultimately hinged on the creation of Rock Falls, the briefly occupied settlement Payne founded with approximately six hundred of his followers in May 1884. Located near the Chikaskia River in present-day Kay County, the town boasted a school, a drugstore that sold liquor, and a printing office for their newspaper, the *Oklahoma War Chief.*[19] The only image of Rock Falls produced for public consumption was that of Payne's cabin, nestled in a densely wooded area that evoked almost a century of log cabin imagery in American culture (figure 3.8). By the 1880s, the log cabin had come to symbolize both the settlement of the American wilderness and the humble origins of great political leaders, including Andrew Jackson, William Henry Harrison, and Abraham Lincoln.[20] Thomas Cole, the dean of American landscape, also associated the log cabin with these themes in influential paintings, such as *Daniel Boone at His Cabin on the Great Osage Lake* (c. 1826; figure 3.9). The association of the log cabin with Boone, the father of westward expansion, only solidified its role in American historical memory. Payne's cabin in the woods acknowledged his place in that national mythology and furthered the boomers' desire to see their leader placed among the pantheon of frontier heroes. The *Wichita Beacon* expressed this sentiment in November 1884, when it predicted that Payne's "name will be forever linked with the history of the state that is sure to be created in the country south of us. What Daniel Boone is to Kentucky, Dave Payne will be to Oklahoma."[21]

By this time, however, Payne's Rock Falls had already met its demise. On August 7, troops burned the settlement, arrested the leaders of the movement, and escorted the boomers out of the Cherokee Outlet. Payne was tried in Topeka for conspiracy but won a brief victory when district judge Cassius G. Foster dismissed the indictment. On November 28, while preparations for another incursion were under way at Wellington,

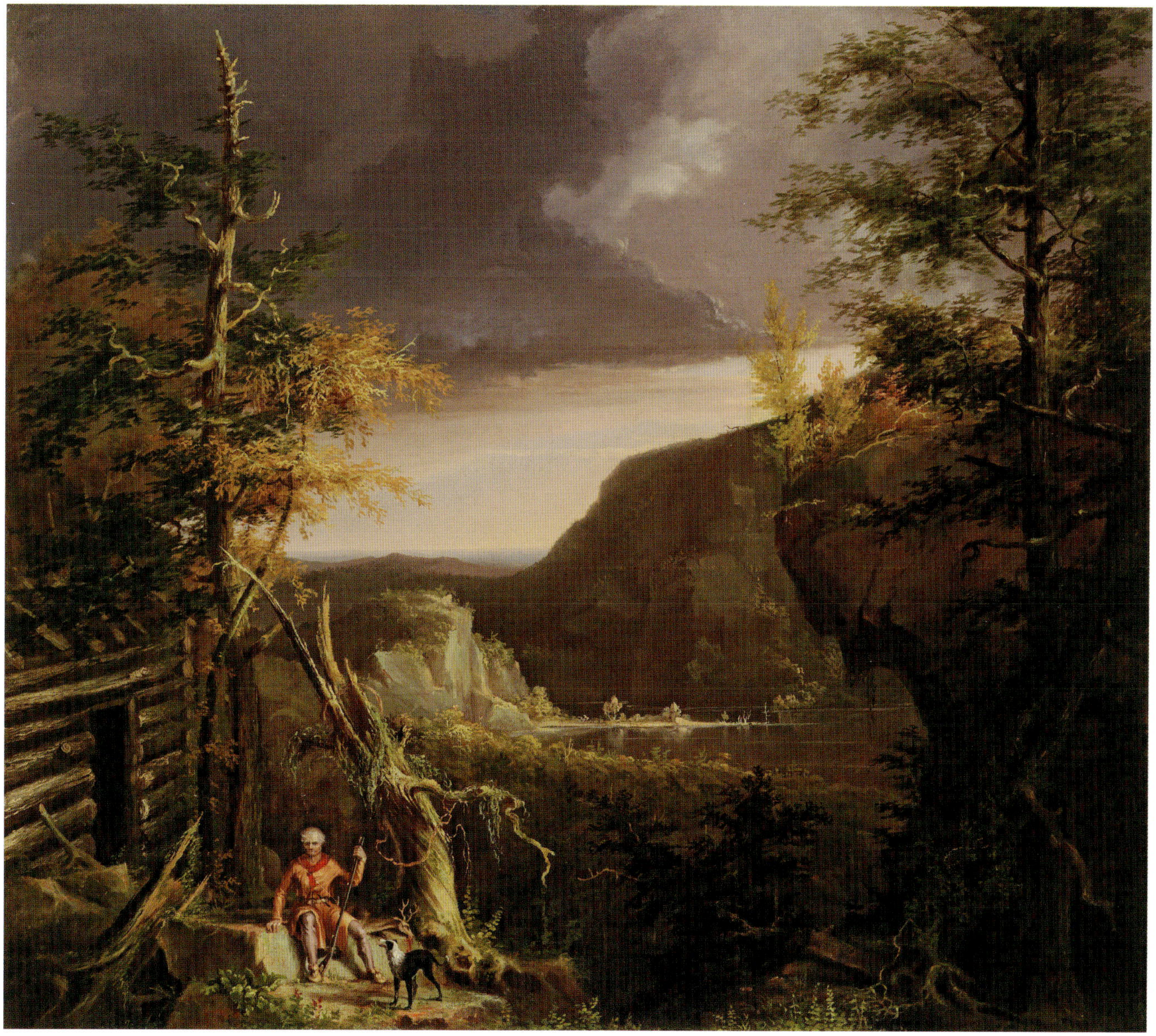

3.9. Thomas Cole, *Daniel Boone at His Cabin at Great Osage Lake*, c. 1826. Oil on canvas, 38 ¼ × 42 ⅝ inches. Mead Art Museum, Amherst College. Museum purchase. Photograph courtesy Bridgeman Images

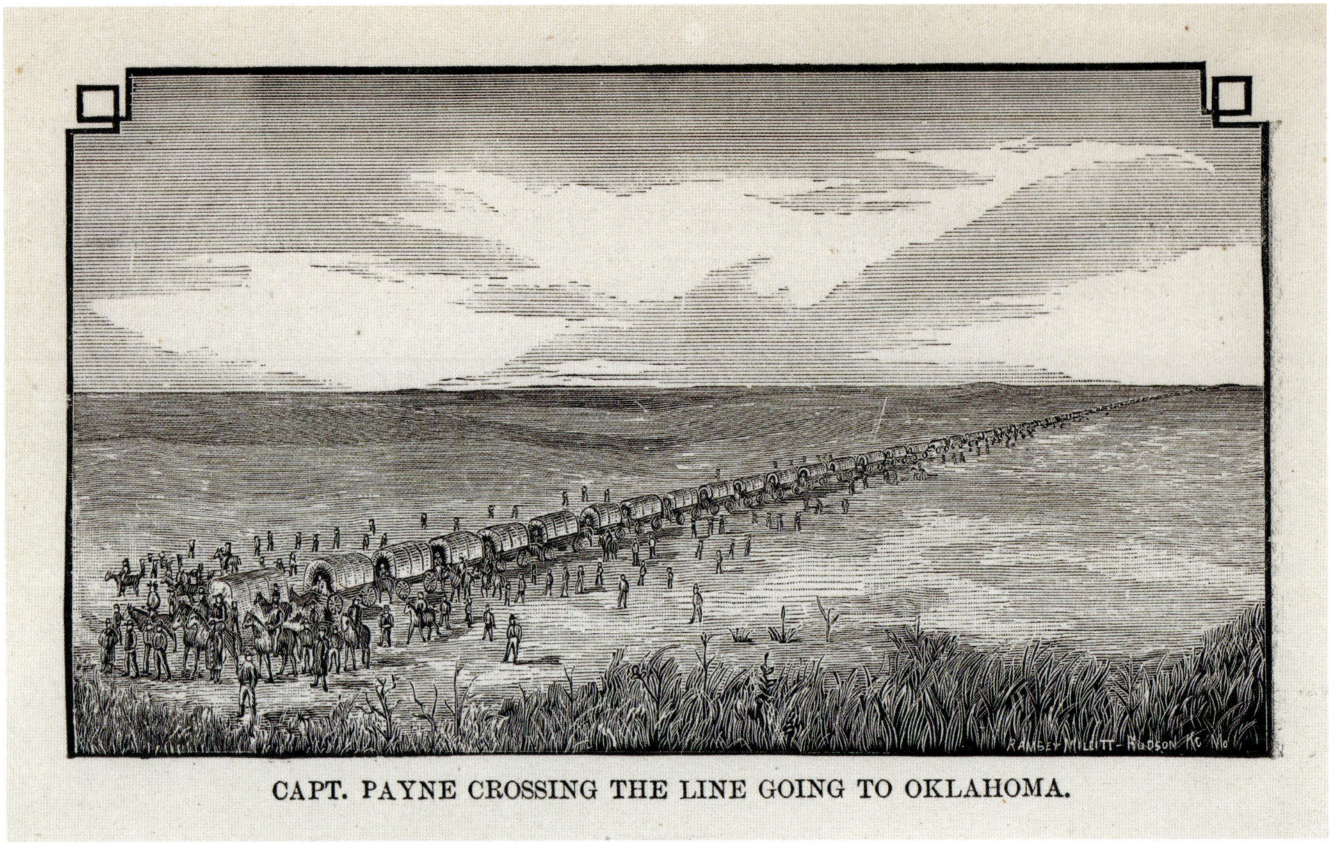

3.10. Unknown artist, *Capt. Payne Crossing the Line Going to Oklahoma*, in A. P. Jackson and E. C. Cole, *Oklahoma! Politically and Topographically Described. History and Guide to the Indian Territory. Biographical Sketches of Capt. David L. Payne, W. L. Couch, Wm. H. Osborn, and Others* (Kansas City, Mo.: Ramsey, Millet, and Hudson, 1885), facing p. 12. Western History Collections, University of Oklahoma Libraries, Norman, Oklahoma

Kansas, Payne suddenly died of heart failure. The movement faltered momentarily but quickly regained momentum, with Payne in the role of martyr to the cause.

By 1885, E. C. Cole, the president of the Oklahoma Colony of Kingman, Kansas, was already recruiting boomers for another settlement. His book with A. P. Jackson, *Oklahoma! Politically and Topographically Described*, offered biographical treatments of Payne and the other leaders of the movement. The book characterized Payne as "one of the most popular men on the Western frontier" and included an image of Payne leading boomers in covered wagons into Oklahoma (figure 3.10). The illustration embodied a motif familiar to most Americans following the Civil War. Since the 1850s, numerous images of pioneers traveling the Oregon Trail had entered popular culture. Albert Bierstadt's painting *Emigrants Crossing the Plains* (1867; figure 3.11) would have been seen by a limited audience in the 1860s, but the visual language Bierstadt employed had already been popularized by the Currier and Ives lithograph *The Rocky Mountains: Emigrants Crossing the Plains* (1866; figure 3.12), by Frances Flora Bond Palmer.[22] Both Palmer and Bierstadt had depicted pioneers seeking the prosperity on the West Coast, to which Bierstadt alludes metaphorically in the golden radiance of twilight.

Cole, who envisioned Oklahoma as no less promising than California or Oregon, described a varied land that seemed to appeal to all tastes: "Its forests and prairies await

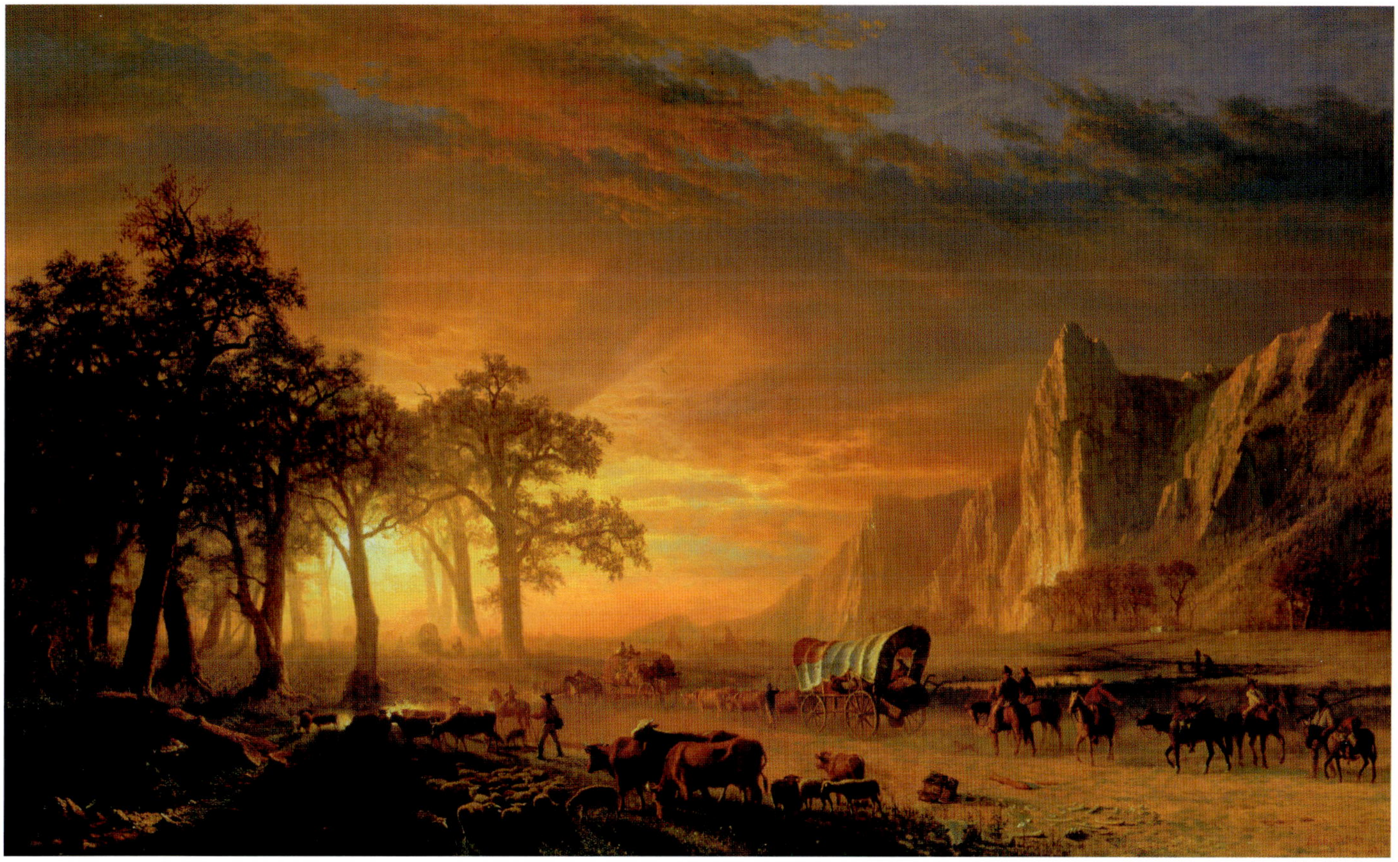

3.11. Albert Bierstadt, *Emigrants Crossing the Plains*, 1867. Oil on canvas, 67 × 102 inches. National Cowboy and Western Heritage Museum, Oklahoma City, Oklahoma (1972.019). Photograph © Dickinson Research Center

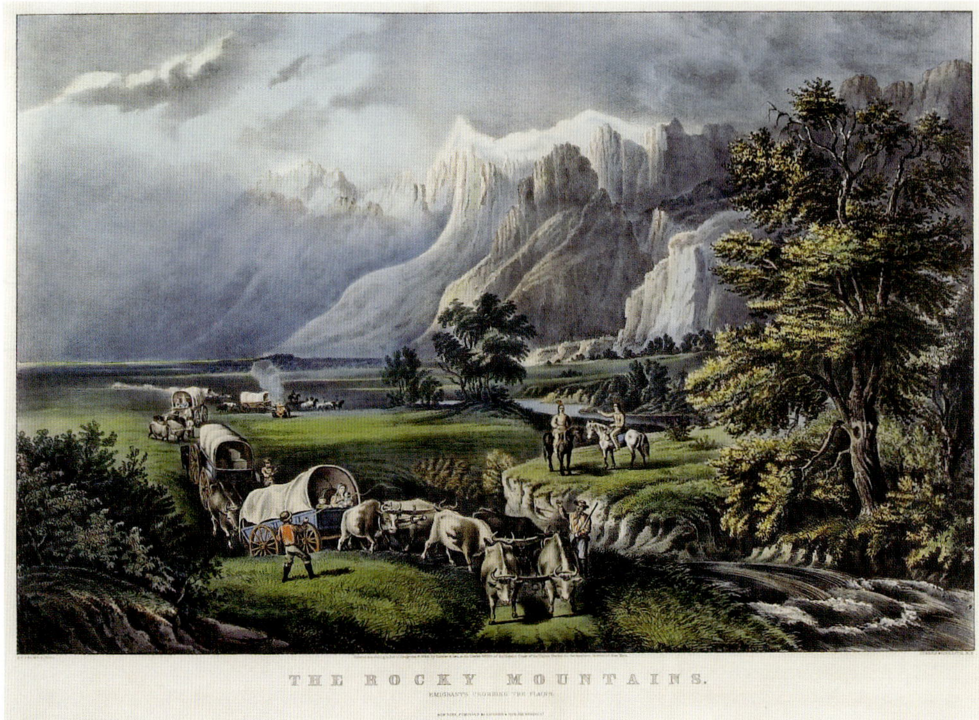

3.12. Frances Flora Bond Palmer (known as F. F. Palmer), *The Rocky Mountains: Emigrants Crossing the Plains*, 1866. Lithograph, published by Currier and Ives, 17 ¼ × 25 ⅝ inches. The Old Print Shop, New York, New York (117)

the laborer and the capitalist; its cataracts and cañons, and crests woo the painter; its mountains, salt beds, and stupendous vegetable productions challenge the naturalist. Its climate invites the invalid, healing the systems wounded by ruder climates. Its fields are large."[23] As if to reinforce his point, the book included the illustration of Payne's cabin, which depicted a landscape potentially alluring for those very reasons.

Payne, Cole, and others had been fairly successful in managing the image of the boomers in the popular press, but the images of boomers that came to dominate the press in the year following Payne's death largely depicted the movement as a series of altercations and misadventures. Cole included one such illustration in his book, *Colonists Chained to Their Own Wagons by the Military and Dragged through the Territory* (figure 3.13). Titled to foster sympathy and outrage, the image focuses on a line of wagons proceeding out of the territory, at a diagonal almost opposite to that depicted in the earlier illustration of Payne's entry. Military personnel drive the wagon, while a chained boomer trails in the rear. The illustration likely represents the removal of settlers from Rock Falls in 1884, but it could depict any of the confrontations between the boomers and the American military that continued after Payne death.

In the months following Payne's death, Captain William L. Couch assumed leadership of the boomers and led another incursion in December 1884, which resulted in the establishment of Camp Stillwater (on the site of present-day Stillwater, Oklahoma). Colonel Edward Hatch, commander of the Ninth Cavalry Regiment, an African American

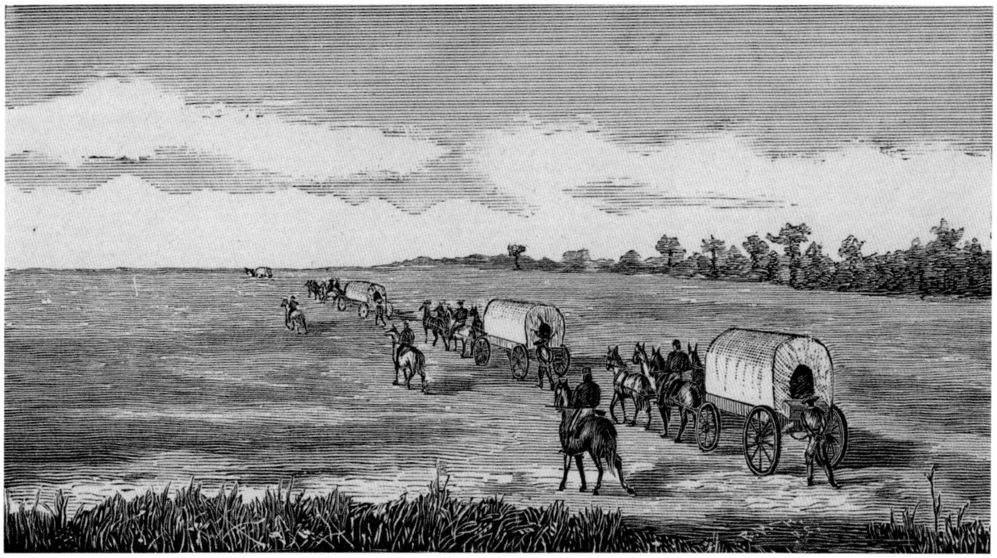

3.13. Unknown, *Colonists Chained to Their Own Wagons by the Military and Dragged through the Territory*, in A. P. Jackson and E. C. Cole, *Oklahoma! Politically and Topographically Described. History and Guide to the Indian Territory. Biographical Sketches of Capt. David L. Payne, W. L. Couch, Wm. H. Osborn, and Others* (Kansas City, Mo.: Ramsey, Millet, and Hudson, 1885), facing p. 16. Western History Collections, University of Oklahoma Libraries, Norman, Oklahoma

outfit popularly known as the Buffalo Soldiers, sent a detachment from Fort Reno under Lieutenant Matthias W. Day to remove Couch. *Harper's Weekly* reported that four hundred armed boomers met Day and stated their intentions to remain on the land. Colonel Hatch, after consulting with Day at Fort Reno, subsequently gave Couch twenty-four hours to leave and threatened to call twelve companies to ready, if necessary.[24] Rather than fire on the boomers, Hatch cut their supply line from Kansas, forcing them to surrender. Frederic Remington's drawing for *Harper's Weekly*, *Ejecting an "Oklahoma Boomer,"* characterized the removal of the boomers as a somewhat comic affair (figure 3.14). Remington lived in Peabody, Kansas, in 1883–84 and had witnessed the travails of the boomers during his own brief excursions into Indian Territory. The drawing also represented one of Remington's first depictions of Buffalo Soldiers and recognized their role in policing Indian Territory. Racial tension between the soldiers and the boomers was often high, and verbal and physical altercations frequently erupted.[25]

Although Remington cast the Stillwater affair as largely peaceful, the popular press frequently emphasized the violent tendencies of the boomers. The potential for violence had created the impression of escalating tensions, prompting *Harper's* to conclude, "from the accounts that come to us there is likely to be an outbreak and bloodshed at any moment."[26] This perspective persisted and influenced James Ingram's 1889 illustration *Indian Territory—The Oklahoma Boomers—United States Scouts Turning Back Invaders* (figure 3.15). Printed in *Frank Leslie's* only months before the first land run, the image represents a verbal, and potentially lethal, confrontation between military scouts and boomers.

With Payne's death and Couch's increasingly frequent trips to Washington to publicize the boomer cause, the movement became disorganized. Some factions had

3.14. T. de Thulstrup, after a sketch by Frederic Remington, *Ejecting an "Oklahoma Boomer,"* front cover of *Harper's Weekly*, March 28, 1885. Oklahoma Historical Society, Oklahoma City, Oklahoma

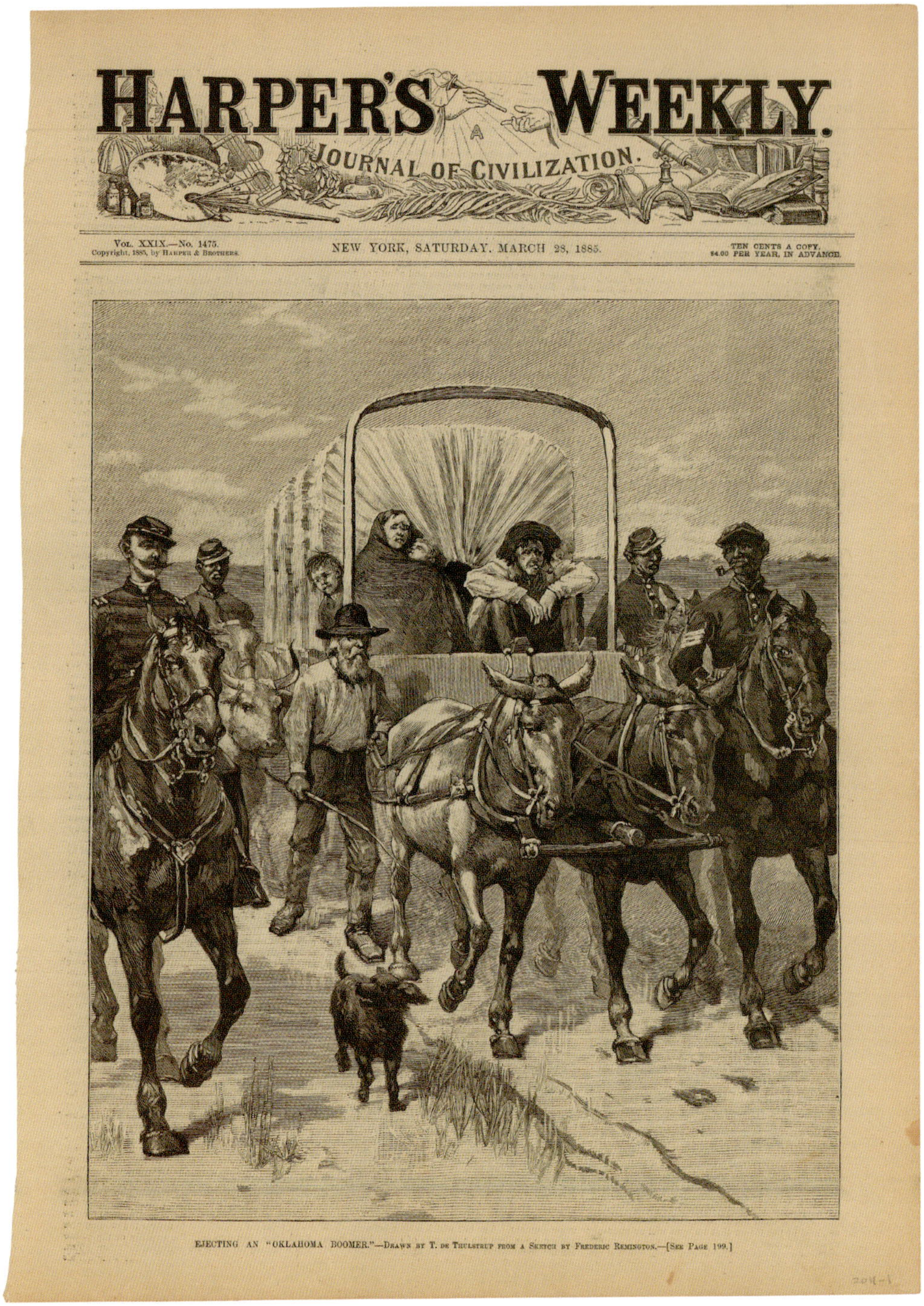

HARPER'S WEEKLY.
A
JOURNAL OF CIVILIZATION.

Vol. XXIX.—No. 1475.
Copyright, 1885, by Harper & Brothers.

NEW YORK, SATURDAY, MARCH 28, 1885.

TEN CENTS A COPY.
$4.00 PER YEAR, IN ADVANCE.

EJECTING AN "OKLAHOMA BOOMER."—Drawn by T. de Thulstrup from a Sketch by Frederic Remington.—[See Page 199.]

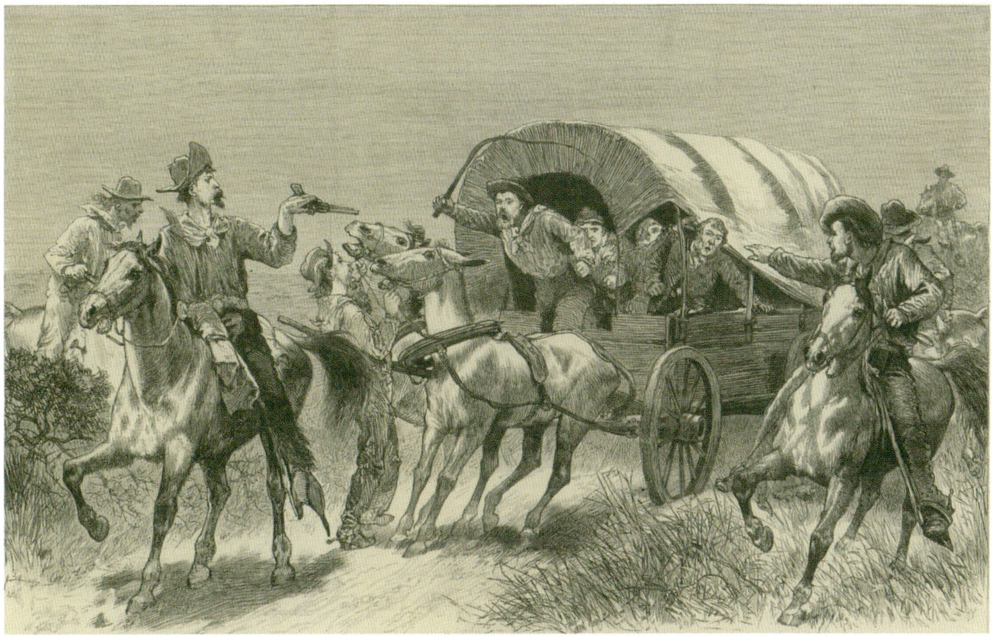

3.15. Unknown artist, after a sketch by James Ingram, *Indian Territory—The Oklahoma Boomers—United States Scouts Turning Back Invaders*, in *Frank Leslie's Illustrated Newspaper*, January 19, 1889, 384. National Cowboy and Western Heritage Museum, Oklahoma City, Oklahoma. Silberman Collection (1996.027.1461.289). Photograph © Dickinson Research Center

aligned with Cole's Oklahoma Colony, while others had located in southern Kansas under the direction of Harry Hill.[27] The Wichita Board of Trade, in hopes of reigniting the plans for Oklahoma settlement, approached a celebrity even more popular than Payne to lead the boomers into Oklahoma: Major Gordon William Lillie, better known by his stage name Pawnee Bill. Lillie had lived in Wellington, Kansas, as a youth, and then worked at the Pawnee Agency on Black Bear Creek in Indian Territory in the late 1870s. When he joined Buffalo Bill's Wild West as a performer in the 1880s, his knowledge of Pawnee language and culture earned him his famous moniker. Lillie's exploits, both real and imagined, became the subject of pulp fiction by the late 1880s, and in 1888, he formed his own show, Pawnee Bill's Historic Wild West, with his new wife, May Manning. The show visited Wichita, Kansas City, Chicago, and Philadelphia with the hope of eventually embarking on an international tour. Lackluster attendance, however, left his operation stranded on the East Coast. It was likely during this time that he had his portrait painted by Philadelphia artist Emil Lenders, who would eventually settle in the Oklahoma Territory and work for the Miller Brothers 101 Ranch (figure 3.16). Lenders depicted Pawnee Bill astride, situating him in the Great Plains with teepees on the nearby ridge. He wears the western garb of the stage and his posters, identifying him firmly as a frontiersman.[28]

The Wichita Board of Trade needed a charismatic figure to lead the boomers out of Kansas anew and proposed that Lillie take charge. The showman agreed and arrived in Wichita on December 22, reportedly to an ovation and a brass band. He felt that his celebrity would help rally the cause, and by the next day, he had already planned a new

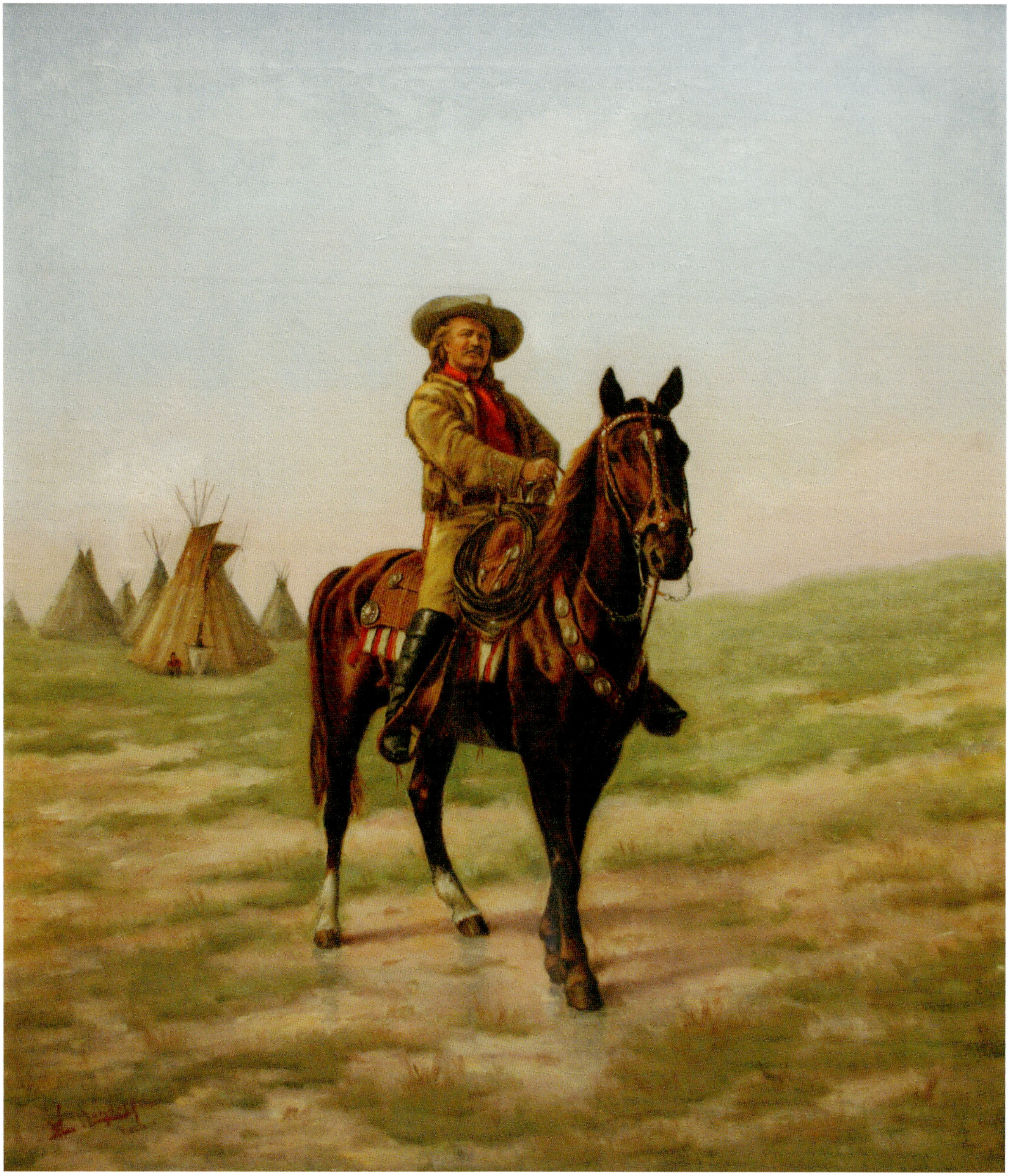

3.16. Emil W. Lenders, *Pawnee Bill*, n.d. Oil on canvas, framed, 24 × 20 ¼ inches. Pawnee Bill Ranch and Museum, Pawnee, Oklahoma

invasion of Oklahoma.[29] As Lillie later explained, the Wichita Board of Trade hired him for his promotional skills. "I began to work on the idea again, applying the psychology of show business," he later recalled. "They employed me to promote the Boomer project, guaranteeing all expenses and immunity of harm."[30]

A consummate showman, Lillie used boisterous, theatrical rhetoric to inspire the boomers and promote the movement. "We will have 10,000 men ready to move," he reported in January 1889, "and I don't see how the 1,500 soldiers—the largest body that can be gotten together—will be able to stop us. There is now no longer any question about it—the men are ready to move. We will go on February 1 and we will take Oklahoma—Congress or no Congress."[31] Harry Hill and other boomer leaders were more cautious and urged Lillie to await the fate of the Springer Bill, which supported the opening of the Unassigned Lands and was currently being considered by Congress.[32]

Despite Lillie's inflammatory rhetoric, Hill must have appealed to his sensibilities, and the invasion was delayed. The Springer Bill stalled in the Senate, but an amendment to Indian Appropriations Act authorized Pres. Grover Cleveland to proclaim the lands open for settlement. This appropriations bill passed, and President Cleveland signed it into law before leaving office—though it would be his successor, Pres. Benjamin Harrison, who ultimately issued the proclamation. Lillie credited the newspaper campaign led by *Wichita Eagle* editor Marsh M. Murdock for prodding Congress: "It was the unceasing advertising which that great newspaper gave the project which brought the tens of thousands of settlers to the border, to settle the territory in one big stampede, one of the most spectacular and epochal events in the history of the United States."[33]

Settlement would occur through a race for the land, heightening the spectacle of the event. On April 22, the day of the run, Lillie moved three thousand settlers to Colonel George Washington Miller's 101 Ranch in the Cherokee Outlet.[34] Lillie approached his role in the event as another opportunity for showmanship, riding the twenty miles to the area around modern-day Kingfisher in sixty-five minutes. He later admitted, "the run was great publicity. The press of the whole country was full of it. This helped the show business wonderfully." By 1890, Pawnee Bill was calling himself "the Chief of the Oklahoma boomers," and his 1902 biography dubbed Oklahoma "a living monument to Pawnee Bill."[35] Lillie's portrait in the book, though somewhat naïve, effectively conveys the frontier personality that the showman cultivated in the press (figure 3.17). He wears a cowboy hat and his hair long, in the tradition of William B. "Wild Bill" Hickok and his mentor Buffalo Bill. His fringed buckskin coat and trousers, as well as his moccasins, are decorated with Plains beadwork, although not Pawnee in origin. His attire conveys a general western persona, one clearly connected to the frontier of American Indian and Euro-American cultures, and to that end, he brandishes his rifle, necessary for

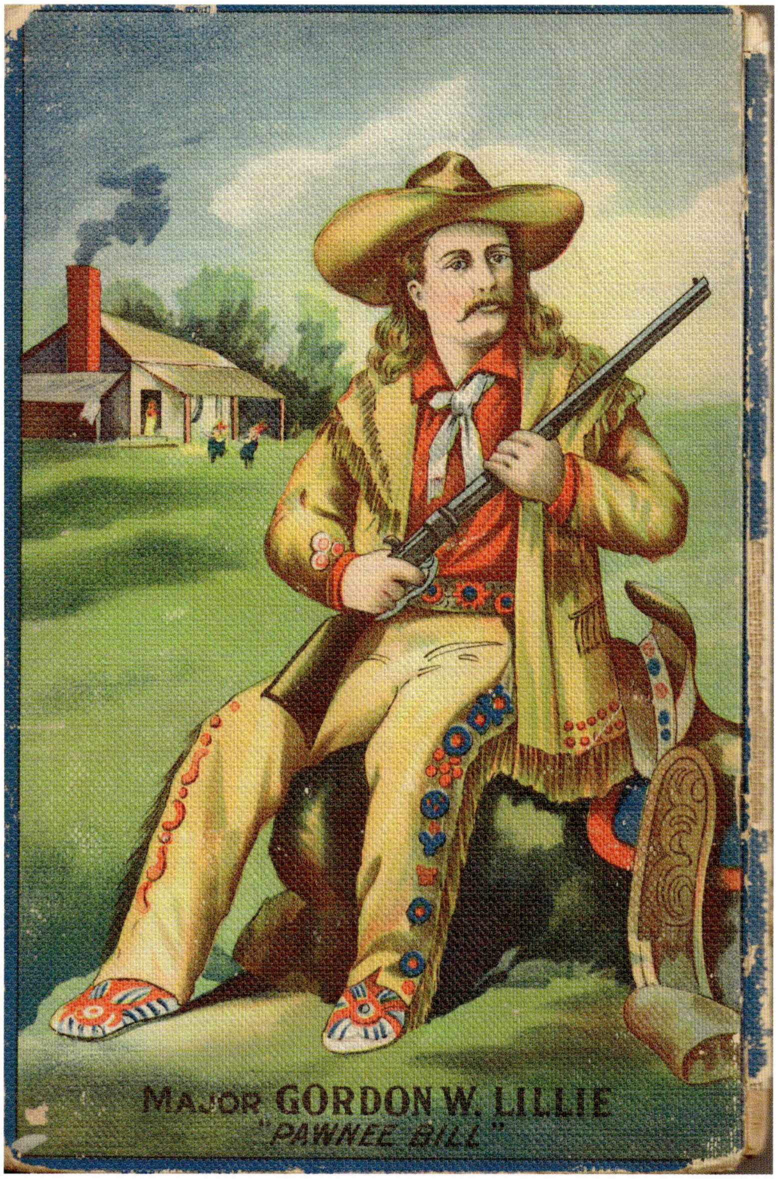

3.17. Unknown artist, *Major Gordon W. Lillie "Pawnee Bill,"* back cover of J. H. DeWolff, *Pawnee Bill (Major Gordon W. Lillie), His Experience and Adventures on the Western Plains, or, From the Saddle of a "Cowboy and Ranger" to the Chair of a "Bank President"* (Pawnee, Okla.: Pawnee Bill's Historic Wild West, 1902). Pawnee Bill Ranch and Museum, Pawnee, Oklahoma

killing game as well as for defending the settlement in the background. The artist has depicted Pawnee Bill as a western stalwart, prepared to protect settlers from an ambiguous Indian threat.

Given Lillie's flamboyant personality, his involvement in the 1889 Land Run contributed to the overall spectacle, and his comments make clear that the settlement of Oklahoma helped advance his career. Hyperbole had elevated the boomers' attempt at a land grab into one of the most significant chapters in westward expansion, and it only enhanced Lillie's western persona. The fact that Lillie had been hired by the Wichita Board of Trade also indicates that both saw the opening of Oklahoma as a business opportunity through expanded markets. Oklahoma promised free land to those willing to compete for it, but as April 22 approached, journalists promoted Oklahoma as much more, calling the territory an "El Dorado of modern times" and the biblical promised land of milk and honey.[36]

When the signal was given, "a wild shout ascended forth from a thousand throats," author Irving Geffs wrote a year later, "and it was greater by far than the glad cry that echoed across the Red Sea when the children of Israel were delivered from the hosts of Pharaoh."[37] Geffs's use of the biblical metaphor in connection with the run was convention by 1890. Even so, it helped to impress readers with the exuberance of the participants.

An eyewitness to the events of April 22, Hamilton S. Wicks, also characterized the run as a singular event in history, especially notable for the zealotry of its participants:

> Here was a unique contest in which thousands participated and which was to occur but once for all time. Truly an historical event! We, the spectators,

> witnessed the spectacle with most intense interest. Away dashed the thoroughbreds, the bronchos, the pintos, and the mustangs at breakneck pace across the uneven surface of the prairie. It was amazing to witness the recklessness of those cow-boy riders: they jumped obstacles; they leaped ditches; they cantered with no diminution of speed through waterpools; and when they came to a ravine too wide to leap, down they would go with a rush, and up the other side with a spurt of energy, to scurry once more like mad over the level plain.[38]

To Wicks, the run was an unparalleled spectacle that he helped to shape for public consumption.

The artists who produced images of the 1889 run for the popular press responded to the event in a similar fashion. Most images depict a wild surge of riders, horses, and wagons, kicking up clouds of dust. The London *Graphic* reprinted a description of the run from the *New York Herald*, and although it is unlikely the *Graphic* sent one of its illustrators to witness the event, the journal published one of the more notable illustrations of the occasion, *The Rush for the Promised Land: Over the Border to Oklahoma, U.S.A.* (figure 3.18).[39] The title evokes the popular promotional language equating Oklahoma with Canaan, and the illustration effectively captured the artifice of the run, which was essentially a carefully managed yet sensational enterprise in the acquisition of land. The artist has organized the jumbled participants, with whips flailing and horses rearing, into a tapering equilateral triangle, the point of which thrusts towards the viewer in the form of the lead rider. By associating the mass of riders that follow with an arrow or spear point, the image implies violence, as the rousing, energetic mass threatens to trample the viewer and anything else in its path in the dangerous race for land.

The aggressive implications of the image are unsurprising, considering the probable inspiration was actually Lady Elizabeth Butler's *Scotland For Ever!* (1881; figure 3.19), which depicts the charge of the Royal Scot Greys at the Battle of Waterloo in 1815. Butler exhibited the history painting in 1881 at the Egyptian Hall in Piccadilly, and it would have been a likely source for any British illustrator. The nationalistic overtones of the painting encourage the defense of empire through heroism. *The Rush for the Promised Land*, in turn, suggests that the participants also acted heroically in their race for land, and that the land run itself has become another chapter in American mythology.

The unknown artist, like other journalists who described the run, is careful to remind the viewer that this is a spectacle designed for consumption. The military personnel placed in charge of supervising the event stand at left, and one soldier looks over his shoulder at both the lead rider and the space beyond the image, thereby including the viewer in the audience gathered to watch the run. Other spectators watch the events

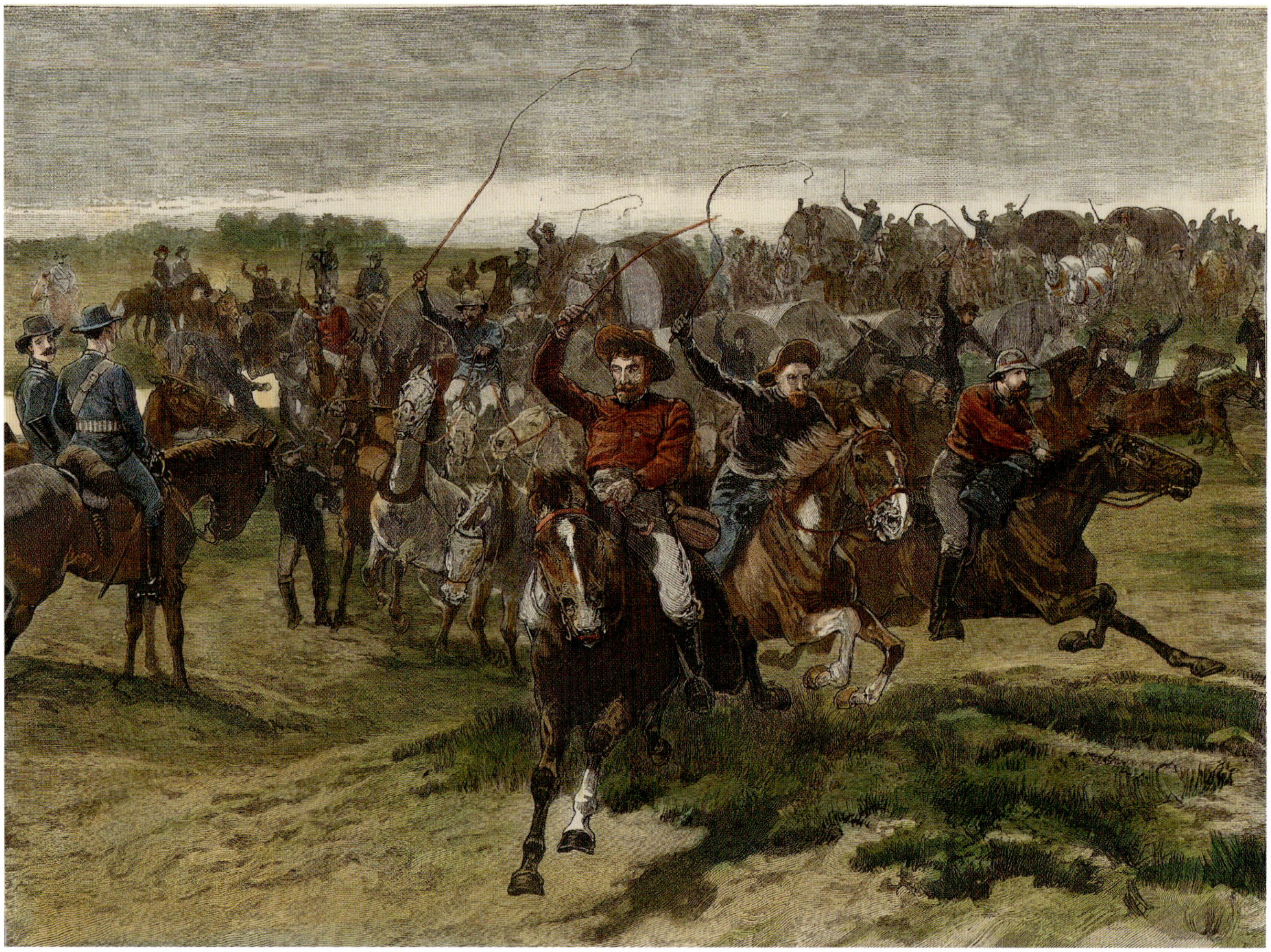

3.18. Unidentified engraver, *The Rush for the Promised Land: Over the Border to Oklahoma, U.S.A.*, in *Graphic*, May 11, 1889, 493. Color added. National Cowboy and Western Heritage Museum, Oklahoma City, Oklahoma (1996.027.1461.290). Photograph © Dickinson Research Center

unfold, clearly attracted by their singularity. By mimicking Butler's famous painting of a canonical event in British history, the *Graphic* artist furthered the historical import of the 1889 Land Run. Using hyperbolic images and language that equated a "free for all" race for land with momentous and mythic moments in world history, the boosters of Oklahoma settlement, whether they were boomers, journalists, or artists, seemed just as interested in selling copy and self-promotion as reporting events.

Although most commentators saw the opening of Oklahoma Territory and the 1889 run as significant events in westward expansion, journalist Richard Harding Davis regarded them as perversions of an idealized pilgrim mythology central to American identity. To Davis the run was little more than a carefully constructed capitalist enterprise, crude in its ideology and violent in its desire for supremacy. In an article written for *Harper's Weekly*, the writer compared the motives and actions of the boomers to those of the Pilgrims:

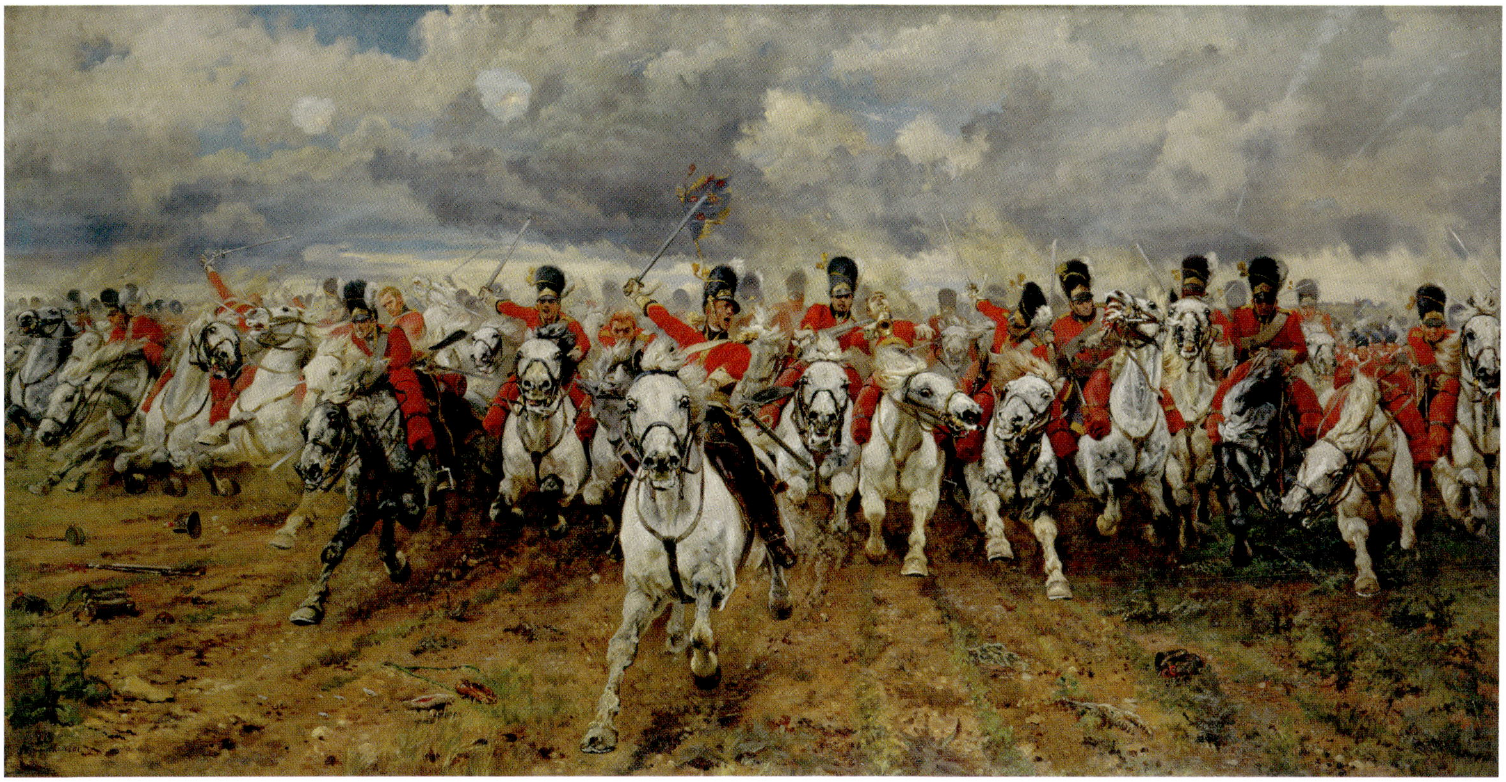

3.19. Elizabeth Southerden Thompson, Lady Butler, *Scotland For Ever!*, 1881. Oil on canvas, 40 × 76½ inches. Leeds Museums and Galleries (Leeds Art Gallery), UK. Photograph courtesy Bridgeman Images

> The history of its pioneers and their invasion of their undiscovered country not only shows how far the West is from the East, but how much we have changed our ways of doing things from the days of the Pilgrim Fathers to those of the modern pilgrims, the "boomers" and "sooners" of the end of the century. We have seen pictures in our school-books, and those which Mr. [George Henry] Boughton has made for us, of the *Mayflower's* people kneeling on the shore, the long, anxious voyage behind them, and the "rock-bound coast" of their new home before them, with the Indians looking on doubtfully from behind the pine-trees. It makes a very interesting picture—those stern-faced pilgrims in their knicker-bockers and broad white collars, with the conscious strength of having resisted persecution and overcome the perils of the sea, and ready to meet the perils of an unknown land. I would like you to place in contrast with this the opening of Oklahoma Territory to the new white settlers three years ago. These modern pilgrims stand in rows twenty deep, separated from the promised land not by an ocean, but by a line scratched in the dirt with the point of a soldier's bayonet. The long row toeing this line is bending forward, panting with excitement, and looking with greedy eyes towards the new Canaan, the women with their dresses tucked up to their knees, the men stripped of coats and waistcoats for the race to follow. And then, a trumpet call, answered by a thousand hungry yells from all along the line, and hundreds of men and women on foot and on horseback break away across the prairie, the stronger pushing down the weak, and those on horseback riding over and in some cases killing those on foot, in a mad, unseemly race for something which they are getting for nothing. These pilgrims do not drop on one knee to give thanks decorously, as did Columbus according to the twenty-dollar bills, but fall on both knees, and hammer stakes into the ground and pull them up again, and drive them down somewhere else at a place they hope will eventually become a corner lot facing the post-office, and drag up the next man's stake, and threaten him with a Winchester because he is on *their* land, which they have owned for the last three minutes. And there are no Indians in this scene. They have been paid $1.25 an acre for the land, which is worth $5 an acre as it is, before a spade has been driven into it or a bit of timber cut, and they are safely out of the way.[40]

Davis not only stripped away the hyperbole surrounding the 1889 run to expose the underlying artifice and greed, but he also provided a useful critique of the images boosters used to justify the opening of Oklahoma. Natives, for example, often appeared in scenes of westward expansion as dispossessed and helpless witnesses to the relentless march of progress. Davis notes, however, that they are absent from the Oklahoma run, having already been cheated out of their land. The visual language of westward expansion has evolved, and the only violence in this conquest takes place between rival claimants, not with angry tribesmen.

The hostility over land claims that Davis and others noted rarely resulted in bloodshed, much to the surprise of the press. A *New York Herald* headline, picked up by other papers, predicted the run was "Bound to Be a Bloody Scramble."[41] Amazed at the relative lack of violence, *Frank Leslie's Illustrated Newspaper* reported, "Some bloodshed and disorder was inevitable, but, considering the comparative lack of restraint, the excitement, and the intense determination to obtain land, the only wonder of the future historian will be that the opening of Oklahoma was not a 'carnival of crime.'"[42] In the weeks after the run, however, the magazine *Puck* continued to exploit the threat of violence to humorous effect. One spoof depicts a customer entering a Kansas hardware store to purchase supplies for his claim, only to be shown farming equipment. When the clerk learns that the claim is in Oklahoma and not Kansas, he invites his customer to "Step right this way and let me show you our repeating rifles. We also carry the finest line of revolvers and bowie knives in the city. They keep Gatling guns over across the street, where my brother works."[43]

Expectations of violence may have been fueled, in part, by the tense relationship that had long existed between the boomers and the military, but the popular perception that both Oklahoma and Indian Territories were dangerous places and a havens for criminals also must have played some role. Such outlaws as William M. "Bill" Doolin, the Dalton Gang, and particularly Belle Starr were connected with Indian Territory in the 1880s. Starr achieved national fame, and her celebrity hints at a much broader interest in the expanded social roles available to women in the Indian and Oklahoma Territories. Whether through the land runs or through outlaw culture, there was a clear perception in the popular press that women had opportunities in the territories to challenge prevailing definitions of gender.

Starr became nationally infamous through the sensational reportage of Richard K. Fox, publisher of the *National Police Gazette*. The periodical delighted in the salacious and, through its illustrations, "became a sort of go-between in Victorian America's transition from rigidly suppressed sexual desires to the rapid onset of modernity and consumerism that turned sex into a commodity."[44] Any tale of a woman breaking with social norms seemed fit to print, and the periodical took notice when Judge Isaac Parker tried Belle and her husband, Sam, for horse thievery in 1886 at his court in Fort Smith, Arkansas. The writer portrayed her as an expert with a gun and a consort to

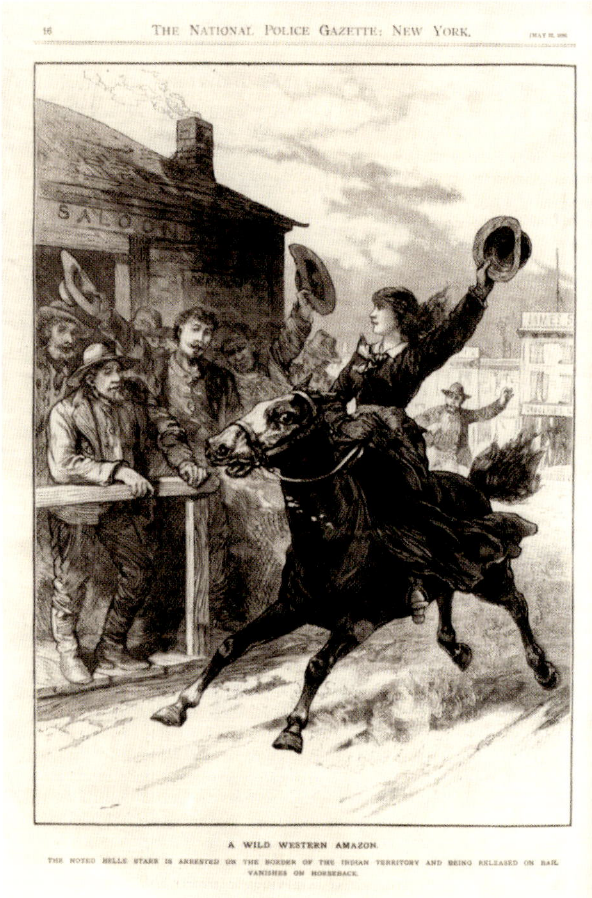

3.20. Unknown artist, *A Wild Western Amazon*, in *National Police Gazette*, May 22, 1886, 16. Library of Congress, Prints and Photographs Division (LC-USZ62–63912)

numerous outlaws and dangerous men, including Quantrill's Raiders and the James and Younger Gang. According to the writer, she was a skilled horsewoman, who often wielded a riding whip as a demonstration of her aggressive tendencies. This propensity for violence and masculine posturing led the journal to dub her a "Wild Western Amazon," and in an accompanying illustration, she rides from Fort Smith after her exoneration with a wild abandon that was scandalous for a lady (figure 3.20).[45] Saluting the cheering crowd that has spilled from the saloon to watch, her familiarity with the onlookers suggests ill repute, and Fox and his writers clearly intended the licentious implications.

Starr's murder in February 1889, a few months before the first land run, offered Fox another opportunity to fluff Starr's legend, and that same year he published *Bella Starr, the Bandit Queen or the Female Jesse James*. Once derided as "a masterpiece of erotic fiction," the book contained little factual data on Starr's life (and even misspelled her first name), but the publication helped to create the legend that persisted for much of the twentieth century.[46] Fox and his unidentified collaborator surpassed the sensationalism and hyperbole pervasive among journalistic reports of the boomers and the 1889 run, depicting Starr in the first passage of the book as both a classic femme fatale and an evolutionary marvel:

> Of all women of the Cleopatra type, since the days of the Egyptian queen herself, the universe has produced none more remarkable than Bella Starr, the Bandit Queen. Her character was a combination of the very worst as well as some of the very best traits of her sex. She was more amorous than Anthony's mistress; more relentless than Pharaoh's daughter, and braver than Joan of Arc. Of her it may well be said that Mother Nature was indulging in one of her rarest freaks, when she produced such a novel specimen of womankind. Bella was not only well educated, but gifted with uncommon musical and literary talents, which were thrown away through the bias of her nomadic and lawless disposition, which early isolated her from civilized life, except at intervals, when in a strange country, and under an assumed name, she brightened the social circle for a week or a month, and then was, perhaps, lost forever.[47]

As this passage suggests, Starr's intellect, talent, and sexual prowess identified her to some degree with the emancipated New Woman, who defied social prescriptions, yet Fox clearly hoped to engender controversy with Belle's barbarity. Far from the virginal or saintly definitions of femininity that dominated popular culture, Starr challenged social norms, and in her numerous contradictions, she was unnatural.[48] Her "nomadic and lawless disposition" seemed more masculine than feminine, and the book knowingly compared her to Joan of Arc. The author furthered the implication that Starr was a manly woman in a later passage, when she enters a riding contest in Oakland with the intention of winning prize saddles by competing in both the male and the female contests. Dressed as a Spaniard, she impresses the crowd with her skill and overhears one rider ask, "Who is that good-looking young Spaniard with black moustache, mounted on the dark stallion?" To win the female competition, she then dressed as an Indian maiden.[49] Cross-dressing, whether gendered or racial, enabled Starr to win the competition, and further emphasized her willingness to violate social norms for personal gain.

Although the anecdote is fictional, it illustrates effectively public fascination with deviant behavior, manly women, and the flexibility of identity in the West, especially in Indian Territory.[50] Scandal may have been the principle interest of the *Police Gazette* and its publisher, but they also praised scrupulous women who challenged social expectations. Cowgirl Lucille Mulhall, daughter of cattleman Colonel Zach Mulhall, first drew the attention of the *Gazette* in 1900 when she roped a steer during a reunion of Theodore Roosevelt and the Rough Riders. Although the anonymous writer did not identify her by name, an illustration of Lucille in sombrero, wooly shirt, and skirt, lasso in hand and riding at a full gallop, must have impressed the readership with her athletic ability, especially because the article added that she began riding broncos at ten and roping steers at fifteen (figure 3.21).[51] Few women wore a sombrero at the time, save perhaps for Fox's Bella Starr, yet Mulhall also wore a leather riding skirt, which emphasized her feminine appearance. The *Gazette* also covered her performance at Madison Square Garden in 1904, and the author was compelled to note, "[Mulhall] wears a pretty riding habit and there is nothing masculine in her appearance." Nevertheless, the correspondent saw her as something of a contradiction, because she effectively straddled the boundaries between the barbarity of the West and civilized culture: "Lucille Mulhall, with all this wild Westernism, is a pretty, cultivated little girl, a brilliant musician, and a warm friend of Miss Alice Roosevelt, who has entertained her at the White House, while Col. Mulhall has been the President's guest."[52] Lucille's pleasing appearance and sophisticated manner earned the respect of the *Gazette*, despite her nontraditional occupation, and her connection to the Roosevelts added further legitimacy to her break with social norms.

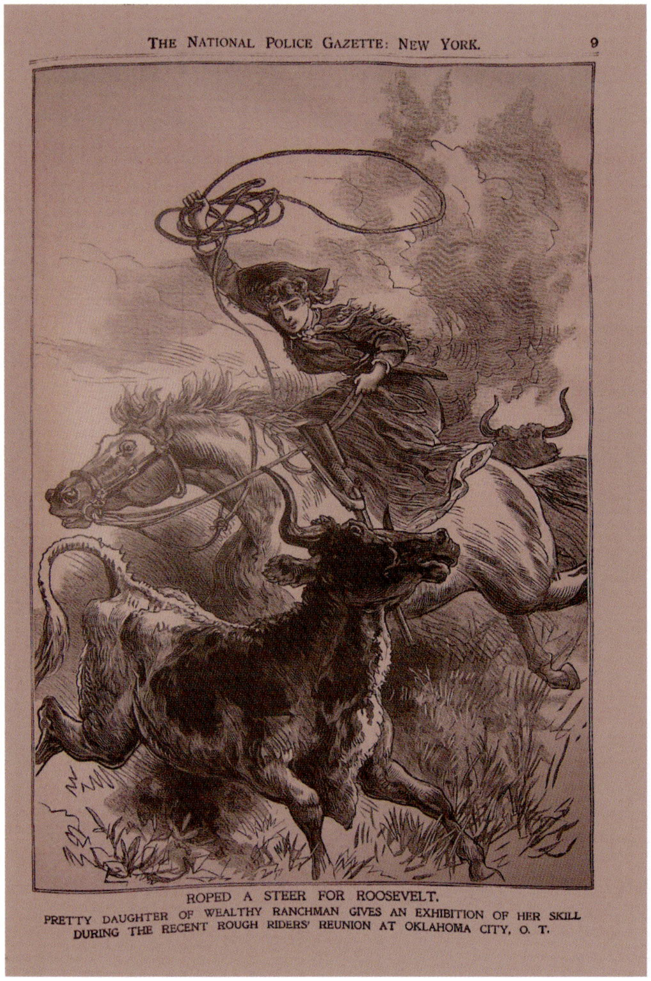

3.21. Unknown artist, *Roped a Steer for Roosevelt*, in *National Police Gazette*, August 4, 1900, 9. National Police Gazette Enterprises, Binghamton, New York

The *Gazette* was hardly alone in perceiving life in uncivilized Oklahoma as a challenge to accepted notions of femininity. The land runs, in particular, provided authors and illustrators with a forum for exploring changing definitions of womanhood, whether through unexpected behavior or through masculine dress. Richard Harding Davis, for example, had clearly intended to shock readers with his observation that women in the 1889 run bunched their dresses above the knee and revealed far too much of their anatomy for proper decorum. Yet, two illustrated short stories released at the turn of the century, Cyrus Townsend Brady's "In Oklahoma" and Henry Milford Steele's "The Run," went even further and used the land runs and the popular imagery of the New Woman as backdrops for gender bending.[53]

In Brady's 1902 short story, Sam and Sue Belle Maxwell leave their failed Kansas farm to participate in the 1889 run in hopes of securing a town lot in Guthrie, but Sam breaks his arm prior to the appointed day. Sue Belle resolves to compete by riding their thoroughbred sorrel, but her gallant husband expresses doubt, arguing "you're a woman."[54] She assuages his concern by wearing his clothes, thereby competing as him.

A skilled rider, Sue Belle takes an early lead during the run and succeeds in securing a corner lot in Guthrie. A cowpuncher arrives soon after and demands the lot, but after realizing that Sue Belle is a woman, he vows to leave peacefully if she gives him a kiss first. Fear of his sexual advances prompts her to cry and relate her predicament. The cowboy agrees to let her have the lot, after a second cowpuncher arrives and threatens his rival for making a woman cry. The Maxwells ultimately settle in Guthrie and gain their elusive fortune.

The illustrations by Howard Chandler Christy depict Sue Belle wearing male attire, including pants and riding boots. In an age when even Lucille Mulhall was expected to wear a dress while performing, Sue Belle openly challenges convention. She rides with full confidence in Christy's *Shouted back to the man* and expresses disdain for a male competitor, who trails closely behind (figure 3.22). In many respects, Sue Belle's attitude and pose compare to those of Belle Starr in *A Wild Western Amazon* in that both flaunt their freedom and power before a male audience. Sue Belle differs, however, in the righteousness of her objectives and the favorable outcomes that implicitly sanction her nontraditional behavior.

The provocative nature of Brady's story is evident when compared with Steele's less adventurous 1901 tale, "The Run." Protagonist Warren Dudley has been suffering from a string of bad luck and hopes to procure a lot in the new town of Perry through the 1893 opening of the Cherokee Outlet. Dudley jumps ahead at the start of the run but is pursued closely by a woman, much to his surprise. When her pony stumbles and breaks its leg, however, Dudley turns back and lends her his horse to finish the run, in the nick of time. Dudley cheers as she rides toward Perry, a scene pictured in the accompanying illustration by Fernand H. Lungren (figure 3.23). Steele's unnamed female protagonist wears a dress, unlike Brady's Sue Belle, but her determination and equestrian skill clearly associate her with the New Woman. For readers in 1901, both her hairstyle and her clothing suggested the influence of the Gibson Girl, the epitome of the New Woman created by Lungren's contemporary Charles Dana Gibson. The Gibson Girl had become a cultural icon of upper-class feminine beauty by the turn of the century, but as Holly Pyne Connor has argued, Gibson's ideal woman was more than just a beautiful visage: "Not only was she attractive, chaste, and interested in romance and marriage, but she was also independent, self-confident, and athletic."[55] Steele's female protagonist certainly exhibits freedom and self-assurance in her bid to win a valuable lot in Perry.

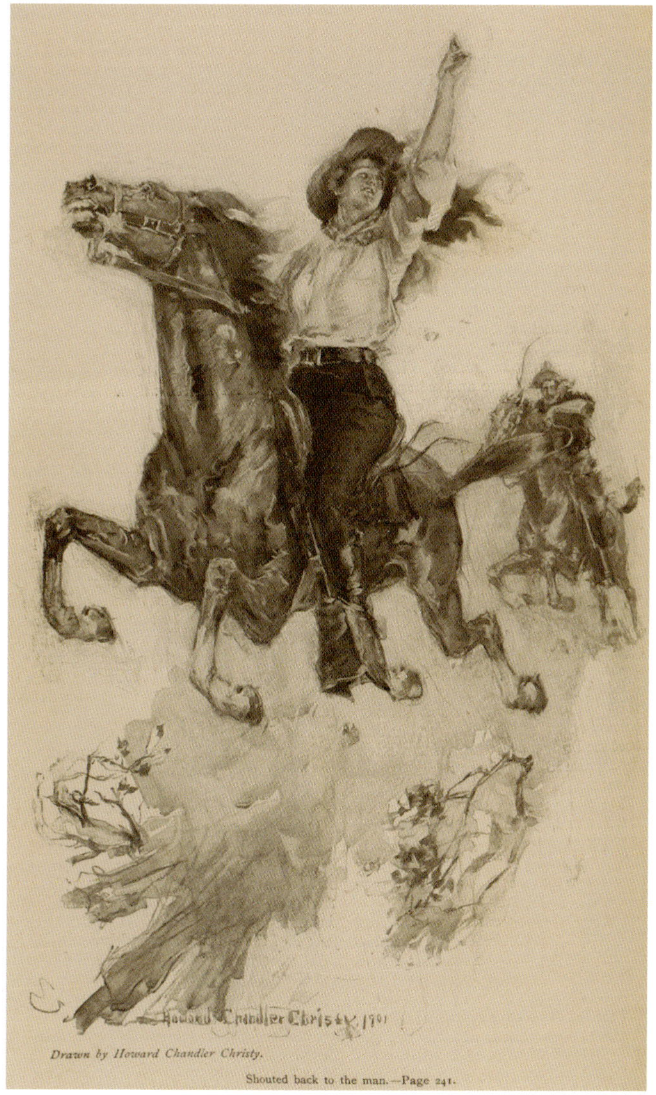

3.22. Howard Chandler Christy, *Shouted back to the man*, in Cyrus Townsend Brady, "In Oklahoma," *Scribner's Magazine* 31, no. 2 (February 1902): 234.

The 1889 and 1893 land runs not only provided an interesting literary vehicle for the treatment of New Womanhood, they also afforded real women social and business opportunities less available in other parts of the country. Women had figured prominently among the runners, according to numerous accounts. The *National Police Gazette* reported that women dressed in buckskin had been among the boomer contingent in the 1889 run, and accounts of the 1893 run took special note of the numerous women, who competed like men while racing for their own parcels.[56] Social decorum had little place in the land run, it seems, and women competed equally for material gain.

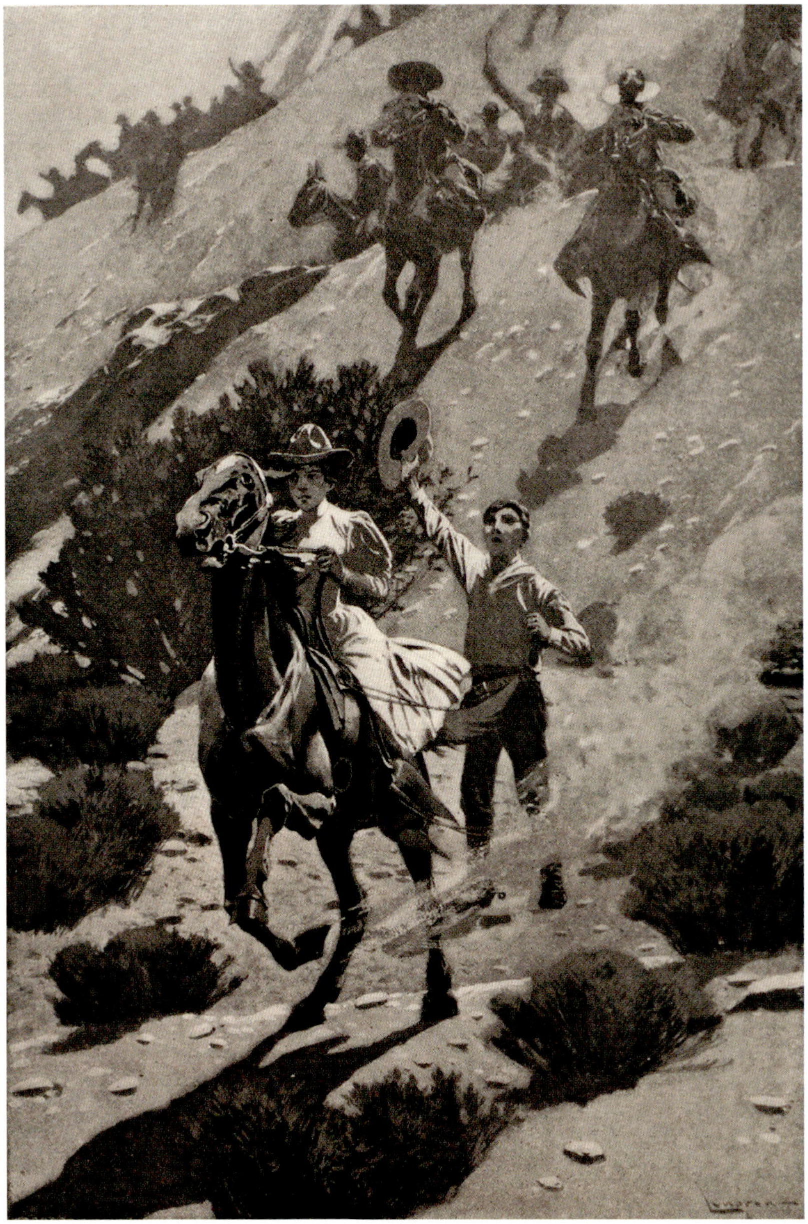

3.23. F. H. Lungren, *The Run*, in Henry Milford Steele, "The Run," *Century Magazine* 61, no. 6 (April 1901): 864. Torreyson Library, University of Central Arkansas, Conway, Arkansas

Among the numerous journalists and photographers who witnessed the opening of the Cherokee Outlet in 1893, Kansas photographer William S. Prettyman captured what would become the most iconic images of the land runs (see figure 3.1). Prettyman, who took part in the run himself, positioned three cameras and operators atop a wooden platform he had constructed near the starting line. The platform gave the photographers an important vantage point above the dust and the action, but technical difficulties spoiled two of the plates.[57]

Although Prettyman's associates produced only one viable photograph, the successful image clearly captured the essence of the run, and it remains the most reproduced photograph of the event. As the line broke, and riders, wagons, and carriages surged forward, individuals were not easily discerned, making it difficult to vouch for the widely heralded diversity of participants. The stationary eyewitnesses that stand at the lower left behind a barbed wire fence leave little doubt as to the spectacular nature of the 1893 run. The raw energy depicted in the Prettyman photograph was also captured by the forward charge in the London *Graphic's* illustration *The Rush for the Promised Land* (see figure 3.18).

Prettyman's recognition of the historical import of the 1893 run and the value of a photographic record reflected a modern awareness of how journalism shapes public opinion and the understanding of the past. Signifiers of speed pervade the scene and anticipate the modernist interest in kineticism and dynamism among artists and writers in the early twentieth century. Although Prettyman's studio had no demonstrable interest in chronophotography, the image of the 1893 run possesses many of the traits implied in the experiments of Étienne-Jules Marey or Thomas Eakins. Moreover, the dematerialization of bodies produced in the photo by both rapid movement and billowing dust, and the concomitant chaos produced by that instantaneous burst and surge of the rush, suggested the dynamism sought by the Italian futurists.[58] The blur and indistinction of the image is understandable given the limitations of dry plate photographic technology, but Prettyman no doubt selected this print with care and with some recognition that these effects conveyed the dynamism of that impassioned rush forward.

While the run itself is clearly the fundamental subject of the Prettyman photograph, the image implies the settlement that will occur as a result. Although there would be one last land run in 1895, the *Dallas Morning News* could not help but see the 1893 run as the conclusion of westward expansion and the triumph of civilization. The paper's correspondent marveled at the haste with which all of this was accomplished: "The wilderness has been conquered, and a half score of cities have been born during a single passage of the sun from zenith to horizon. Civilization, at one bound, is master of the ground, and frontier and frontiersmen, in the old sense of the words, are no more."[59] The *Kansas City Star* reported that the recent happenings in Oklahoma were unprecedented in American history, an observation shared by William Willard Howard, who had been impressed by the speed with which the town of Guthrie had been founded and occupied. In *Harper's Weekly*, he reported:

> In some respects the recent settlement of Oklahoma was the most remarkable things of the present century. Unlike Rome, the city of Guthrie was built in a day. To be strictly accurate in the matter, it might be said that it was built in an afternoon. At twelve o'clock on Monday, April 22d, the resident population of

to the following depiction of the first Oklahoma City election. Figures with ballots fill the frame and give pictorial form to the idea that Oklahoma City developed from unspoiled wilderness to a populated urban center in the course of a day. To emphasize this point, the second image, titled *an election for city officers*, precedes the final image at left, titled *held in the evening*, which includes a sun setting on the prairie. The image returns to the theme of primal wilderness and includes a lone teepee to underscore the narrative of progress. A final vignette of an overflowing ballot box surrounded by mounds of paper votes, located at the bottom of the poster, concludes the brief chronicle of Oklahoma City's founding and population boom, attended by the phrase *and 10,000 ballots cast*. The narrative of progress drawn through the five vignettes is not merely a story of urban development, however, and the juxtaposition of the "poor Indian" with the ballot box alludes to the triumph of both civilization and the democratic ideal. American republicanism, with leaders elected through popular suffrage, is easily transplanted to the wilderness, erecting the political framework for civilization in less than a day.

The narrative of the poster and accompanying newspaper reports make clear that the rapid development of Guthrie and Oklahoma City can be credited in part to the republican government model. Irving Geffs, who published in 1890 the first chronicle of Oklahoma City, agreed: "This wonderful gathering of people—this 'nation born in a day'—is a mighty argument for a republican form of government, a government founded on the consent of men."[62] Geffs had been with U.S. troops stationed in Oklahoma City on the day of the 1889 run, and he remained as a freelance journalist and an eyewitness to the growth of the city.

The swift creation of community infrastructure also played a significant role in the evolution of both cities. The reports of both Howard and the *Dallas Morning News* noted that lots had been staked and streets planned by the end of the first day. Some credit belongs to the organizational prowess of the military and some to the efficacy of American city planning and building construction in the late nineteenth century. Balloon framing provided a relatively simple form of building construction, especially with the plentiful supplies of milled lumber in standardized sizes and cut iron nails available at the end of the century. The use of studs, or long framing members, required little carpentry skill or time for the construction of the building, and less than two weeks after the 1889 run, the *New York Times* reported that approximately fifty wooden buildings had been erected in both Guthrie and Oklahoma City. All of the buildings were constructed so that they might be easily moved to conform to ongoing refinements to the city plans.[63]

Guthrie and Oklahoma City both followed a simple gridiron plan that was largely in place the first night of settlement. A surveyor, or even a layman, could stake out an area for development in a relatively short time and with little expense. Streets, parks, and other public spaces could be inserted into the lattice of verticals and horizontals with little difficulty, and the grid could be expanded easily as the city grew. Jon A. Peterson has noted that the gridiron plan promoted economic growth as well as real estate speculation:

> Lot buyers familiar with the grid in one place automatically knew its economic advantages elsewhere: the great allure of corner properties and riverfronts, the ease of building on the standard deep and narrow lots, the surety of title conferred by easily recorded boundaries. For all these reasons, the grid also reinforced the gambling ethos so pervasive in American culture, enabling buyers and sellers to treat the city as a giant game board for wagering on the future value of each lot. The grid, in sum, had proven cheap, fast, reliable, and widely understood, as readily applicable to the muddy flats of Chicago and Oklahoma City as to the slopes of San Francisco—a perfecting marketing formula for headlong growth.[64]

Rampant speculation was present in Oklahoma City, according to Richard Harding Davis, who reflected on the state of affairs in 1892.[65] By contrast, Hamilton S. Wicks, writing only months after the 1889 run, viewed capitalism as the primary reason Guthrie had prospered so quickly. He also delighted in signs of modernity that had appeared so soon after the prairie had been settled.[66]

This rapid modernization, which delivered the amenities of modern life, is apparent in Thaddeus Mortimer Fowler's 1891 panoramic map, *Guthrie—Oklahoma's Capital and Largest City* (figure 3.25). The map describes Guthrie as "The busy, bustling metropolis of Oklahoma," and "the great *Commercial, Educational, Religious, Social* and *Political* center of Oklahoma," at only two and a half years of age. Despite the youth of the city, Guthrie demonstrated significant industrial and commercial improvement in the vignettes arrayed around the panorama of the gridiron plan. The map was also careful to note that Guthrie's economy exhibited "steady, substantial growth but no boom," to counter perceptions from the outside. As if to encourage the impression that Guthrie was primed for economic development, the Atchison, Topeka, and Santa Fe Railway and the Cottonwood and Cimarron Rivers are pictured as potential engines of progress.

Publisher O. C. Seely would reiterate many of the claims promoted in Fowler's map in his 1894 book *Oklahoma Illustrated*. Seely argued that Guthrie's development had

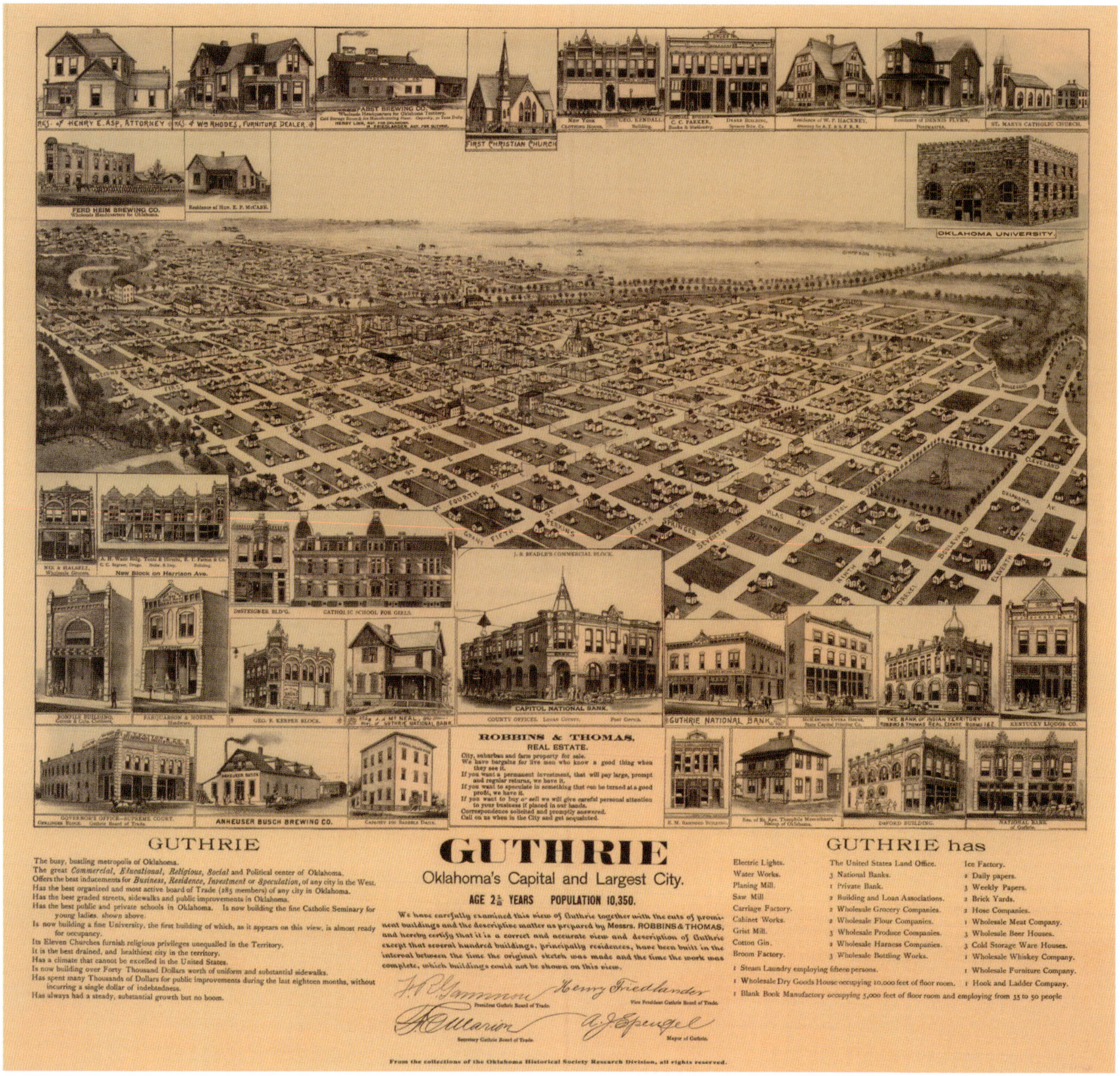

3.25. Thaddeus Mortimer Fowler, *Guthrie: Oklahoma's Capital and Largest City*, 1891. Lithograph, 23 × 25 inches. Oklahoma Historical Society, Oklahoma City, Oklahoma. Frederick S. Barde Collection (CTPMAP.Guthrie.0001)

"excelled that of any other city in the United States during the same length of time," and he added to Hamilton Wicks's list a telephone exchange and the imminent paving of city streets with asphalt.[67] Guthrie could also boast technological advance in the artificial ice plant owned by Pabst Brewing Company and cultural refinement in the opening of the Murray and Williams Jewelry and Music Store.

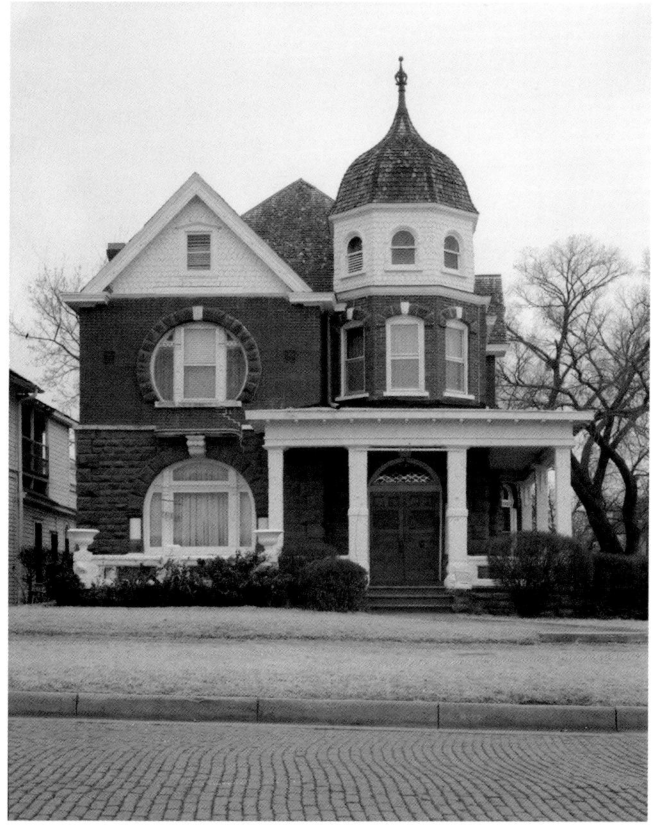

3.26. Joseph Pierre Foucart, *North (Front) Façade, P. J. Heilman House, 401 East Cleveland Avenue, Guthrie, Logan County, Oklahoma*, local red sandstone and brick, 1895. Library of Congress, Prints and Photographs Division (HABS OKLA, 42-GUTH,1E–1). Photograph by William E. Barrett (OK-15-1)

But by the time Seely published, the Guthrie cityscape had already taken a cosmopolitan turn through the influence of Belgian-born architect Joseph Pierre Foucart. After completing his training in Ghent, he worked briefly in Paris before immigrating to the United States in 1888. He settled in Guthrie in June 1889, and by the following year, his designs—characterized by domes, turrets, horseshoe and keyhole arches, and rusticated sandstone—appeared on city streets. Architectural historian Arn Henderson has argued that Foucart drew on a range of eclectic influences, including the work of gothic revivalist Eugène Viollet-le-Duc, the Romanesque revival of H. H. Richardson, and Russian and Islamic traditions.[68] Foucart's revivalist architecture spoke to contemporary, cosmopolitan tastes and helped to make Guthrie a modern city, keeping pace with mainstream architecture in most of the country. By the time of Seely's publication, Foucart had also completed plans for a domestic mansion, the P. J. Heilman house, which finished construction in 1895 (figure 3.26). The Heilman house possesses many of the features of the fashionable Queen Anne style with its stylistic hybridity, including horseshoe windows, rusticated sandstone, a wrap-around porch, and a Russian dome. Foucart used decorative latticework, keyhole windows, and asymmetrical lines in the interior, reminiscent of both gothic and Islamic design without being clearly illustrative of either.

The Heilman house would have been well suited to any affluent neighborhood in a metropolitan area, and its appearance in Guthrie spoke to the growing prosperity of Oklahoma Territory. High society accompanied the development. Marion Tuttle Rock, who wrote the first history of Oklahoma, noted that there were no class distinctions early on, but society quickly established itself: "Society in Oklahoma, and more especially in the capital city, in its rapid development, its refining influences, and its

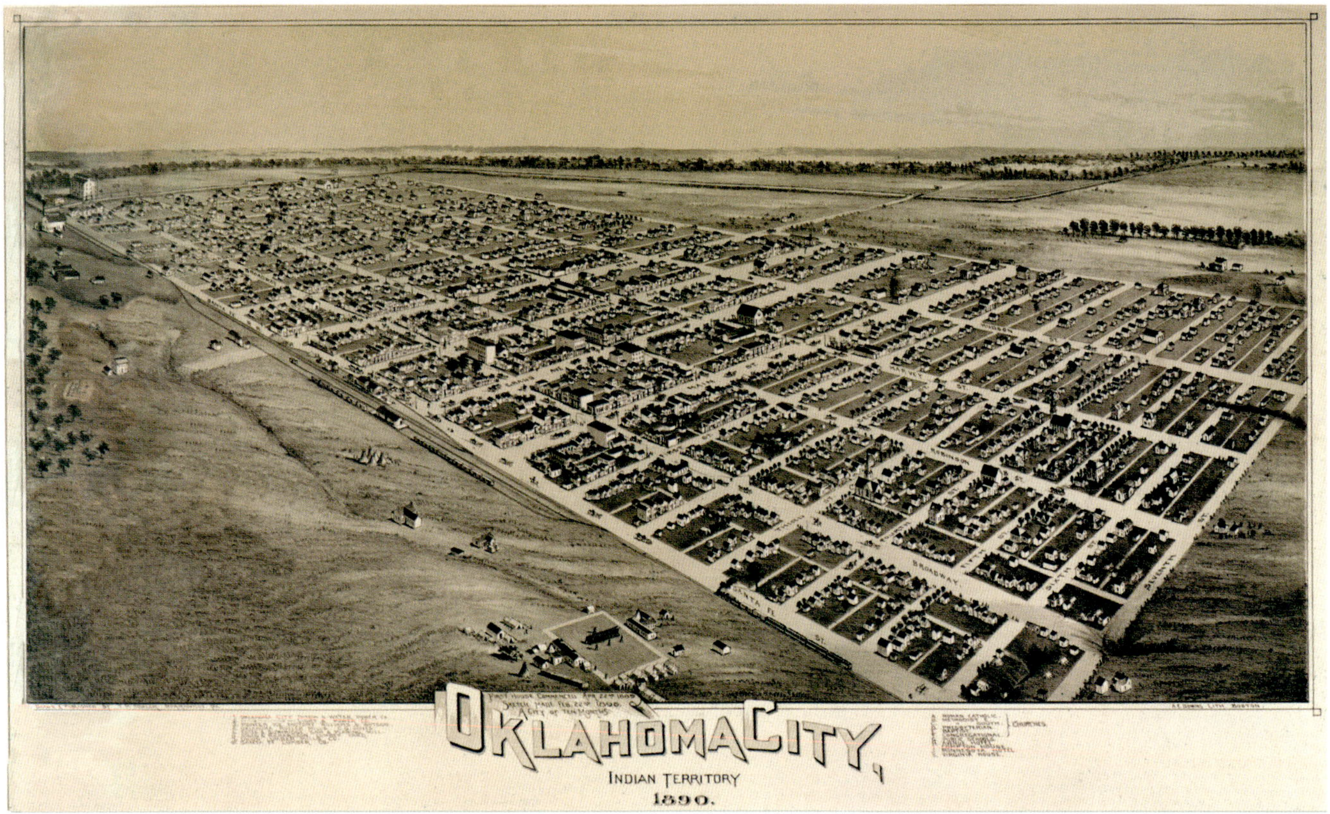

3.27. Thaddeus Mortimer Fowler, *Oklahoma City, Indian Territory*, 1890. Lithograph, 14 × 23 inches. Oklahoma Historical Society, Oklahoma City, Oklahoma (CTPMAP.OKC.0005)

advanced culture, is one of the most remarkable instances ever witnessed in the growth of civilization."[69] Like other writers, Rock cast Guthrie as a spectacular episode in the bloom of modern civilization, although she provided little proof of her assertion apart from portraits of many members of high society.

Seely reported that Oklahoma City had seen similar development, in addition to a boom in industry, which included two flour mills and factories producing bricks, brooms, carriages, candy, and ice. Oklahoma City also boasted five breweries, three daily and five weekly newspapers, eighteen hotels, and an opera house.[70] This is borne out, to some degree, by Fowler's 1890 panoramic map, *Oklahoma City, Indian Territory* (figure 3.27). Completed ten months after settlement, it lacks some of the detail in the Guthrie panorama, but some of the businesses, churches, and hotels mentioned by Seely are already apparent. The Santa Fe Railroad is also pictured in the panorama, indicating Oklahoma City's accessibility and potential for economic advancement. Most striking, however, is Fowler's inclusion of multiple teepees on the western side of the city, which impart some degree of geographical specificity. Yet their presence also signals the growing dependence the Plains tribes were forced to adopt following the so-called Plains Indian Wars and the division of Indian lands into allotments, after the passage of the Dawes Act in 1887. Fowler's map suggests, perhaps unintentionally, that the Plains tribes have been domesticated and brought under the influence of civilization.

The narrative of Oklahoman progress constructed by Seely, Tuttle, Wicks, and other commentators would continue to drive the territorial mythology in the years preceding statehood. Oklahomans, they claimed, had transformed the empty prairie into a populated territory with modern metropolitan centers, industry, and high society. Both the prairies and the Native tribes had been subjugated in the service of modernity, and much of the imagery created prior to statehood encouraged this perception. Naïve artist Augusta Isabella Corson Metcalfe spent much of her career painting the farm and ranch life of western Oklahoma Territory. Her family had settled in the Washita River valley in 1893, and Metcalfe began recording her experiences of prairie life in her early twenties. She lived on a working ranch for the majority of her life and created her works of art in her spare time. Eventually known as "the Sagebrush Artist," she became one of the first practicing artists in the territories and, later, the state. Her image of a cattle drive suggests the taming of the prairie for economic ends (figure 3.28). The vast herd will be sold, likely to markets in the north or south to satisfy growing demand for beef.

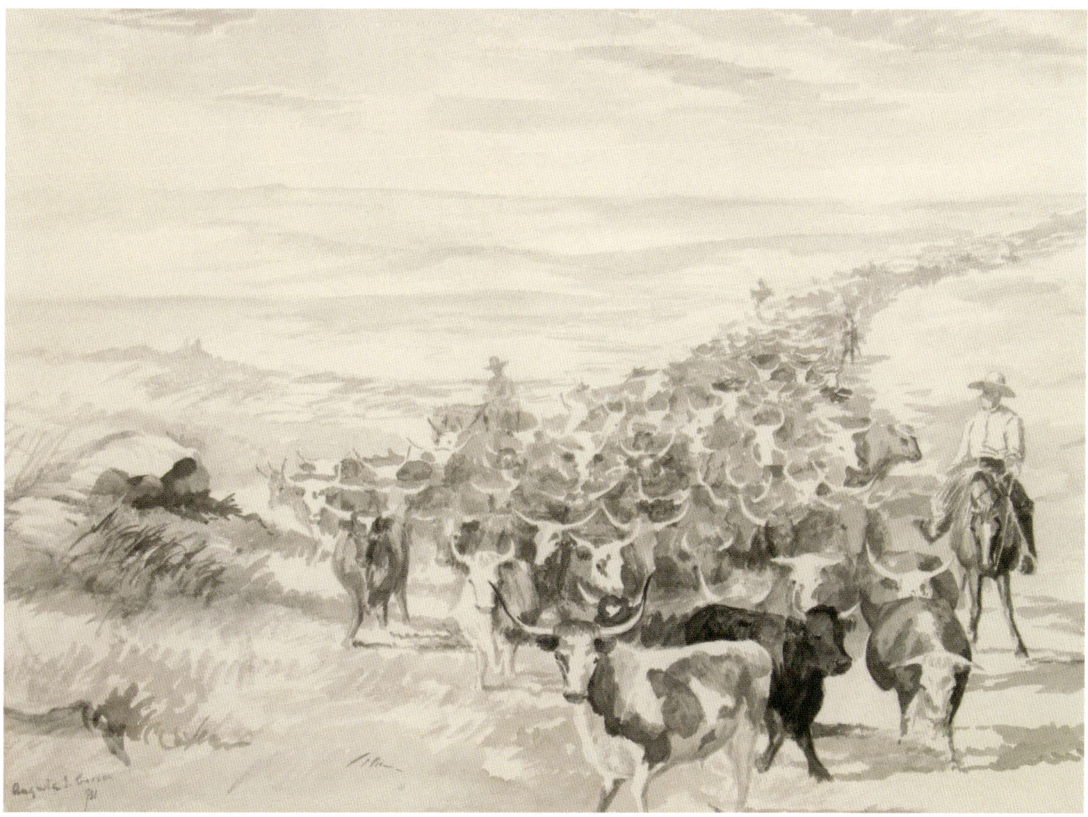

3.28. Augusta Isabella Corson Metcalfe, *Cattle Drive*, 1901. Ink wash on board, 11 × 14 inches. Metcalfe Museum, Durham, Oklahoma

The cowboy culture depicted in Metcalfe's image would continue to have a long life in Oklahoma before and after statehood, although the working cowboys she represented were often overshadowed by the popular performers of Wild West shows and rodeos, which both preserved and mythologized the life of the cowboys even as their culture was changing at the turn of the century. Nostalgia for a vanishing way of life was essential to the success of the Wild West shows, and the recent past was made spectacle.[71] Pawnee Bill was not the only performer in the territory who understood the popular appeal of the western mythos, and he encouraged the Miller Brothers, who lived on the sprawling 101 Ranch north of Guthrie, to create their own Wild West show. For several years prior to statehood, their Big Round-Up, which included rodeo performances, attracted sizable crowds. The performances boasted nascent celebrities such as Tom Mix, who would soon become one of the most popular actors in silent films, and Willie M. "Bill" Pickett, who had achieved acclaim for bull dogging, in which he wrestled bulls to the ground by biting their upper lip.[72]

Pickett and his siblings had organized the Pickett Brothers Broncho Busters and Rough Riders Association in the 1890s, but it was Bill who became a popular regional sensation. He first performed with the 101 Ranch in 1905 and then signed a contract with the outfit in 1907. By that time, Emil Lenders had developed an association with the ranch, and his 1907 untitled painting is almost certainly a portrait of Pickett (figure 3.29). There were few African Americans on the ranch payroll who enjoyed the popularity of Pickett, and the hat, yellow neckerchief, and red shirt compare closely to the attire pictured in later posters for the 1921 production *The Bull-Dogger*. Lenders chose a quiet moment in which Pickett adjusts the saddle on his mount, possibly his favorite horse, Spradley, instead of performing the theatrical bull-dogging maneuver that had brought him acclaim in rodeos and Wild West shows.

Bull dogging is a novel and somewhat artful innovation of cowboy wrangling techniques, yet the theatrical context of Pickett's performance is strikingly spectacular. Pickett gained some measure of celebrity, which was no small feat for a man of African American and Cherokee descent at the turn of the century. Spectacle often trumped social norms in the territories, and Pickett's skill afforded him opportunities unavailable to most African Americans at that time.

Modernity in Oklahoma and Indian Territories also meant proper management of natural resources, and the attendant potential for sustained economic growth also provided proof that the territories were ready for statehood. Indian Territory had to prove ready for statehood to Congress, and the documents forwarded to Washington, D.C., included *Souvenir of Tulsa, I.T.* (figure 3.30).[73] The burgeoning city chose to emphasize its economic and industrial progress, represented chiefly by cotton farming

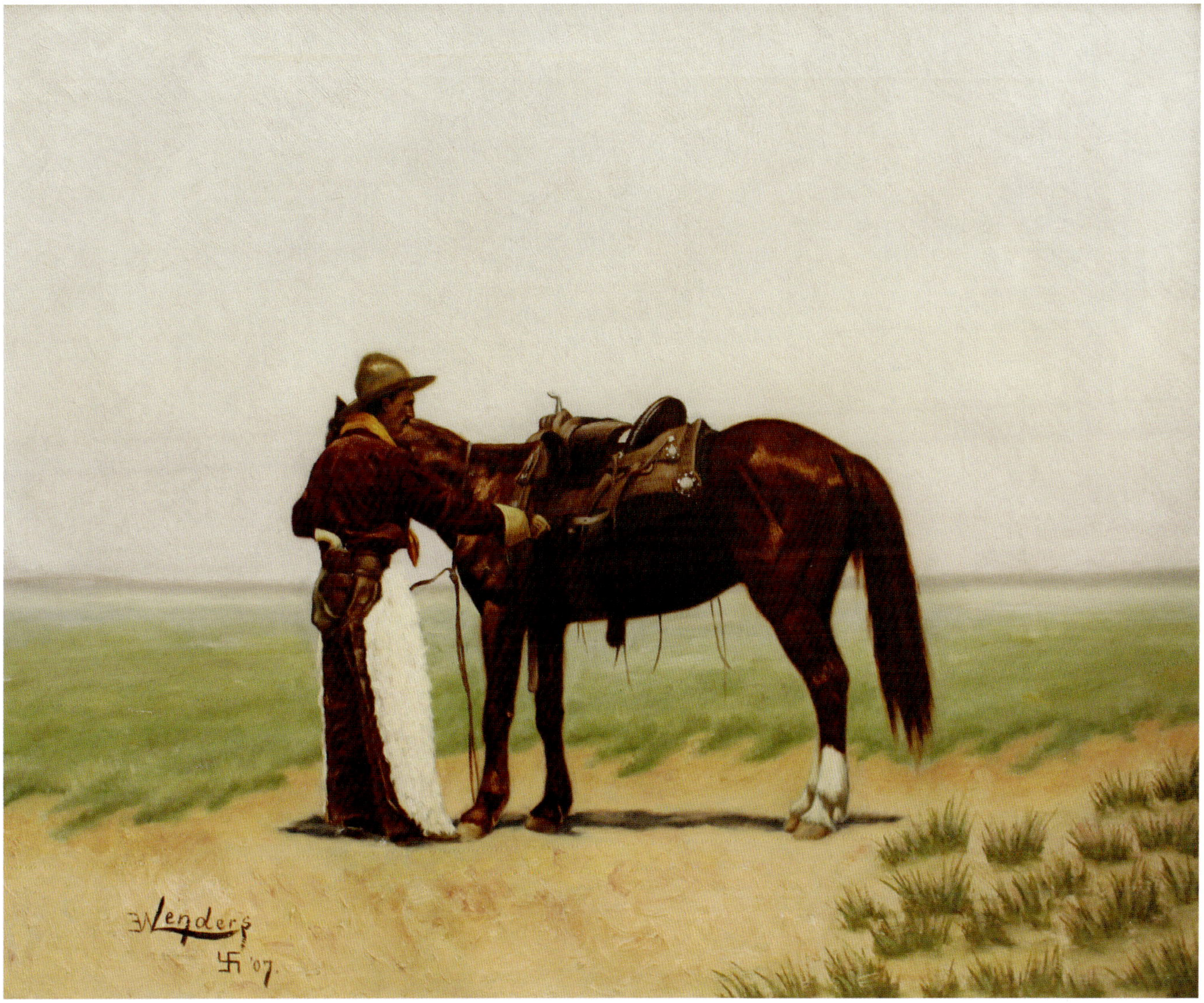

3.29. Emil W. Lenders, *Untitled (Portrait of Willie M. "Bill" Pickett)*, 1907. Oil on canvas, 22½ × 26½ inches. President David L. Boren and Molly Shi Boren, University of Oklahoma

and petroleum drilling and refining. The latter eventually became synonymous with the city and led to incredible growth over the century.

Calls for statehood began soon after the conclusion of the land runs, but there was significant disagreement as to how this would be granted. Whereas Oklahoma Territory had been opened for settlement in 1889, some tribal leaders in Indian Territory were reluctant to join their neighbor in statehood, fearing the loss of their land and sovereignty. As early as 1902, tribal leaders began meeting to discuss the idea of creating a separate state. These meetings culminated with the Sequoyah Constitutional Convention in Muskogee on August 21, 1905.[74] The notion of a state of Sequoyah, named for the creator of the Cherokee syllabary, found uneven support among the tribes and little interest in Congress, and President Theodore Roosevelt ultimately ruled that both territories would have to be admitted as a single state.

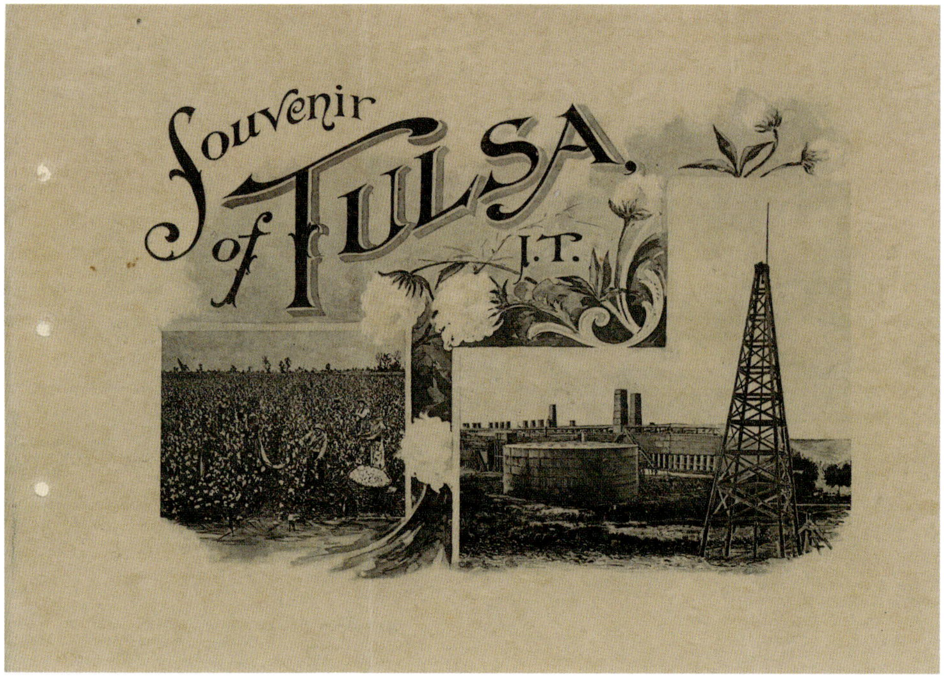

3.30. Unknown artist, cover of *Souvenir of Tulsa, I.T.,* 1906. National Archives, Washington, D.C., www.archives.gov/legislative/features/oklahoma

The statehood ceremony, held on November 16, 1907, in Guthrie, included a mock marriage in which Indian Territory was pledged as the faithful bride to Oklahoma Territory. The notion that Indians had become the domestic dependents of the American presence in Oklahoma, suggested eighteen years earlier in Fowler's panoramic map of Oklahoma City, was given ceremonial form. Muskogee resident Anna Trainor Bennett, wife of former U.S. marshal Leo Bennett, represented Indian Territory and was married symbolically to the groom of Oklahoma Territory, Charles G. Jones of Oklahoma City. By the standards of the day, a feminized Indian Territory became the figurative dependent to the masculine Oklahoma Territory.

Given the spectacular, and sometimes theatrical, nature of Oklahoma settlement, it is of little surprise that the ceremony accompanying statehood would dramatize the climax of westward expansion. Boosters for settlement and statehood, from David Payne to Pawnee Bill, had employed spectacle as an ideological device for furthering their cause. Collectively, they constructed a common mythology in print and image that positioned Oklahoma as the apogee of American expansion: an American Canaan promising limitless wealth and possibilities, settled in a series of spectacular land runs with no parallel in human history and transformed seemingly overnight into the site of a modern, progressive society. It was no accident that author Alexander Cantonwine, fully conscious of this narrative, subtitled his 1911 history of Oklahoma "The Building of an Empire."[75] Cantonwine, like those journalists, writers, and artists before him, could not help but associate the state with the success of American imperial desire, and he celebrated Oklahoma's place in the conclusion of that national mythology.

Notes

1. Some lands were sold prior to the land run or won in a lottery, but the primacy of the land run in the settlement of Oklahoma Territory is unquestionable.
2. William Willard Howard, "The Rush to Oklahoma," *Harper's Weekly*, May 18, 1889, 391.
3. "A Land-Rush in the United States," *Graphic*, October 28, 1893, 535.
4. Quoted in Stan Hoig, *The Oklahoma Land Rush of 1889* (Oklahoma City: Oklahoma Historical Society, 1984), 245–46.
5. A full examination of the boomers is beyond the scope of this chapter. For a more complete history of the boomer movement, see Stan Hoig, *David L. Payne: The Oklahoma Boomer* (Oklahoma City: Western Heritage Books, 1980); Michael W. Lovegrove, "Free Homes: David L. Payne and the Oklahoma Boomer Movement, 1879–1884" (Master's thesis, University of Oklahoma, Norman, 1996); and Carl Coke Rister, *Land Hunger: David L. Payne and the Oklahoma Boomers* (Norman: University of Oklahoma Press, 1942).
6. Boudinot published his article in the *Chicago Times* on February 17, 1879. He had been a Cherokee Nation representative to the Confederacy and supported the idea of opening the territory to non-Indian settlement. Payne and Boudinot would become friends. For further information on Boudinot, see Hoig, *David L. Payne*, 47–66.
7. Lovegrove's thesis notes the importance of the press to the boomer movement; "Free Homes," 82.
8. John Forbes, "Oklahoma on Toast," *Kansas City Times*, May 4, 1879, 1.
9. "Carpenter as Moses," *Kansas City Times*, May 18, 1879, 1. The David L. Payne Papers in the Western History Collection, University of Oklahoma, Norman, consists chiefly of typewritten transcripts of the newspaper articles Payne and his family collected on the boomer movement. A survey of the articles indicates that words and phrases such as "boom" and "On to Oklahoma" were used continuously in boomer literature.
10. For the purposes of this chapter, Indian Territory refers chiefly to the territory set aside by the 1834 Indian Intercourse Act for Native tribes living in the Midwest or forcibly removed to the area. Over the course of the nineteenth century, Indian Territory was gradually reduced, until the 1880s, when it had boundaries comparable to modern Oklahoma. Oklahoma Territory refers to the land within Indian Territory that was carved out for settlement following the 1890 Oklahoma Organic Act. From 1890 to 1907, Indian and Oklahoma Territories coexisted until statehood united them as Oklahoma.
11. "Invading the Indian Territory," *Frank Leslie's Illustrated Newspaper*, January 1, 1881, 303; and Rister, *Land Hunger*, 79.
12. "Invading the Indian Territory," 303. Also reported in A. P. Jackson and E. C. Cole, *Oklahoma! Politically and Topographically Described. History and Guide to the Indian Territory. Biographical Sketches of Capt. David L. Payne, W. L. Couch, Wm. H. Osborn, and Others* (Kansas City, Mo.: Ramsey, Millet, and Hudson, 1885), 14; and Rister, *Land Hunger*, 83.
13. "Payne, a Dime Novel Reader," *Cherokee Advocate* (Tahlequah, C.N.), May 19, 1880.
14. The article originally appeared in the *St. Louis Republican*, then was picked up in Indian Territory as "Wonderful Shooting," *Cheyenne Transporter* (Darlington, I.T.), October 25, 1880, 4.
15. *Buffalo Bill's Wild West : America's national*

entertainment, led by the famed scout and guide Buffalo Bill (Hon. W. F. Cody). . . . (Hartford, Conn.: Calhoun, 1884), n.p. John M. Burke, *"Buffalo Bill" from Prairie to Palace; An Authentic History of the Wild West, with sketches, stories of adventure, and anecdotes of "Buffalo Bill," the hero of the plains* (Chicago: Rand, McNally, 1893), 172. Rister, in *Land Hunger*, 154, notes that Payne refused Buffalo Bill's invitation to join the Wild West.

16. "'Oklahoma' Payne," *National Police Gazette*, November 10, 1883, 6.
17. "The Occupation of Oklahoma," *London Daily News*, May 4, 1889, 5.
18. Payne's heritage is first reported in Jackson and Cole, *Oklahoma!*, n.p. and 17. Rister, in *Land Hunger*, 5, repeats the assertion that Payne's mother, Celia, was a cousin to Davy Crockett.
19. Grant Harris, one of the printers hired for the *Oklahoma War Chief* office in Rock Falls, recounted his brief time in the camp in 1927. Editorial, *Chronicles of Oklahoma* 5, no. 4 (December 1927): 363–70.
20. See Alex W. Bealer, *The Log Cabin: Homes of the North American Wilderness* (Barre, Mass.: Barre Publishing, 1978); and Clinton Alfred Weslager, *The Log Cabin in America; from Pioneer Days to the Present* (New Brunswick, N.J.: Rutgers University Press, 1969). Harrison never actually lived in a log cabin, but in the 1840 presidential election, the Whigs successfully used the image of the log cabin to suggest that Harrison was a common man of modest means, like many of his constituents.
21. *Wichita (Kans.) Beacon* article from November 19, 1884, quoted in Rister, *Land Hunger*, 187.
22. Patricia Hills offers an excellent survey of the pictorial imagery of westward expansion in "Picturing Progress in the Era of Westward Expansion," in *The West as America: Reinterpreting Images of the Frontier, 1820–1920*, ed. William H. Truettner (Washington, D.C.: Smithsonian Institution Press, 1991), 97–147.
23. Jackson and Cole, *Oklahoma!*, n.p.
24. Frederic Remington, "Oklahoma," *Harper's Weekly*, March 28, 1885, 199. Although Remington's authorship is not listed in *Harper's*, he is credited in James K. Ballinger, *Frederic Remington* (New York: Abrams, 1989), 22–23.
25. Remington's illustration was redrawn for publication by Thure de Thulstrup. For an account of the Buffalo Soldiers and the boomers, see Charles L. Kenner, *Buffalo Soldiers and Officers of the Ninth Cavalry, 1867–1898* (Norman: University of Oklahoma Press, 1999), 46 and 198–205.
26. Remington, "Oklahoma," 199.
27. "In Favor of Holding Back," *Wichita (Kans.) Eagle*, February 3, 1889, 2.
28. One of Pawnee Bill's first treatments in popular fiction was Prentiss Ingraham, "Pawnee Bill, the Prairie of Shadower, or, the Gold Queen's Secret. A Romantic Story of Real Border Life," *Beadle's Half Dime Library*, April 17, 1888. "New Attractions," *Wichita Eagle*, May 1, 1888, 5; and John Hudson, "Says Wichita Eagle Was Real Founder of Oklahoma," *Wichita (Kans.) Eagle*, November 29, 1931, 21.

    Although Lenders's portrait of Pawnee Bill is undated, the artist identified the location of his studio as "Philadelphia" on the surface of the painting. The portrait also lacks the Thunderbird cartouche that Lenders used to identify his Thunderbird Ranch near Bliss and thus place the location of the portrait in Oklahoma Territory. It is likely that the portrait was painted circa 1889.
29. Hudson, "Says Wichita Eagle," 21; "Up Again," *Wichita (Kans.) Eagle*, December 23, 1888, 5.

30. Jason Stevens, "To Pawnee Bill, Last Living Boomer Chief," *Daily Oklahoman* (Oklahoma City), April 23, 1939, 2.

31. "Will Take Oklahoma," *Abilene (Kans.) Weekly Reflector*, January 24, 1889, 2.

32. "Pawnee Bill Preparing," *Iola Register* (Iola, Kans.), January 18, 1889, 2. The Springer Bill was authored by William M. Springer, representative from Illinois, and a proponent of opening the Unassigned Lands. Springer proposed the bill in 1888, but it was not enacted. Congress considered the bill in early 1889, and it passed the House of Representatives, only to stall (temporarily) in the Senate.

33. Hudson, "Says Wichita Eagle," 21.

34. "Outposts of the Boomers," *New York Times*, April 16, 1889, 1.

35. Lillie's run was reported in an unidentified article in *New York World*, May 5, 1889, folder 6, box 10, Gordon W. Lillie Papers, Western History Collection, University of Oklahoma, Norman. Lillie quoted in Stevens, "To Pawnee Bill," 2. Lillie's identification as "Chief of the Oklahoma Boomers" appeared in "Oklahoma Outlines," *Wichita (Kans.) Daily Eagle*, August 26, 1890, 4; J. H. De Wolff, *Pawnee Bill (Major Gordon W. Lillie): His Experience and Adventures on the Western Plains, or, From the Saddle of a "Cowboy and Ranger" to the Chair of a "Bank President"* (Pawnee, Okla.: Pawnee Bill's Historic Wild West, 1902). As if to cement Lillie's position in the mythology of the Old West, the biography also included chapters on Geronimo, George Armstrong Custer, and the Pony Express.

36. "Bound to Be a Bloody Scramble," *Dallas Morning News*, April 21, 1889, 2. The article originally appeared in the *New York Herald*.

37. Irving Geffs, *The First Eight Months of Oklahoma City* (Oklahoma City: McMaster, 1890), 7.

38. Hamilton S. Wicks, "The Opening of Oklahoma," *Cosmopolitan* 7, no. 5 (September 1889): 465.

39. The illustration accompanied the article "The Rush for the Promised Land," *Graphic*, May 11, 1889, 493–94.

40. Richard Harding Davis, "The West from a Car Window," *Harper's Weekly*, April 23, 1892, 389.

41. "Bound to Be a Bloody Scramble."

42. "Untitled," *Frank Leslie's Illustrated Newspaper*, May 4, 1889, 199.

43. "Holding a Claim," *Puck*, May 15, 1889, 199.

44. Guy Reel, *The National Police Gazette and the Making of the Modern American Man, 1879–1906* (New York: Palgrave Macmillan, 2006), 3. Burton Rascoe recalled that the *National Police Gazette* "was found in bordellos, saloons, gambling houses, poolhalls, livery stables and barber-shops"; *Belle Starr, the Bandit Queen* (Lincoln: University of Nebraska Press, 2004), 3.

45. "Our Pictures: The Chief Events of the Week Pictorially Delineated," *National Police Gazette*, May 22, 1886, 2.

46. Rascoe, *Belle Starr*, 19.

47. Richard K. Fox, *Bella Starr, the Bandit Queen or the Female Jesse James* (Austin, Tex.: Steck, 1960), 5.

48. Henry Adams coined the term "American Virgin" to describe feminine ideals in *Education of Henry Adams: An Autobiography* (Boston: Houghton and Mifflin, 1918), 385. Later, Bram Dijkstra described the desire for "vestal purity" in both married and unmarried women in the United States and Europe as "The Cult of the Household Nun." Dijkstra, *Idols of Perversity: Fantasies of Feminine Evil in Fin-de-Siècle Culture* (New York: Oxford University Press, 1986), 14.

49. Fox, *Bella Starr*, 35.

50. Mary W. Blanchard, "The Manly New Woman," in *Off the Pedestal: New Women in the Art of Homer, Chase, and Sargent*, ed.

Holly Pyne Connor (Newark, N.J.: Newark Museum, 2006), 92. See also Sandra L. Myres, "The Madonnas of the Prairies and Calamity Jane: Images of Westering Women," in *Westering Women and the Frontier Experience, 1800–1915* (Albuquerque: University of New Mexico Press, 1982), for a further discussion of the binary opposition that culture often imposed on women in the West.

51. "Roped a Steer for Roosevelt," *National Police Gazette*, August 4, 1900, 6.
52. "Woman Champion," *National Police Gazette*, June 24, 1905, 6.
53. Cyrus Townsend Brady, "In Oklahoma," *Scribner's Magazine* 31, no. 2 (February 1902): 231–43; Henry Milford Steele, "The Run," *Century Magazine* 61, no. 6 (April 1901): 864–68.
54. Brady, "In Oklahoma," 238.
55. Holly Pyne Connor, "Not at Home: The Nineteenth-Century New Woman," in Connor, *Off the Pedestal*, 4.
56. "Booms!" *National Police Gazette*, April 13, 1889, 3; and "A Land-Rush in the United States," *Graphic*, October 28, 1893, 535. The *New York Times* also reported that "men and women of all nationalities and colors" were present at the 1893 run. "Into the Promised Land," *New York Times*, September 17, 1893, 1.
57. Robert E. Cunningham, ed., *Indian Territory: A Frontier Photographic Record by W. S. Prettyman* (Norman: University of Oklahoma Press, 1957), 30–33.
58. For a discussion of Étienne-Jules Marey and his significance, see Marta Braun, *Picturing Time: The Work of Étienne-Jules Marey (1830–1904)* (Chicago: University of Chicago Press, 1992). For one of the few sources on the futurist interest in photography, see Giovanni Lista, *Futurism and Photography* (London: Merrell, 2001).
59. "Magic of the Rush," *Dallas Morning News*, September 17, 1893, 2.
60. "Staking Out Claims," *Kansas City Star*, April 22, 1889, 1; and Howard, "The Rush to Oklahoma," 391.
61. "In the Promised Land," *Dallas Morning News*, April 23, 1889, 6.
62. Geffs, *First Eight Months*, 7.
63. "The Oklahoma Settlers," *New York Times*, May 2, 1889, 1. George E. Woodward helped to encourage the spread of balloon framing in 1860 with a series of articles published in *Cultivator* and with his 1865 book *Woodward's Country Homes*. By 1889, balloon framing had been adopted by farmers across the Midwest as the most practical solution for farmhouses. See Fred W. Peterson, "Anglo-American Wooden Frame Farmhouses in the Midwest, 1830–1900: Origins of Balloon Frame Construction" in *People, Power, Places*, vol. 8 of *Perspectives in Vernacular Architecture*, ed. Sally McMurry and Annmarie Adams (Knoxville: University of Tennessee Press, 2000), 3–16.
64. Jon A. Peterson, *The Birth of City Planning in the United States, 1840–1917* (Baltimore, Md.: Johns Hopkins University Press, 2003), 8–9. Also see John W. Reps, *Cities of the American West: A History of Frontier Urban Planning* (Princeton, N.J.: Princeton University Press, 1979).
65. Davis, "The West from a Car Window," 391.
66. Wicks, "The Opening of Oklahoma," 469. Wicks observed,

    As soon as it became apparent to capitalists that this enterprise was in reality the beginnings of a great city, preparations were made for the erection of a number of brick blocks; and at the time of writing this article—less than one hundred days from the date of the opening—Guthrie presents the appearance of a model Western city, with broad and regular streets and alleys; with handsome store and office buildings; with a system of parks and boulevards, unsurpassed in point of number, extent, and beauty by any city twice its size and population in the West; with a number of fine iron bridges spanning the Cottonwood River, which runs through its midst; with a system of water-works that furnishes hydrants at the corners of all the principle streets, and keeps several large sprinkling carts continually busy; with an electric-light plant on the Westinghouse system of alternating currents, capable not only of thoroughly lighting the whole city, but of furnishing the power for running an electric railway, for which the charter has already been granted by the city council, and a large sum of money put up as a forfeiture by the company that accepted it.

67. *Oklahoma Illustrated. A Book of Practical Information* (Guthrie, Okla.: O. C. Seely, 1894), 15 and 61.

68. Arn Henderson, "Joseph Foucart, Territorial Architect," in *Of the Earth: Oklahoma Architectural History*, ed. Howard L. Meredith and Mary Ellen Meredith (Oklahoma City: Oklahoma Historical Society, 1980), 72–86; and Henderson, "Low-Style/High-Style: Oklahoma Architectural Origins and Image Distortion," in *The Culture of Oklahoma*, ed. Howard F. Stein and Robert F. Hill (Norman: University of Oklahoma Press, 1993), 160–85.

69. Marion Tuttle Rock, *Illustrated History of Oklahoma* (Topeka, Kans.: C. B. Hamilton, 1890), 118.

70. *Oklahoma Illustrated*, 113.

71. For an expanded discussion of the Wild West show and nostalgia, see Joy S. Kasson, *Buffalo Bill's Wild West: Celebrity, Memory, and Popular History* (New York: Hill and Wang, 2000).

72. On the history of the 101 Ranch, see Ellsworth Collings, *The 101 Ranch* (Norman: University of Oklahoma Press, 1937). The primary source on Bill Pickett is Bailey C. Hanes, *Bill Pickett, Bull Dogger: The Biography of a Black Cowboy* (Norman: University of Oklahoma Press, 1977).

73. Center for Legislative Archives, "Oklahoma Statehood, November 16, 1907," National Archives, accessed January 14, 2016, www.archives.gov/legislative/features/oklahoma.

74. "State of 'Sequoyah,'" *New York Times*, October 5, 1905, 8.

75. Alexander Cantonwine, *Star Forty-Six, Oklahoma* (Oklahoma City: Pythian Times Publishing, 1911).

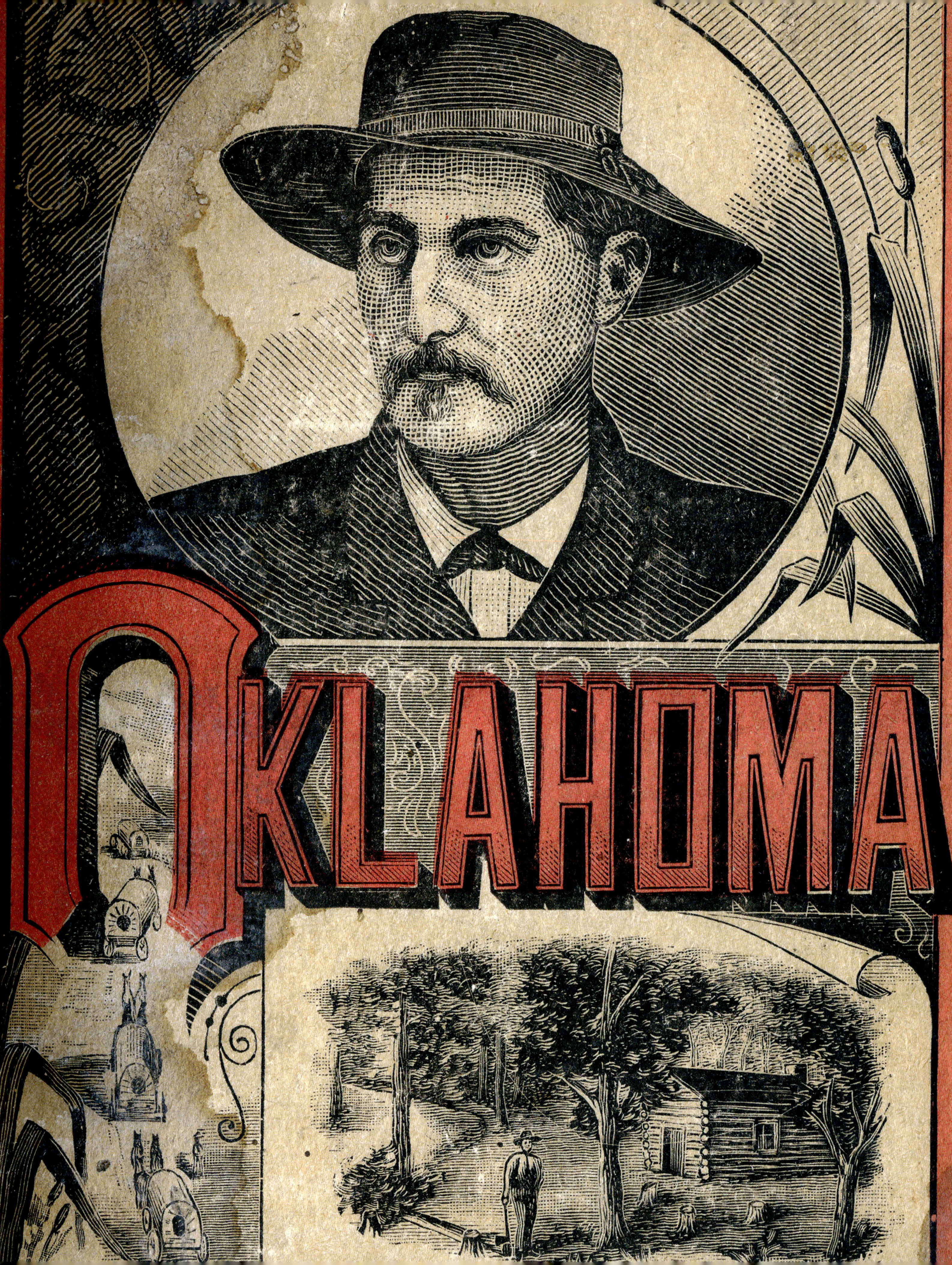
OKLAHOMA

ACKNOWLEDGMENTS

Picturing Indian Territory, the book, the exhibition, and the electronic database available at the Charles M. Russell Center are the products of many hands stretching over more than a decade. The following institutions and individuals have played a role in the success of this ongoing project.

CHARLES M. RUSSELL CENTER

School of Art and Art History, University of Oklahoma, Norman, Oklahoma

Charles M. Russell Center Staff

B. Byron Price, Director
Sharon R. Burchett, Assistant to the Director
Carol Nunley, Librarian
Lauren Belteau Gerfen, Librarian
Alyssa M. Giles, Librarian

Robert S. and Grayce B. Kerr Fellows

Tammi J. Hanawalt
Chelsea M. Herr
Hadley E. Jerman
James Peck
Melynda Seaton
Thomas B. Smith
Heather Elizabeth White

Graduate Research Assistants and Interns

Courtney L. Abbott
Katherine M. Baker
Courtney R. Covington
Caroline J. Fernald
Mary S. Hanson
Katie McLaughlin
Kimberly Riley

FRED JONES JR. MUSEUM OF ART

University of Oklahoma, Norman, Oklahoma

Mark Andrew White, Wylodean and Bill Saxon Director and Eugene B. Adkins Curator
Gail Kana Anderson, Deputy Director
Michael Bendure, Director of Communication
Tracy Bidwell, Chief Registrar
Selena Capraro, Associate Registrar
Brynnan Light-Lewis, Assistant Registrar

WESTERN HISTORY COLLECTIONS

University of Oklahoma Libraries, Norman, Oklahoma

John R. Lovett, Curator
Jacquelyn Reese, Librarian
Tara Reynolds, Staff Assistant
Kathryn Shauberger, Student Photo Assistant

RESEARCH ASSISTANCE

Autry National Center of The American West, Los Angeles, California
Marva Felchlin, Director, Libraries and Archives of the Autry

Billy Ireland Cartoon Library and Museum, The Ohio State University Libraries, Columbus, Ohio
Susan Liberator, Assistant Curator

FACING
(Detail) Unknown artist, front cover of A. P. Jackson and E. C. Cole, *Oklahoma! Politically and Topographically Described, History and Guide to the Indian Territory. Biographical Sketches of Capt. David L. Payne, W. L. Couch, Wm. H. Osborn, and Others* 1885 (See figure 3.8, page 86)

Boston College, Chestnut Hill, Massachusetts
Judith Bookbinder, Co-Director, The Becker Collection

Buffalo Bill Center of the West, Cody, Wyoming
Peter H. Hassrick, Director Emeritus and Senior Scholar
Marcy Robinson, Housel Director, McCracken Research Library
Jaclyn Rubino, Research Assistant

Cowan's Auctions, Cincinnati, Ohio
Evan Sikes, Marketing Communications

Historic Deerfield Library, Deerfield, Massachusetts
Heather Harrington, Associate Librarian

Howard Chandler Christy Art Studio, Blue Rock, Ohio
Jaye and Melodie Hayes, Owners

Leeds Art Gallery, Leeds, England
Sheel Douglas, Administrative Assistant

Lilly Library, Indiana University, Bloomington, Indiana
David K. Frasier, Reference Librarian

Little Bighorn Battlefield National Monument, Crow Agency, Montana
Cindy (Norum) Hagen, Archeologist and Librarian

Lovejoy Library, Southern Illinois University, Edwardsville, Illinois
Debbie Hard, Interlibrary Loan
Deirdre Johnson, Interlibrary Loan

Charles G. Markantes, Independent Scholar, Tarrytown, New York

Missouri History Museum Library and Research Center, St. Louis, Missouri
Emily Jaycox, Librarian
Jason D. Stratman, Assistant Librarian, Reference

Museum of Fine Arts Boston, Boston, Massachusetts
Sue Bell, MFA Images

Museum of Nebraska Art, Kearney, Nebraska
Gina Garden

Museum of the Western Prairie, Altus, Oklahoma
Jennie Buchanan, Director

National Academy Museum and School, New York, New York
Diana Thompson, Curator, Nineteenth- and Early-Twentieth-Century Art

National Archives at Kansas City, Kansas City, Missouri
Dee A. Harris, Exhibits Specialist, Office of Legislative Archives, Presidential Libraries, and Museum Services

Poteau Main Street Matters, Poteau, Oklahoma
Eric Standridge, Director

Sotheby's, New York, New York
William Tylee Ranney Abbott, Associate Specialist, Fine Arts

The State Historical Society of Missouri, Columbia, Missouri
Erika Van Vranken, Reference Specialist

St. Louis Mercantile Library at the University of Missouri–St. Louis, St. Louis, Missouri
Charles E. Brown, Assistant to the Director and Head of Reference

Thomas Jefferson Library, University of Missouri–St. Louis, St. Louis, Missouri
Mary Zettwoch, Head, Interlibrary Loan

Robert J. Titterton, Independent Scholar, Morrisville, Vermont

U.S. Geological Survey Library, Denver, Colorado
Jenny M. Stevens, Librarian

Washita Battlefield National Historic Site, Cheyenne, Oklahoma
Kathryn Harrison, Park Ranger

IMAGES

Academy of Natural Sciences of Drexel University, Philadelphia, Pennsylvania
Daniel A. Thomas Collection Manager, Library
Jennifer A. Vess, Archivist, Library
Douglas L. Wechsler, Director, VIREO

American Philosophical Society, Philadelphia, Pennsylvania
Michael P. Miller, Manuscripts Processor

Amon Carter Museum of American Art, Fort Worth, Texas
Jana Hill, Collection Information and Imaging Manager

Art, Design, and Architecture Museum, University of California, Santa Barbara, California
  Susan Lucke, Registrar

Art Institute of Chicago Images, Chicago, Illinois
  Jackie Maman, Image Licensing Coordinator

J. N. Bartfield Galleries, New York, New York
  Michael Frost
  Manny Garcia

Brandywine River Museum of Art, Chadds Ford, Pennsylvania
  Virginia H. O'Hara, Curator of Collections

The Bridgeman Art Library Ltd., New York, New York
  Kajette Solomon, Former Account Manager
  Leslie Wong, Junior Account Manager

Brooklyn Museum, Brooklyn, New York
  Alexander L. Wallace, Library Assistant

The Butler Institute of American Art, Youngstown, Ohio
  Rebecca Davis, Registrar
  Pat McCormick, Archivist and Asst. Registrar

Circus World, Baraboo, Wisconsin
  Peter Shrake, Archivist, Robert L. Parkinson Library and Research Center

The Coeur d'Alene Art Auction, Hayden, Idaho
  Michael Eric Scott, Project Manager

Cooper Hewitt, Smithsonian Design Museum, New York, New York
  Greg Herringshaw, Photo Services

Desert Caballeros Western Museum, Wickenburg, Arizona
  Mary Ann Igna, Curator and Deputy Director

Ann Cowan Dixon Archives and Special Collections, Harding University, Searcy, Arkansas
  Hannah Wood, Archives and Special Collections Librarian/Instructor

Ralph Duke Photographer, Amarillo, Texas
  Ralph Duke

Eiteljorg Museum of American Indians and Western Art, Indianapolis, Indiana
  James H. Nottage, Vice President, Chief Curatorial Officer and Gund Curator of Western Art, History and Culture

Forsyth Galleries, Texas A&M University, College Station, Texas
  Heather Ann Bennett, Collections Manager
  Amanda Dyer, Curator, Forsyth Galleries, and Assistant Director

Gilcrease Museum, Tulsa, Oklahoma
  Sandra Freeman, Director of Operations and Secretary to the Gilcrease Museum National Board
  Michelle Maxwell, Rights and Reproduction Manager
  Diana M. Cox, Intellectual Property and Copyright Manager
  Robert B. Pickering, Director of Curatorial Affairs and Public Programs
  Dana Yarbrough, Account Clerk
  Robert Stevens Cross, Photographer

Heritage Auctions, Dallas, Texas
  Eric Bradley, Public Relations Associate

Kansas City Public Library, Kansas City, Missouri
  Courtney Butler, MVSC Library Associate

Kansas City Star, Kansas City, Missouri
  Jack Beasley, Inventory Manager

Kansas State Historical Society, Topeka, Kansas
  Lisa Keys, Research/Collections Division
  Nancy Sherbert, Curator of Photographs and Acquisitions Coordinator, Research Collections

Kenneth Spencer Research Library, The University of Kansas, Lawrence, Kansas
  Karen S. Cook, Special Collections
  Kathy A. Lafferty, Public Services and Reference, Copy Services Manager, Digital Lab Manager

Metcalfe Museum, Durham, Oklahoma
  Lloydelle Lester, Museum Director
  Sarah Hammer, Accession Analyst
  Steve St. Clair, Photo and Image Producer
  Vicki St. Clair, Photo and Image Producer

Museum of American Illustration, at the Society of Illustrators, New York, New York
  Eric Fowler, Collections Manager

National Anthropological Archives, National Museum of Natural History, Smithsonian Institution–Museum Support Center, Suitland, Maryland
Adam Minakowski, Reference Archivist
Daisy Njoku, Media Resource Specialist

National Cowboy and Western Heritage Museum, Oklahoma City, Oklahoma
Gerrianne Schaad, Director, Donald C. and Elizabeth M. Dickinson Research Center
Holly Hasenfratz, Digital and Institutional Archivist, Donald C. and Elizabeth M. Dickinson Research Center

National Gallery of Art, Washington, D.C.
Barbara Bernard, Division of Imaging and Visual Services

National Museum of American Illustration and Frederick Law Olmsted Park, Newport, Rhode Island
Gina Tripodi

National Police Gazette Enterprises, LLC, Binghamton, New York
William A. Mays

The Newberry Library, Chicago, Illinois
John Powell, Digital Imaging Services Manager

Newton Gresham Library, Sam Houston State University Huntsville, Texas
Lynn M. McMain, Head of Reference and Instructional Services
James Williamson, Digital Resources Librarian

Oklahoma Historical Society, Oklahoma City, Oklahoma
Chad Williams, Director Research Division
Patricia Nunes Jones, Technical Services Manager
Terry Zinn, Photo Processing Manager

The Old Print Shop, Inc., New York, New York
Harry Shaw Newman II
Robert K. Newman

Panhandle-Plains Historical Museum, Canyon, Texas
Michael R. Grauer, Associate Director for Curatorial Affairs, Curator of Art and Western Heritage
Mary Moore, Registrar

Pawnee Bill Ranch, Pawnee, Oklahoma
Erin Brown, Curator of Collections

Philbrook Museum of Art, Tulsa, Oklahoma
Darcy Marlow, Assistant Registrar
Thomas E. Young, Librarian

Princeton University Library, Princeton, New Jersey
Stephen Ferguson, Acting Associate University Librarian for Rare Books and Special Collections
AnnaLee Pauls, Photoduplication Coordinator, Rare Books, and Special Collections
Gabriel Swift, Reference Librarian for Special Collections, Rare Books, and Special Collections

The Frederic Remington Art Museum, Ogdensburg, New York
Laura A. Foster, Director

School of Art and Art History, University of Oklahoma, Norman, Oklahoma
Eric H. Anderson, Professor, Visual Communications

Smithsonian American Art Museum, Washington, D.C.
Robin T. Dettre, Coordinator, Inventories of American Painting and Sculpture
Erin Clements Rushing, Digital Images Librarian/Intern Coordinator
Riche Sorensen, Rights and Reproductions Coordinator

Southwest Collection/Special Collections Library, Texas Tech University, Lubbock, Texas
Monte L. Monroe, Archivist
Bojana Ristic
Randy Vance

St. Louis Public Library, St. Louis, Missouri
Katie LaBarbera, Information Services Manager

The Texas Collection, Baylor University, Waco, Texas
Amie Oliver, Librarian/Curator of Print Materials

Torreyson Library, University of Central Arkansas, Conway, Arkansas
Kaye M. Talley, Assistant Director
Timothy Purkiss, Interlibrary Loan Supervisor

University of Michigan Library, Ann Arbor, Michigan
Christina Powell

University of Oklahoma Libraries, Norman, Oklahoma
Barbara Laufersweiler, Coordinator of Digitization
Brian C. Shults, Digital Archivist
Alexis Beaman, Interlibrary Loan
Sara H. Huber, Interlibrary Loan
Abigail Stout, Interlibrary Loan
Amy Lantrip, Student Photo Assistant
Vicki Michener, Government Documents
Molly Murphy, Document Delivery Librarian

Virginia Museum of Fine Arts, Richmond, Virginia
Howell W. Perkins, Image Rights Licensing Coordinator

Washington University Libraries, Washington University, St. Louis, Missouri
Deb Ehrstein, Interlibrary Loan and Reserves Librarian

William Reese Company, New Haven, Connecticut
William Reese

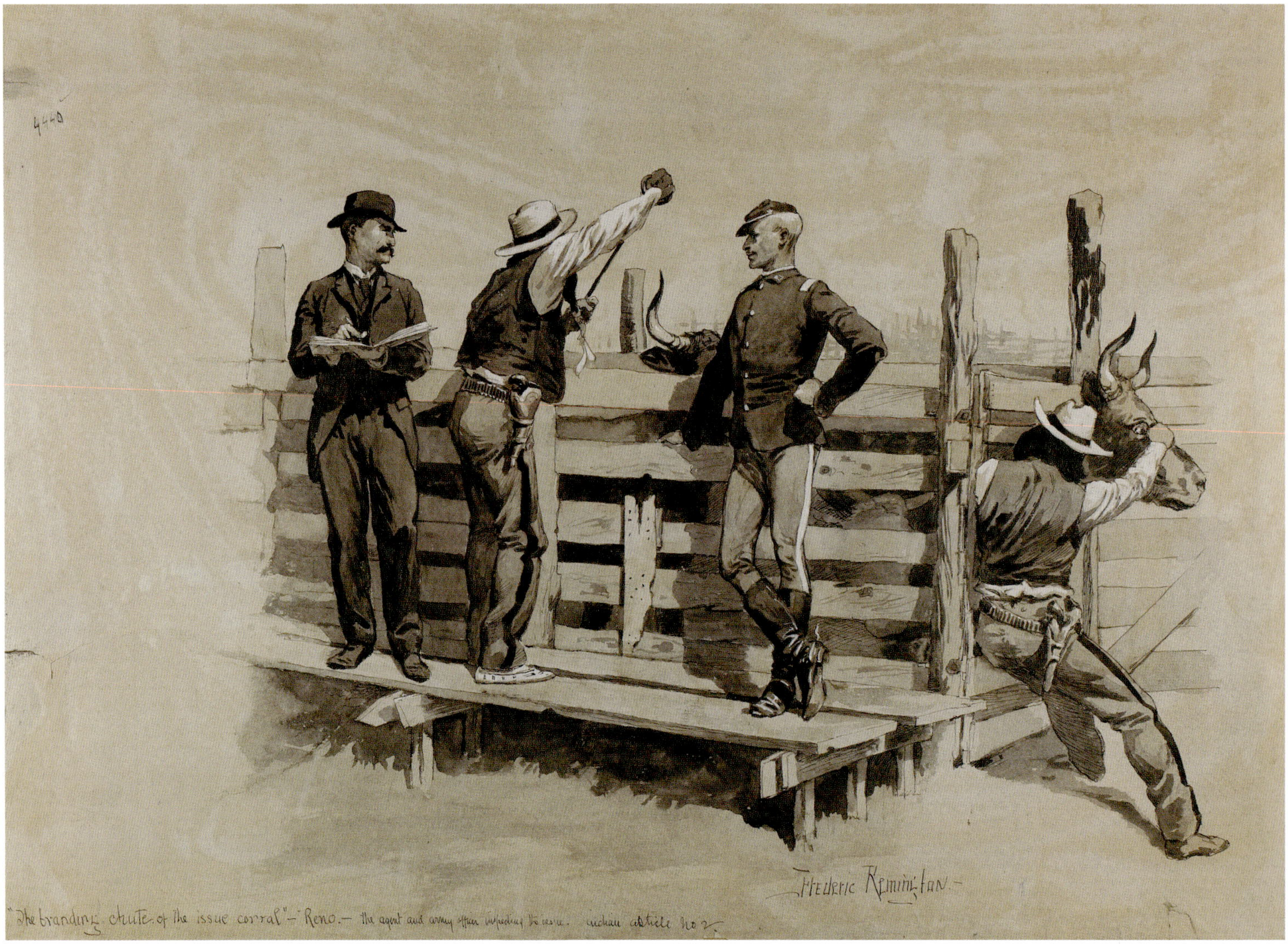

Frederic Remington, *The Branding Chute*, n.d. Pen and black ink and brush and black wash, heightened with white gouache, over traces of graphite, on tan laid paper with blue fibers, laid down on Masonite, 18 × 24 inches. The Art Institute of Chicago, Chicago, Illinois. George F. Harding Collection (1982.1586)

BIBLIOGRAPHY

ARCHIVAL COLLECTIONS

Ayer, Edward E., Collection. Newberry Library, Chicago, Illinois.

Champney, James W., Champney Sketches Mss. Manuscript Collections. Lilly Library, Indiana University, Bloomington, Indiana.

Lillie, Gordon W., Papers. Western History Collection. University of Oklahoma, Norman, Oklahoma.

Outer Banks Historical Society. James Wells Champney Sketchbooks, 1862–1863. Manteo, North Carolina.

Scott, Julian. Photograph Collection. Firestone Library, Princeton University, Princeton, New Jersey.

University of Oklahoma College of Fine Arts Collection. Publications 1901–1992. Western History Collection. University of Oklahoma, Norman, Oklahoma.

———. Records 1910–1967. Western History Collection. University of Oklahoma, Norman, Oklahoma.

Zogbaum, Rufus. Diary, September 25, 1888, to October 20, 1888. Rufus F. Zogbaum Papers, 1883–1908. American Heritage Center, University of Wyoming, Laramie, Wyoming.

BOOKS AND ARTICLES

Allgood, Samuel Y. "Historic Spots and Actions in the Washita Valley Up to 1870." *Chronicles of Oklahoma* 5, no. 2 (June 1927): 221–33.

American Water Color Society. *Illustrated Catalogue of the Twenty-Third Annual American Water Color Society*. New York: American Water Color Society, 1890.

Anderson, Nancy K. *Frederic Remington: The Color of Night*. Washington, D.C.: National Gallery of Art in association with Princeton University Press, 2003.

Anderson, William Brett. "Oklahoma and American Indian Imagery." PhD diss. University of Kansas, 2011.

"The Arrival of the Mail in Camp." *Harper's Weekly*, October 5, 1889, 792.

"An Art Display." *Oklahoman* (Oklahoma City), December 4, 1904, 22.

"Artist Farny." *Cincinnati Enquirer*, June 24, 1900, 17.

Baird, W. David, and Danney Goble. *The Story of Oklahoma*. Norman: University of Oklahoma Press, 1994.

Baker, T. Lindsay, comp. and ed. "The Survey of the Headwaters of the Red River, 1876." *Panhandle-Plains Historical Review* 58 (1985): 1–121.

Baker, William E. "A History of Cimarron County." *Chronicles of Oklahoma* 31, no. 3 (Autumn 1953): 255–67.

Baltzer, Charles. *Henry F. Farny*. Cincinnati, Ohio: Indian Hill Historical Museum Association, 1975.

Barba, Preston Albert. *Balduin Möllhausen, the German Cooper*. Menasha, Wisc.: Banta, 1914.

"Battle of Honey Springs, July 17, 1863." *Frank Leslie's Illustrated Newspaper*, August 29, 1863, 364.

"The Battle of Washita—The Attack on Black Kettle's Cheyenne Camp, Washita River, Indian Territory, by the Seventh Regiment Cavalry Under Major-General George A. Custer, Nov. 27th." *Frank Leslie's Illustrated Newspaper*, December, 26, 1868, 233.

"The Battle of the Washita—General Custar's [*sic*] Report to General Sheridan." *Frank Leslie's Illustrated Newspaper*, December, 26, 1868, 235.

Beadle, John H. *The Undeveloped West: Or, Five Years in the Territories. . . .* Philadelphia: National Publishing, 1873.

Bealer, Alex W. *The Log Cabin: Homes of the North American Wilderness*. Barre, Mass.: Barre Publishing, 1978.

Bell, John R. *The Journal of Captain John R. Bell, Official Journalist for the Stephen H. Long Expedition to the Rocky Mountains, 1820*. Vol. 6 of The Far West and the Rockies Historical Series, edited by Harlan M. Fuller and LeRoy R Hafen. Glendale, Calif.: A. H. Clark, 1957.

Belle Starr, the Bandit Queen. Lincoln: University of Nebraska Press, 2004.

Blackstone, Sarah J. *The Business of Being Buffalo Bill: Selected Letters of William F. Cody, 1879–1917*. New York: Greenwood, 1988.

Blanchard, Mary W. "The Manly New Woman." In *Off the Pedestal: New Women in the Art of Homer, Chase, and Sargent*, edited by Holly Pyne Connor, 91–124. Newark, N.J.: Newark Museum, 2006.

"Book Notices." *New York Evening Post*, June 20, 1873, 2.

"Booms!" *National Police Gazette*, April 13, 1889, 3.

"Boston and Vicinity." *Boston Evening Journal*, January 29, 1874, 2.

"Bound to Be a Bloody Scramble." *Dallas Morning News*, April 21, 1889, 2.

Braddock, Alan. "Shooting the Beholder: Charles Schreyvogel and the Spectacle of Gun Vision." *American Art* 20, no. 1 (Spring 2006): 36–59.

Brady, Cyrus Townsend. "In Oklahoma." *Scribner's Magazine* 31, no. 2 (February 1902): 231–43

Braun, Marta. *Picturing Time: The Work of Étienne-Jules Marey (1830–1904)*. Chicago, Ill.: University of Chicago Press, 1992.

Bryce, J. Y. "Temporary Markers of Historic Points." *Chronicles of Oklahoma* 8, no. 3 (September 1930): 282–90.

"Buffalo Bill's Nephew Hurt." *New York Times*, May 1, 1909, 9.

Buffalo Bill's Wild West: America's national entertainment, led by the famed scout and guide Buffalo Bill (Hon. W. F. Cody). . . . Hartford, Conn.: Calhoun Printing Company, 1884.

Bunce, Mrs. Oliver Bell. "Champney the Pastellist." *Decorator and Furnisher* 29, no. 6 (March 1897): 165–68.

"Burbank's Real American Reds." *Decatur (Ill.) Daily Review*, October 27, 1901.

Burke, Bob, Betty Crow, and Sandy Meyers. *Art Treasures of the Oklahoma State Capitol*. Oklahoma City: Oklahoma State Senate Historical Preservation Fund, 2003.

Burke, John M. *"Buffalo Bill" from Prairie to Palace: An Authentic History of the Wild West, with Sketches, Stories of Adventure, and Anecdotes of "Buffalo Bill," the Hero of the Plains*. Chicago, Ill.: Rand, McNally, 1893.

Busby, Orel. "Buffalo Valley: An Osage Hunting Ground." *Chronicles of Oklahoma* 40, no. 1 (Spring 1962): 22–35.

Bushnell, David I., Jr. "John Mix Stanley, Artist Explorer." *Annual Report of the Board of*

Regents of The Smithsonian Institution . . . 1924, 506–12. Washington: GPO, 1925.

"Camp Supply, Indian Territory." *Harper's Weekly*, February 27, 1869, 140.

"A Captured Trader." *Harper's Weekly*, July 6, 1889, 547.

"Carpenter as Moses." *Kansas City Times*, May 18, 1879, 1.

Carter, Denny. *Henry Farny*. New York: Watson-Guptill, 1978.

Catlin, George. *Letters and Notes on the Manners, Customs, and Condition of the North American Indians*. 2 vols. London: David Bogue, 1844.

Catlin-Legutko, Cinnamon. "George Catlin and Archaeology: Data Drawn from the Canvas." *Chronicles of Oklahoma* 81, no. 3 (Fall 2003): 260–73.

Cawelti, John G. *America as Art*. Washington, D.C.: Smithsonian Institution Press, 1976.

Center for Legislative Archives. "Oklahoma Statehood, November 16, 1907." National Archives. Accessed January 22, 2014. www.archives.gov/legislative/features/oklahoma.

Chalmers, Claudine. *Chronicling the West for Harper's: Coast to Coast with Frenzeny and Tavernier in 1873–1874*. Norman: University of Oklahoma Press, 2013.

"Cheyenne Scouts in Oklahoma." *Harper's Weekly*, April 6, 1889, 267.

Conrad, David E. "The Whipple Expedition on the Great Plains." *Great Plains Journal* 2, no. 2 (Spring 1962): 42–66.

"A Court Martial in the Field." *Harper's Weekly*, March 2, 1889, 168–69.

Coward, John M. "Making Images on the Indian Frontier: The Adventures of Special Artist Theodore Davis." *Journalism History* 36, no. 3 (Fall 2010): 150–59.

Cunningham, Robert E., ed. *Indian Territory: A Frontier Photographic Record by W. S. Prettyman*. Norman: University of Oklahoma Press, 1957.

Custer, George Armstrong. *My Life on the Plains; or, Personal Experiences with Indians*. New York: Sheldon, 1874. Reprint edition, Norman: University of Oklahoma Press, 1962.

Davis, Richard Harding. "The West from a Car Window." *Harper's Weekly*, April 23, 1892, 386.

Davis, Theodore R. "How a Battle Is Sketched." *St. Nicholas* 16 (July 1889): 661–68.

Dearinger, David. *Paintings and Sculpture in the Collection of the National Academy of Design, 1826–1925*. Vol. 1, *1826–1925*. New York: Hudson Hills Press, 2004.

De Wolff, J. H. *Pawnee Bill (Major Gordon W. Lillie): His Experience and Adventures on the Western Plains, or, From the Saddle of a "Cowboy and Ranger" to the Chair of a "Bank President."* Pawnee, Okla.: Pawnee Bill's Historic Wild West, 1902.

Dippie, Brian W. *Catlin and His Contemporaries: The Politics of Patronage*. Lincoln: University of Nebraska Press, 1990.

———. *Custer's Last Stand: The Anatomy of an American Myth*. Lincoln: University of Nebraska Press, 1976.

———. "Drawn to the West." *Western Historical Quarterly* 35, no. 1 (Spring 2004): 4–26.

Dodge, Theodore A. "Some American Riders." First Paper. *Harper's New Monthly Magazine* 82, no. 492 (May 1891): 849–62.

Doherty, Kathleen. "Möllhausen, Heinrich Balduin." *Handbook of Texas Online*. Texas State Historical Association. June 15, 2010. www.tshaonline.org/handbook/online/articles/fmobt.

Drury, Clifford M. *Diary of Titian Ramsay Peale*. Los Angeles, Calif.: Glen Dawson, 1957.

Editorial. *Chronicles of Oklahoma* 5, no. 4 (December 1927): 363–70.

"Elbridge Ayer Burbank—1858–1949." *Pony Express*, 1966. Available within the *Elbridge Ayer Burbank Timeline*. Harvard-Diggens Library. www.harvard-diggins.org/Burbank/index2.htm.90.

Elbridge Ayer Burbank: A Chronology. Harvard-Diggens Library. Accessed February 5,

2015. www.harvard-diggins.org/Burbank/chronology.htm.

Evans, Charles. "Itemized List of the Whipple Collection." *Chronicles of Oklahoma* 28, no. 3 (Autumn 1950): 231–34.

Everett, Dianna. "Shepherd, Nellie Ellen." *Encyclopedia of Oklahoma History and Culture*. Accessed November 23, 2015. www.okhistory.org/publications/enc/entry.php?entry=SH024.

"Farmer Painter to Address Chautauqua." *Oklahoman* (Oklahoma City), July 26, 1906, 6.

Forbes, John. "Oklahoma on Toast." *Kansas City Times*, May 4, 1879, 1.

Ford, Lisa, Tim Rowse, and Anna Yeatman, eds. *Between Indigenous and Settler Governance*. London: Routledge, 2012.

Foreman, Grant, ed. *A Pathfinder in the Southwest: The Itinerary of Lieutenant A. W. Whipple during His Explorations for a Railway Route from Fort Smith to Los Angeles in the Years 1853–1854*. Norman: University of Oklahoma Press, 1941.

"The Forts in Texas." *Harper's Weekly*, March 16, 1861, 173.

Foster, George E. "Among the Cherokees." *Frank Leslie's Popular Monthly*, February 1888, 231–38.

———. "A Zig-Zag Journey through the Indian Territory." *Frank Leslie's Illustrated Newspaper*, August 11, 1888, 417, 410.

Fox, Richard K. *Bella Starr, the Bandit Queen or the Female Jesse James*. Reprint, Austin, Tex.: Steck, 1960.

Franks, Kenny A. "Among the Plains Tribes in Oklahoma with Frederic Remington." *Chronicles of Oklahoma* 52, no. 4 (Winter 1974–1975): 419–38.

Geffs, Irving. *The First Eight Months of Oklahoma City*. Oklahoma City: McMaster, 1890.

Gerdts, William H. *Art Across America*. 3 vols. New York: Abbeville Press, 1990.

"Gleanings from American Art Centers." *Brush and Pencil* 12, no. 3 (June 1903): 209–12, 215–17.

Goetzmann, William H. *Army Exploration of the American West, 1803–1863*. New Haven, Conn.: Yale University Press, 1959.

Goetzmann, William H., and William N. Goetzmann. *The West of the Imagination*. New York: Norton, 1986.

Grauer, Michael R. "Charles Franklin 'Frank' Reaugh." In *Windows on the West: The Art of Frank Reaugh*, edited by Peter F. Mears, 5–12. Austin, Tex.: Harry Ransom Center, 2015.

"The Great South." *Harrisburg (Pa.) Patriot*, January 14, 1874, 2.

Hagan, Francis J. "Deer Stalking in the Indian Territory." *Outing Magazine* 19, no. 1 (October 1891): 21–28.

Haltman, Kenneth. *Looking Close and Seeing Far: Samuel Seymour, Titian Ramsay Peale, and the Art of the Long Expedition, 1818–1823*. University Park: Pennsylvania State University Press, 2008.

Harrel, Melvin. "My Life in the Indian Territory of Oklahoma—Augusta Metcalf." *Chronicles of Oklahoma* 33, no. 1 (Spring 1955): 49–62.

Haverstock, Mary Sayre, comp. and ed. *Artists in Ohio, 1787–1900: A Biographical Dictionary*. Kent, Ohio: Kent State University Press, 2000.

Henderson, Arn. "Joseph Foucart, Territorial Architect." In *Of the Earth: Oklahoma Architectural History*, edited by Howard L. Meredith and Mary Ellen Meredith, 72–86. Oklahoma City: Oklahoma Historical Society, 1980.

———. "Low-Style/High-Style: Oklahoma Architectural Origins and Image Distortion." In *The Culture of Oklahoma*, edited by Howard F. Stein and Robert F. Hill, 160–85. Norman: University of Oklahoma Press, 1993.

Hills, Patricia. "Picturing Progress in the Era of Westward Expansion." In *The West as America: Reinterpreting Images of the Frontier,*

1820–1920, edited by William H. Truettner, 97–147. Washington, D.C.: Smithsonian Institution Press, 1991.

Hogarth, Paul. *Artists on Horseback: The Old West in Illustrated Journalism, 1857–1900*. New York: Watson-Guptill, 1972.

Hoig, Stan. *David L. Payne: The Oklahoma Boomer*. Oklahoma City: Western Heritage Books, 1980

———. *The Oklahoma Land Rush of 1889*. Oklahoma City: Oklahoma Historical Society, 1984.

"Holding a Claim." *Puck*, May 15, 1889, 199.

Howard, William W. "The Rush to Oklahoma." *Harper's Weekly*, May 18, 1889, 391–94.

Howell, Edgar M. *Hermann Stieffel: Soldier Artist of the West*. Contributions from The Museum of History and Technology, Paper 12, U.S. National Museum Bulletin 225. Washington, D.C.: Smithsonian Institution, 1960.

Hubert, Philip G., Jr. "Rufus S. [*sic*] Zogbaum." *Book Buyer* 12 (April 1895): 132–35.

Hudson, John. "Says Wichita Eagle Was Real Founder of Oklahoma." *Wichita (Kans.) Eagle*, November 29, 1931, 21.

Hyde, Ann Farrar. *An American Vision: Far Western Landscape and National Culture, 1820–1920*. New York: New York University Press, 1990.

"Indian Prisoners Taken by Custer." *Harper's Weekly*, December 26, 1868, 826.

"Indian Scouts." *Harper's Weekly*, May 25, 1889, 111.

"The Indians His Models." *Kansas City Star*, May 26, 1901, 20.

"Indians Make Fine Models." *Reno (Nev.) Evening Gazette*, February 18, 1899.

"The Indian War." *Harper's Weekly*, January 16, 1869, 41–42.

"In Farny's Studio." *Cincinnati Tribune*, October 6, 1895, 22.

"In Favor of Holding Back." *Wichita (Kans.) Eagle*, February 3, 1889, 2.

Ingraham, Prentiss. "Pawnee Bill, the Prairie of Shadower, or, the Gold Queen's Secret: A Romantic Story of Real Border Life." *Beadle's Half Dime Library*, April 17, 1888.

"In the Promised Land." *Dallas Morning News*, April 23, 1889, 6.

"Into the Promised Land." *New York Times*, September 17, 1893, 1.

"Invading the Indian Territory." *Frank Leslie's Illustrated Newspaper*, January 1, 1881, 303.

"Issuing Beef to The Indians at Medicine Bluff Creek." *Harper's Weekly*, March 27, 1869, 204–205.

Jackson, A. P., and E. C. Cole. *Oklahoma! Politically and Topographically Described. History and Guide to the Indian Territory. Biographical Sketches of Capt. David L. Payne, W. L. Couch, Wm. H. Osborn, and Others*. Kansas City, Mo.: Ramsey, Millet, and Hudson, 1885.

Jacob, Richard T. "Military Reminiscences of Captain Richard T. Jacob." *Chronicles of Oklahoma* 2, no. 1 (March, 1924): 9–36.

Jacobson, O. B., and Jeane d'Ucel. "Art in Oklahoma." *Chronicles of Oklahoma*, pt. 1, 31 (Summer 1953): 122–40; pt. 2, 32 (Autumn 1954): 263–77.

James, Edwin, comp. *Account of an Expedition from Pittsburgh to the Rocky Mountains, Performed in the Years 1819 and 20 by Order of The Hon. J. C. Calhoun, Sec'y. of War, Under the Command of Major Stephen H. Long*. Vols. 14–17, edited by Reuben G. Thwaites. Cleveland, Ohio: A. H. Clark, 1905.

"James Wells Champney, 1843–1903." National Academy Museum. Accessed August 23, 2015. www.nationalacademy.org/collections/artists/detail/230.

Jensen, Don. "O'Neill and the Band: The Baxter Springs Massacre, Part 1." Kansas Genealogy Trails, March 2011, http://genealogytrails.com/kan/cherokee/oneillandtheband.html.

———. "O'Neill and the Band: The Baxter Springs Massacre, Part 2," Civil War Wisconsin, April 2011, http://civilwarwisconsin.com/campfire-stories/43-oneill-and-the-band-part-two.html.

Jones, Ralph. "Honey Springs, Battle of." *Encyclopedia of Oklahoma History and Culture.* Accessed December 12, 2015. www.okhistory.org/publications/enc/entry.php?entry=HO025.

"Journalism." *New York Commercial Advertiser,* February 14, 1873, 1.

Kelly, James C., and Estill Curtis Pennington. *The South on Paper: Line, Color and Light.* Spartan, S.C.: Hicklin, 1985.

Kenner, Charles L. *Buffalo Soldiers and Officers of the Ninth Cavalry, 1867–1898.* Norman: University of Oklahoma Press, 1999.

Kinietz, W. Vernon. *John Mix Stanley and His Indian Paintings.* Ann Arbor: University of Michigan Press, 1942.

King, Edward. *The Great South.* Hartford, Conn.: American Publishing, 1875.

———. "The Great South: The New Route to the Gulf." *Scribner's Magazine* 6, no. 3 (July 1873): 257–88.

Knecht, Robert L. "Ado Hunnius, Great Plains Cartographer." Master's thesis, Emporia State University, Kansas, 1987.

"A Land-Rush in the United States." *Graphic,* October 28, 1893, 535.

"Leaf from a Sketch-Book." *Harper's Weekly,* November 8, 1873, 994.

Ledbetter, Roy C. "Frank Reaugh: Painter of Longhorn Cattle." *Southwestern Historical Quarterly* 54, no. 1 (July 1950): 13–25.

Lista, Giovanni. *Futurism and Photography.* London: Merrell, 2001.

Litton, Gaston. *History of Oklahoma at the Golden Anniversary of Statehood.* 4 vols. New York: Lewis Historical Publishing, 1957.

Lombardi, William V. Review of *A Journal of Travels into the Arkansas Territory during the Year 1819,* by Thomas Nuttall. *Interdisciplinary Studies in Literature and Environment* 20, no. 1 (Winter 2013): 195–96.

Lovegrove, Michael W. "Free Homes: David L. Payne and the Oklahoma Boomer Movement, 1879–1884." Master's thesis, University of Oklahoma, 1996.

Maciejunes, Nannette, and M. Melissa Wolfe. "Like Going Home: Henry Farny's American West." *Timeline Magazine,* January–February 1995, 2–25.

"Magic of the Rush." *Dallas Morning News,* September 17, 1893, 2.

Markantes, Charles G. "James E. Taylor, Artist and Correspondent." *Research Review: The Journal of the Little Big Horn Associates* 12, no. 1 (Winter 1998): 2–13.

McCracken, Harold. *The Frederic Remington Book: A Pictorial History of the West.* Garden City, N.Y.: Doubleday, 1966.

McDermott, John F. *Samuel Seymour: Pioneer Artist of the Plains and the Rockies.* Washington, D.C.: Government Printing Office, 1951.

McGarry, Susan Hallsten. "Tulsans Collect." *Gilcrease Magazine of American History and Art* 12, no. 1 (1990): 3–37.

Meserve, John Bartlett. "The Perrymans." *Chronicles of Oklahoma* 15, no. 2 (June 1937): 166–84.

Metcalf, Augusta. "My Life in Indian Territory—Augusta C. Metcalf." *Chronicles of Oklahoma* 33, no. 1 (1955): 49–62.

Meyn, Susan Labry. *Henry Farny Paints the Far West.* Cincinnati, Ohio: Cincinnati Art Museum, 2007.

Miller, David H. "Baduin Möllhausen: A Prussian's Image of the American West." PhD diss., University of New Mexico, 1971.

———. "A Prussian on the Plains: Balduin Möllhausen's Impressions." *Great Plains Journal* 12, no. 2 (Spring, 1973): 174–93.

Möllhausen, Baldwin. *Diary of a Journey from the Mississippi to the Coasts of the Pacific with a United States Government Expedition.* 2 vols. Translated by Mrs. Percy Sinnett. London:

Longman, Brown, Green, Longmans, and Roberts, 1858. Reprint edition, New York: Johnson Reprint, 1969.

Mothershead, Harmon. "The Journal of Ado Hunnius, Indian Territory, 1876." *Chronicles of Oklahoma* 51 (Winter 1973–1974): 451–72.

"Music and Art Page." *Dallas Morning News*, March 3, 1901, 19.

Myres, Sandra L. "The Madonnas of the Prairies and Calamity Jane: Images of Westering Women." In *Westering Women and the Frontier Experience, 1800–1915*, 1–11. Albuquerque: University of New Mexico Press, 1982.

"New Attractions." *Wichita (Kans.) Eagle*, May 1, 1888, 5.

"New England News Summary." *Massachusetts Spy* (Worcester), January 3, 1873, 2.

"New Publications." *Boston Evening Journal*, January 22, 1873, 4.

Newsom, J. A. *The Life and Practice of the Wild and Modern Indian: The Early Days of Oklahoma, Some Thrilling Experience*. Oklahoma City: Harlow, 1922.

"New York Letters." *Sunday Oregonian* (Portland), May 22, 1887, 1.

Nichols, Roger L., and Patrick L. Halley. *Stephen Long and the American Frontier Exploration*. Newark: University of Delaware Press, 1980.

"Notes." *Chronicles of Oklahoma* 12, no. 3 (September, 1934): 367–68.

"Notes." *Chronicles of Oklahoma* 13, no. 4 (December 1935): 485–88.

"Notes and Documents." *Chronicles of Oklahoma* 26, no. 2 (1948): 245–46.

"Notes and Documents." *Chronicles of Oklahoma* 31, no. 1 (Spring 1953): 96–111.

Nuttall, Thomas. *A Journal of Travels into the Arkansas Territory during the Year 1819*. Philadelphia, Pa.: Palmer, 1821.

"The Occupation of Oklahoma." *London Daily News*, May 4, 1889, 5.

"Official Reception of the Whipple Collection." *Chronicles of Oklahoma* 28, no. 4 (Winter 1950–1951): 433–44.

"Oklahoma." *Harper's Weekly*, March 28, 1885, 199.

Oklahoma Illustrated. A Book of Practical Information. Guthrie, Okla.: O. C. Seely, 1894.

"Oklahoma Outlines." *Wichita (Kans.) Daily Eagle*, August 26, 1890, 4.

"'Oklahoma' Payne." *National Police Gazette*, November 10, 1883, 6.

"The Oklahoma Settlers." *New York Times*, May 2, 1889, 1.

"The Old Regiment." *Harper's Weekly*, June 7, 1890, 443.

Olds, Frederick A. "Historians and Art: An Oklahoma Case Study." *Chronicles of Oklahoma* 52, no. 2 (1974): 196–206.

"Our Pictures: The Chief Events of the Week Pictorially Delineated." *National Police Gazette*, May 22, 1886, 2.

"Outposts of the Boomers." *New York Times*, April 16, 1889, 1.

Packer, C. L. "Had Brush—and Traveled." *Tulsa Sunday World*, April 24, 1966, 10–11.

Padget, Martin. *Indian Country: Travels in the American Southwest, 1840–1935*. Albuquerque: University of New Mexico Press, 2004.

"A Painter on the Plains." *Cincinnati Commercial Gazette*, October 28, 1894, 22.

"Paintings Worth $50,000 at Fair." *Oklahoman* (Oklahoma City), September 17, 1918, 4.

Palmer, Barbara. "Coming into the Country." *Oklahoma Today* 43 (September–October 1993): 22–35.

Palmquist, Peter E., and Thomas R Kailbourn. *Pioneer Photographers from the Mississippi to the Continental Divide: A Biographical Dictionary, 1839–1865*. Stanford, Calif.: Stanford University Press, 2005.

Parke-Bernet Galleries. *The American West, 1869–1871: Watercolors and Drawings by Vincent Colyer: Arizona, New Mexico, Indian Territory, Kansas, Texas, Indians, Southwestern Nature Studies*. New York: Parke-Bernet Galleries, 1967.

"Pawnee Bill Preparing." *Iola Register* (Iola, Kans.), January 18, 1889, 2.

"Payne, a Dime Novel Reader." *Cherokee Advocate* (Tahlequah, C.N.), May 19, 1880.

"Personal Mention." *Harvard (Ill.) Herald*, February 6, 1908, 5.

"Personal Mention." *Harvard (Ill.) Herald*, March 12, 1908, 5.

Peterson, Fred W. "Anglo-American Wooden Frame Farmhouses in the Midwest, 1830–1900: Origins of Balloon Frame Construction." In *People, Power, Places*, vol. 8 of Perspectives in Vernacular Architecture, edited by Sally McMurry and Annmarie Adams, 3–16. Knoxville: University of Tennessee Press, 2000.

Peterson, Jon A. *The Birth of City Planning in the United States, 1840–1917*. Baltimore, Md.: Johns Hopkins University Press, 2003.

Pratt, Mary Louise. *Imperial Eyes: Travel Writing and Transculturation*. 2nd ed. London: Routledge, 2008.

Price, B. Byron. "Rufus Fairchild Zogbaum: A Champion of the West." *Persimmon Hill* 20 (Summer 1992): 38–41.

———. "The Utopian Experiment: The Army and the Indian, 1890-1897." *By Valor and Arms* 3 (1977): 15–35.

Quintana, Marlou J. *The Realistic Expressions of Henry Farny: A Retrospective*. Santa Fe, N. Mex.: Gerald Peters Gallery, 1981.

Reel, Guy. *The National Police Gazette and the Making of the Modern American Man, 1879–1906*. New York: Palgrave Macmillan, 2006.

Remington, Frederic. "Artist Wanderings Among the Cheyennes." *Century Magazine* 38, no. 4 (August 1889): 536–45.

———. *Crooked Trails*. New York: Harper, 1898.

———. "On the Indian Reservations." *Century Magazine* 38, no. 3 (July 1889): 394–405.

Reps, John W. *Cities of the American West: A History of Frontier Urban Planning*. Princeton, N.J.: Princeton University Press, 1979.

Rister, Carl Coke. "A Federal Experiment in Southern Plains Indian Relations, 1835–1845." *Chronicles of Oklahoma* 14, no. 4 (December, 1936): 434–55.

———. *Land Hunger: David L. Payne and the Oklahoma Boomers*. Norman: University of Oklahoma Press, 1942.

Rock, Marion Tuttle. *Illustrated History of Oklahoma*. Topeka, Kans.: C. B. Hamilton, 1890.

———. *The Oklahoma State Capitol Art Edition*. Guthrie, Okla.: Logan County Historical Society, 1980.

"Rock Mary Report." *Chronicle of Oklahoma* 38 (Summer 1960): 130, 132.

"Roped a Steer for Roosevelt." *National Police Gazette*, August 4, 1900, 6.

Royce, Ernest. *Burbank and the Indians*. Edited by Frank J. Taylor. Caldell, Idaho: Caxton, 1944.

"The Rush for the Promised Land." *Graphic*, May 11, 1889, 493–94.

Schimmel, Julia Ann. "John Mix Stanley and Imagery of the West in Nineteenth-century American Art." PhD diss., New York University, 1983.

"Scribner's Monthly for 1874." *New-York Tribune*, December 11, 1873, 6.

Shirk, George H. "Peace on the Plains." *Chronicles of Oklahoma* 28, no. 1 (Spring 1950): 2–41.

Sikes, Graydon R. "Henry Farny's Paintings of American Indians, 1894–1916: Images of Conflict between Indians and Whites Evolve into Symbolic Representations of the Demise of the Western Frontier." Master's thesis, University of Cincinnati, Ohio, 2005.

Spurr, David. *The Rhetoric of Empire: Colonial Discourse in Journalism, Travel Writing, and Imperial Administration*. Durham, N.C.: Duke University Press, 1993.

"Staking Out Claims." *Kansas City Star*, April 22, 1889, 1.

"State of 'Sequoyah.'" *New York Times*, October 5, 1905, 8.

Steele, Henry Milford. "The Run." *Century Magazine* 61, no. 6 (April 1901): 864–68.

Stevens, Jason. "To Pawnee Bill, Last Living Boomer Chief." *Daily Oklahoman* (Oklahoma City), April 23, 1939, 2.

Stoddard, Francis R. "Amiel Weeks Whipple." *Chronicles of Oklahoma* 28, no. 3 (Autumn 1950): 226–34.

"Studies and Studio." *Boston Evening Journal*, January 27, 1874.

Taft, Robert. *Artists and Illustrators of the Old West, 1850–1900*. New York: Scribner, 1953.

———. "The Pictorial Record of the Old West. Artists of Indian Life: Henry Farny." *Kansas Historical Quarterly* 18, no. 1 (February, 1950): 1–19.

———. "The Pictorial Record of the Old West: Heinrich Balduin Möllhausen," *Kansas Historical Quarterly* 16, no. 3 (August 1948): 222–44.

Tate, Michael. "Randolph B. Marcy: First Explorer of the Wichitas." *Great Plains Journal* 15 (Spring 1976): 80–113.

"Territorial Fair." *Oklahoma Times Journal* (Oklahoma City), October 2, 1894, 4.

Titterton, Robert J. *Julian Scott: Artist of the Civil War and Native America*. Jefferson, N.C.: McFarland, 1997.

Tomer, John S., and Michael Brodhead, eds. *A Naturalist in Indian Territory: The Journals of S. W. Woodhouse, 1849–50*. Norman: University of Oklahoma Press, 1992.

Troccoli, Joan Carpenter. *First Artist of the West: George Catlin Paintings and Watercolors*. Tulsa, Okla.: Gilcrease Museum, 1993.

———. "The Sketchbooks of Emil Lenders: Down to the Soles of the Moccasins." *Gilcrease Journal* 1, no. 1 (1993): 30–47.

Tyler, Ron. "Discovered Lands, Invented Pasts: A Review Essay." *Montana* 42, no. 3 (1992): 81–85.

———. "Illustrated Government Publications Related to the American West, 1843–1863." In *Surveying the Record: North American Scientific Exploration to 1930*, edited by Edward C. Carter II, 147–72. Philadelphia: American Philosophical Society, 1999.

———. *Prints of the West*. Golden, Colo.: Fulcrum, 1994.

Untitled. *Frank Leslie's Illustrated Newspaper*, May 4, 1889, 199.

"Up Again." *Wichita (Kans.) Eagle*, December 23, 1888, 5.

Vennum, Thomas. *American Indian Lacrosse: Little Brother of War*. Baltimore, Md.: Johns Hopkins University Press, 2007.

Viola, Herman. "The American Indian: Genre Paintings of Catlin, Stanley, Wimar, Eastman, and Miller." In *American Frontier Life*, edited by Ron Tyler, 131–65. New York: Abbeville, 1987.

Wardell, M. L. "Protestant Missions among the Osages 1820 to 1838." *Chronicles of Oklahoma* 2, no. 3 (September, 1924): 285–97.

"Watching the Storm." *Harper's Weekly*, March 21, 1874, 267.

Weslager, Clinton Alfred. *The Log Cabin in America: From Pioneer Days to the Present*. New Brunswick, N.J.: Rutgers University Press, 1969.

"The Whitcomb Riley of Art in Topeka." *Topeka Daily Capital*, July 30, 1906, 8.

White, Robert R. "Artists of Territorial New Mexico, 1846–1912." PhD diss., University of New Mexico, 1993.

Wicks, Hamilton S. "The Opening of Oklahoma." *Cosmopolitan* 7, no. 5 (September 1889): 460–70.

"Will Take Oklahoma." *Abilene (Kans.) Weekly Reflector*, January 24, 1889, 2.

Wingo, Rebecca S. "Charles Schreyvogel (1861–1912)." *The Artistic Legacy of Buffalo*

Bill Cody. Accessed September 29, 2015. http://rebeccawingo.com/bonner/schreyvogel.php.

Wise, Lu Cell. *Oklahoma's Blending of Many Cultures, Illustrated in Oklahoma's Art*. N.p.: L. C. Wise and the American Revolution Bicentennial Authority, 1974.

"Woman Champion." *National Police Gazette*, June 24, 1905, 6.

"Wonderful Shooting." *Cheyenne Transporter* (Darlington, I.T.), October 25, 1880, 4.

Wright, Muriel H., and George H. Shirk. "Artist Möllhausen in Oklahoma, 1853." *Chronicles of Oklahoma* 31, no. 4 (Winter 1953–1954): 392–441.

———. "The Journal of Lieutenant A. W. Whipple." *Chronicles of Oklahoma* 28, no. 3 (Autumn 1950): 235–83.

Young, Denny, and Susan Meyn. *The Vanishing Frontier: Henry F. Farny, 1847–1916*. Cincinnati, Ohio: Taft Museum, 1997.

Zogbaum, Rufus. "Life at an Indian Agency," *Harper's Weekly*, January 4, 1890, 11–12.

GOVERNMENT DOCUMENTS

Colyer, Vincent. "Report of the Hon. Vincent Colyer, United States Special Indian Commissioner, on the Indian tribes and reservations of Eastern Kansas, Indian Territory, Northern Texas, New Mexico, Northeastern Arizona, and Southeastern Colorado, obtained by personal observation and inspection among these tribes during the year 1869." *Report of the Commissioner of Indian Affairs Made to the Secretary of the Interior for the Year 1869*, 70–88. Washington, D.C.: Government Printing Office, 1870.

Marcy, Randolph Barnes. *Exploration of the Red River of Louisiana, in the Year 1852*. 32nd Cong., 2d Sess., S. Doc. No. 54. Washington D.C.: Beverly Tucker, 1854.

U.S. Congress. *The Statutes at Large and Proclamations of the United States of America from December 1869–March 1871*. Vol. 16, edited by George P. Sanger. Boston: Little, Brown, 1871.

U.S. Department of the Interior. Census Office. *Indians Taxed and Indians Not Taxed in the United States (except Alaska) at the Eleventh Census*. Washington D.C.: Government Printing Office, 1894.

Whipple, Amiel W. *Reports of Explorations and Surveys to Ascertain the Most Practicable and Economical Route for a Railroad from the Mississippi River to the Pacific Ocean*. Vol. 3, 33rd Cong., 2nd Sess., S. Doc. No. 78. Washington, D.C.: Beverly Tucker, 1856.

INDEX

Page numbers in *italics* indicate illustrations.